European Yearbook of Constitutional Law

Volume 6

The *European Yearbook of Constitutional Law* (EYCL) is an annual publication devoted to the study of constitutional law. The yearbook provides a forum for in-depth analysis and discussion of new developments in constitutional law in Europe and beyond. The founding editors were Professor Ernst Hirsch Ballin and Dr Gerhard van der Schyff. Each issue is dedicated to a specific theme. Papers are subject to editorial and double-blind peer review. The yearbook is published by T.M.C. ASSER PRESS in cooperation with Springer Publishers.

Contact

To get in touch, please send an e-mail to eycl@tilburguniversity.edu

Maartje De Visser · Ingrid Leijten ·
Jurgen de Poorter · Gerhard van der Schyff ·
Maarten Stremler · Sophie Vonk
Editors

European Yearbook of Constitutional Law 2024

Varieties of Constitutionalism

ASSER PRESS

Springer

Editors
Maartje De Visser
Yong Pung How School of Law
SMU School of Law
Singapore, Singapore

Ingrid Leijten
Department of Public Law and Governance
Tilburg Law School
Tilburg, The Netherlands

Jurgen de Poorter
Department of Public Law and Governance
Tilburg Law School
Tilburg, The Netherlands

Gerhard van der Schyff
Department of Public Law and Governance
Tilburg Law School
Tilburg, The Netherlands

Maarten Stremler
Faculty of Law, Department of Public Law
Maastricht University
Maastricht, The Netherlands

Sophie Vonk
Department of Public Law and Governance
Tilburg Law School
Tilburg, The Netherlands

ISSN 2405-6111 ISSN 2405-612X (electronic)
European Yearbook of Constitutional Law
ISBN 978-94-6265-698-7 ISBN 978-94-6265-699-4 (eBook)
https://doi.org/10.1007/978-94-6265-699-4

This T.M.C. ASSER PRESS imprint is published by the registered company Springer-Verlag GmbH, DE, part of Springer Nature.
The registered company address is: Heidelberger Platz 3, 14197 Berlin, Germany

Contents

Editors and Contributors

About the Editors

Maartje De Visser is Professor at the Yong Pung How School of Law, Singapore. Her current research focuses on constitutional engagement by courts and non-judicial actors, transnational judicial dialogues in Europe and Asia, and means to improve constitutional literacy.

Ingrid Leijten is Professor of Dutch and European Constitutional Law in the Department of Public Law and Governance at Tilburg University, The Netherlands. Her research primarily deals with the changing role and meaning of fundamental rights against the background of broader (comparative) constitutional law developments.

Jurgen de Poorter is State Councillor in the Dutch Council of State and Professor of Administrative Law in the Department of Public Law and Governance at Tilburg University, The Netherlands. His research focuses in particular on constitutional dialogues, public interest litigation and methods of judicial lawmaking.

Gerhard van der Schyff is Associate Professor in the Department of Public Law and Governance at Tilburg University, The Netherlands. His research interests include constitutional law and fundamental rights, especially from a comparative and European perspective.

Maarten Stremler is Assistant Professor of Constitutional Law at the Faculty of Law at Maastricht University, The Netherlands. His research interests are Dutch and European constitutional law, comparative constitutional law and constitutional theory.

Sophie Vonk is a doctoral researcher in the Department of Public Law and Governance at Tilburg University, The Netherlands. Her research deals with the relation between innovation in democracy and fundamental rights protection.

Contributors

Kushagr Bakshi Law School, University of Michigan, Ann Arbor, MI, USA

Thibault Carrère Department of Law, Avignon University, Avignon, France

Maria Francesca Cavalcanti Department of Public Law and Governance, School of Law, Tilburg University, Tilburg, The Netherlands

Chris Monaghan School of Law, University of Worcester, Worcester, UK

Ronald Tinnevelt Department of the Philosophy of Law, Radboud University, Nijmegen, The Netherlands

Mark Tushnet Harvard University, Cambridge, MA, USA

Eklavya Vasudev Public International Law and Human Rights, Friedrich-Alexander University Erlangen-Nuremberg, Erlangen, Germany

Sergio Verdugo Law School, IE University, Madrid, Spain

Chapter 1
Introduction: Reflections on Varieties of Constitutionalism

Maartje De Visser, Jurgen de Poorter, Ingrid Leijten, Gerhard van der Schyff, Maarten Stremler and Sophie Vonk

Contents

Abstract This opening chapter explains the importance of exploring constitutions through an ideological prism to reckon with the normative outlook of such texts. It notes that it is possible, fruitful and arguably even necessary to accept that there are varieties in such an outlook that go beyond the classic liberal constitutional democratic paradigm. The chapter also offers an overview of the contributions included in the remainder of this edition of the Yearbook that help to diversify the toolkit that scholars may use in deciding on the appropriate adjective(s) to pair with the notion of constitutionalism. Finally, the chapter includes a call for scholars to be explicit about the conceptual approach that they adopt. More particularly, there would be a

We would like to thank Terēze Lība Tiesniece (student-assistant at Tilburg Law School) for her valuable assistance in editing the manuscript.

M. De Visser (✉)
Yong Pung How School of Law, Singapore Management University, Singapore, Singapore
e-mail: mdevisser@smu.edu.sg

J. de Poorter · I. Leijten · G. van der Schyff · S. Vonk
Department of Public Law and Governance, Tilburg University, Tilburg, The Netherlands
e-mail: j.c.a.depoorter@tilburguniversity.edu

I. Leijten
e-mail: a.e.m.leijten@tilburguniversity.edu

G. van der Schyff
e-mail: g.vdrschyff@tilburguniversity.edu

S. Vonk
e-mail: s.e.c.vonk@tilburguniversity.edu

M. Stremler
Faculty of Law, Maastricht University, Maastricht, The Netherlands
e-mail: m.stremler@maastrichtuniversity.nl

M. De Visser et al. (eds.), *European Yearbook of Constitutional Law 2024*, European Yearbook of Constitutional Law 6, https://doi.org/10.1007/978-94-6265-699-4_1

need to explain the reasons for recognising a given form of constitutionalism, why it is considered appropriate to use that form to describe or analyse the practice of constitutionalism in a certain country or group of countries as well as how various forms of constitutionalism relate to one another, which extends to engaging with the conceptions, applications and taxonomies put forward by others working on these topics.

Keywords Adjectival constitutionalism · Conceptual pluralism · Constitutionalism · Ideology · Liberal constitutionalism · Varieties of constitutionalism

1.1 Constitutions Through an Ideological Prism

Written constitutions are believed to be unavoidable trappings of modern nationhood, much like the issuance of passports or the printing of money, and most states eagerly adopt such documents to assert their sovereignty and independence for reasons of both domestic as well as international legitimacy.[1] The spread of constitutions has proceeded regardless of regime type, and the existence of a fundamental text—a supreme law of the land—is ubiquitous among all the countries of the world, both those that identify as liberal democracies as well as in those that have—at times vastly—different aims and aspirations. Given this reality, the scholarly tendency has been to understand the term 'constitution' in a formalistic or purely descriptive fashion, irrespective of the normative values that a particular supreme law subscribes to. Matters of ideology do come to the fore, however, when thinking about the notion of 'constitutionalism', which deals with the legitimation, authorisation and limitation of state power, the attainment of fundamental values and the polity's chosen identity. While it has long been common practice to associate constitutionalism with a normative outlook that is linked to the expectations of the role of a constitution in liberal democracies, there is a growing acknowledgment that it is possible, fruitful or even necessary to pluralise the concept of constitutionalism further.[2]

This edition of the *Yearbook* is therefore devoted to an exploration of varieties of constitutionalism. This topic offers an important provocation for scholars, as it suggests that concepts that are central to our field may lack a single, unified understanding or be applied differently in different spatial settings. As Chen has correctly observed, "a multitude of definitional approaches are possible."[3] There has, indeed, been a veritable explosion of monikers to describe the many varied notions and practices of constitutionalism. A 2023 study by Kapiszewski, Groen and

---

[1] Generally, on the legitimacy of constitutions: Fallon 2005, Harel and Shinar 2022. For the idea of constitutional legitimacy over time, see Dupré and Yeh 2013.

[2] Chen 2022; Tushnet 2016.

[3] Chen 2022, p. 61.

Newman identified a striking 1,621 adjective-constitutionalism combinations.[4] This begs the question what has prompted the identification of so many combinations. Without attempting to be exhaustive, some possible causes include the proliferation of constitution-making exercises across the world, notably from the middle of the twentieth century onwards as well as during the first decades of the twenty-first century.[5] Realisation has progressively dawned that the outcome of such exercises has not always followed the ideology of the liberal-democratic model originally adopted and today still used by many Western countries, which could be perceived as necessitating the deployment of adjectives to clarify that one is confronted with a distinctive or even unique approach to constitutional ideology. There is also an emerging awareness that the liberal-democratic model of constitutionalism is not a monolith but perhaps rather a broad church that may contain varieties within it that scholars can profitably unpack and analyse. Linked to these explanations we could point to an increase in heterogeneity in how constitutionalism is conceptualised and practiced, with new modes coming into operation, resulting in a scholarly desire to ensure that the terminology used accurately reflects what happens on the ground.[6] The constitutionalisation of international law may further have provided an impetus to resort to qualifiers such as global constitutionalism[7] or a specific kind of regional constitutionalism, with due reference to the existence of regional institutions—notably courts—that pursue a specific ideological agenda.

Following on from the above, there are a couple of purposes that may be pursued in having recourse to adjectives in relation to the concept of constitutionalism, that may shade into one another. The first of these is to signal the precise nature of constitutionalism that one is dealing with. The aim is descriptive precision, identifying core features of the ideological proclivities under study. One example are the works devoted to Confucian constitutionalism, which consider among others how Confucian philosophical thought and concepts—such as rituals or *li*—are given expression in written constitutions and are part of the constitutional identity of several East Asian jurisdictions.[8] A second purpose is to devise taxonomies that allow us to make more sense of how the constitutional world is organised and operates. Consider for instance the question of the identity of the actor(s) principally responsible for ensuring that the constitution is heeded by state authorities. In this regard, a three-fold schematic is in play, in the form of judicial constitutionalism, which envisages a starring role for the courts through the exercise of judicial review;[9] political constitutionalism, which contemplates that majoritarian institutions ought to take the lead

[4] Kapiszewski et al. 2023; Voermans 2023.

[5] Elkins et al., "Comparative Constitutions Project" (2009). Available at: https://comparativeconstitutionsproject.org/.

[6] Kapiszewski et al. 2023.

[7] Peters 2015; Lang and Wiener 2023.

[8] Bui 2024; Kim 2023; Ginsburg 2006; Hahm 2003.

[9] On the rise in prominence of judicial constitutionalism, see Hirschl 2007; Stone Sweet 2000.

in ensuring compliance with constitutional rules and values;[10] and popular constitutionalism, which casts the people as authoritative interpreters of the constitution.[11] Another common taxonomical approach is to distinguish between liberal constitutionalism and other modalities that are not rights-centric and court-centric, with such counterpoints including illiberal constitutionalism, which itself has been subdivided into religious, socialist and communitarian constitutionalism,[12] authoritarian constitutionalism[13] and hybrid constitutionalism "in which features of both constitutionalism and authoritarian practices that subvert or are inconsistent with such constitutionalism exist simultaneously."[14]

This brings us back to the question of the normativity inherent in most usages of the concept of constitutionalism. As Tushnet, a contributor to this volume and one of the leading voices in this regard has observed, it seems misguided to equate constitutionalism with liberal constitutionalism. As he aptly points out, "Not only do other constitutionalisms exist, but some of them are as normative defensible, under appropriate circumstances, as liberal constitutionalism is."[15] For those working on constitutional law and constitutional theory, then, this raises critical questions about identifying and accounting for the attributes that make a particular form of constitutionalism appealing and, to the extent that this form is not the paradigmatic liberal one, how that form is different from liberal constitutionalism.

1.2 Pluralising Scholarly Thinking as Regards the Varieties of Constitutionalism

As the aspirations, substance and implementation of constitutions are not uniform across jurisdictions, including on account of the influence of national political and social developments, there is concomitant need for scholars to reckon with the ideological choices that have been made and decide, with due care, on the adjective(s) to be paired with the notion of constitutionalism that best capture those choices. It is therefore encouraging to see that there are deliberate and ongoing efforts to diversify the toolkit that is available to scholars in this regard. The chapters included in the *Yearbook* are a contribution to these efforts and, taken together, illustrate the plethora of options that colleagues could rely on.

In Chap. 2 Mark Tushnet seeks to advance our analytic understanding by suggesting a classificatory system of constitutionalism's varieties. He discusses different ways in which one can go about this exercise, from nominalism to genealogy and expands on an approach that entails relating constitutionalism to classic features

[10] Bellamy 2009; Greally 2024.

[11] Kramer 2004; Tushnet 1999; Donnelly 2012.

[12] Thio 2021.

[13] Tushnet 2015; Pozas-Loyo and Ríos-Figueroa 2022; Alviar García and Frankenberg 2019.

[14] Chen 2010, p. 880.

[15] Tushnet 2016.

of its domain, i.e. the degree of entrenchment of constitutional provisions and the role of courts. He shows how those features can be profitably used to signal the existence of a given form of constitutionalism and structure our thinking. For instance, the question of what is entrenched can give us classically liberal constitutionalism, while a consideration of the significance of courts can yield "superstrong" constitutionalism or political constitutionalism. Tushnet also addresses the question of regional constitutionalism, putting forth the view that it is often difficult to identify distinctiveness in constitutional ideas or institutions that would justify the application of region-specific labels. He ends on a cautionary note, observing that linking constitutionalism to other nouns means that the former should be seen as part of a broader conceptual domain and that our categorisations may be "no better than we can classify those other norms."

Illustrating the different meanings of the term 'constitutionalism', in Chap. 3 Thibault Carrère investigates the concept of 'republican constitutionalism'. In this regard, we are confronted by the question whether constitutionalism is 'irredeemably liberal'? In other words, is liberal constitutionalism, understood as natural rights whose enforcement depends on impartial constitutional judges, the only kind of constitutionalism that matters? We learn that alongside the liberal definition of constitutionalism, there exists also a republican definition. The latter, based on a conceptualisation of liberty as 'non-domination' rather than 'non-interference', results in a constitutionalism which emphasises the protection of the constitution through elected institutions and the people. In this way, our conception of constitutionalism shifts from the courts to political deliberation in an attempt to reconcile law and politics.

Chris Monaghan, in Chap. 4, explores the concept of 'muddling-through constitutionalism' in the United Kingdom, highlighting the flexibility and adaptability of the UK's unwritten constitution in times of political crisis. The UK's constitution evolves through conventions, statutes, and court decisions, allowing it to survive challenges without formal overhaul. Its stability depends on political actors, especially the Prime Minister and the monarch. Monaghan argues that Boris Johnson's premiership put this system to test by challenging constitutional norms, but that the system ultimately self-corrected, with political actors and institutions stepping in to preserve democratic principles. Monaghan concludes that the UK's 'muddling-through' constitution is not inherently weak, which would necessitate the adoption a written constitution. Instead, historical examples show that this constitution can survive without the need for fundamental constitution reform.

In Chap. 5, Ronald Tinnevelt engages with possible safeguards for constitutional democracy in the face of the threats posed by illiberal and authoritarian forces, which have been on the rise in recent decades. He focuses on the notion of militant constitutionalism, with a view to clarifying its meaning and the underlying conceptions of the rule of law and constitutionalism that this notion is premised on. Ensuring the resilience of constitutional democracy, he argues, is not only a matter of having well-functioning formal institutions, but also dependent on informal instruments as well as the political and legal culture in a given jurisdiction. More precisely, Tinnevelt identifies four possible elements that make up such supportive constitutional practices: acceptance of and dialogue regarding unwritten rules and norms; public and professional mentality; legal trust; and civic and professional education. As such, his chapter offers a powerful account of the conditions that should be in place to ensure that models of constitutional democracy survive if not thrive.

In Chap. 6, Kushagr Bakshi compares two paradigms of constitutionalism, illustrated through LGBTQ+ rights cases: traditional liberal-democratic constitutionalism and transformative constitutionalism. The former, dominant in the United States and Europe, treats privacy as a negative right, limiting state interference but not imposing obligations to ensure equality. This shields LGBTQ+ individuals from state intrusion but fails to guarantee full legal recognition, as seen in privacy-based rulings on same-sex marriage. In contrast, transformative constitutionalism, seen in India, South Africa, and Brazil, embraces substantive equality, imposing positive obligations on the state to dismantle discrimination. These courts reject the notion that private relationships are beyond constitutional scrutiny and instead subject social norms to constitutional morality, ensuring more robust protection. Bakshi highlights how courts can shift between both paradigms, with some US and European rulings adopting elements of substantive equality. Ultimately, Bakshi argues that transformative constitutionalism, by recognising indirect discrimination and imposing duties on the state, provides stronger and more meaningful legal protections for LGBTQ+ individuals.

Eklavya Vasudev, in Chap. 7, also focuses on the role played by the courts in giving effect to a particular variety of constitutionalism. He considers how the Indian Supreme Court integrates international law in its rulings and uses its environmental case law as the laboratory to study how the resultant integration has played out. While such a judicial practice can be said to align with the global orientation of the Indian Constitution, Vasudev highlights the challenges and risks attendant on what he calls "gatekeeper" constitutionalism vis-à-vis international law. His argument is that the Indian Supreme Court should be more discerning and cautious in the exercise of its gatekeeper role to ensure that it keeps within its constitutional limits and that rulings are internally consistent, clear and actionable. Vasudev's chapter provides a cautionary note for other courts, both in the Global South and beyond, that may also increasingly practice gatekeeper constitutionalism and engage with norms that emanate from outside the domestic order, including to give effect to the aspirations and outlook of the domestic constitution.

Varieties of constitutionalism can also be linked to religion. This is what Maria Francesca Cavalcanti does in Chap. 8, comparing Greece, Israel and Lebanon in this respect. Investigating the role between the constitutional order and religion in these countries' legal systems, she finds that although they affirm the principle of laicity, religion plays an important role at the institutional level. By analysing how religion shapes the constitutional order in these countries, Cavalcanti contributes to a broader discussion relating to the challenges that come with religious pluralism. Indeed, the chapter is explicitly placed against the background of growing religious diversity and the challenges this brings to liberal constitutionalism as we have come to understand it. After delving into the specifics of the three States under comparison when it comes to constitutionalism and religion, Cavalcanti presents intercultural accommodation as a possible solution to accommodate religious diversity.

Lastly, in Chap. 9, Sergio Verdugo interrogates a particular regional version of constitutionalism that has been popularised by several scholars and judges based in or writing on Latin America: the idea of a *ius constitutionale commune* as a transformative normative project that envisages the realisation of an egalitarian approach to the protection of human rights through judicial means, with a prominent role in the final instance for the Inter-American Court of Human Rights. Verdugo is sceptical about the reliance that this project places on judges and considers that the delivery of its stated goals may even be retarded on account of the method of judicialisation. He accordingly calls on the protagonists of the *ius constitutonale commune* to critically reflect on the means and institutional actors best suited to deliver social reform and improved engagement with human rights in Latin American settings. His plea underscores the need for advocates of particular forms of constitutionalism to be duly sensitive to prevailing political and social realities to ensure that their ideological agenda will work in practice and yield minimal risks or drawbacks.

1.3 Reckoning with Conceptual Pluralism

Writing in 2013, Ginsburg and Simpser observed that there is "no scholarly consensus capable of supplying us with a single correct definition" of constitutionalism.[16] This observation continues to ring true. If anything, understandings of the concept have arguably become even more diverse in the intervening decade, including on account of the identification of more varieties of constitutionalism. As alluded to in the preceding sections, this diversification may be a boon for the discourse. At the same time, however, it arguably gives rise to an obligation for scholars to be explicit about the conceptual approach that they adopt. More particularly, there would be a need to explain the reasons for recognising a given form of constitutionalism, why it is considered appropriate to use that form to describe or analyse the practice of constitutionalism in a certain country or group of countries as well as how various forms of constitutionalism relate to one another, which extends to engaging with the conceptions, applications and taxonomies put forward by others working on these topics. It should be recognised here that scholars may well disagree with each other and for instance draw the line between liberal and other forms of constitutionalism differently or argue for the applicability of one or the other form in making sense of constitutionalism in a given jurisdiction. This, to be sure, is not problematic, provided that readers can make out the underlying thinking that has produced the difference in views. Doing so is instrumental to ensure that the relevant literature will be marked by clarity and—ideally, at least in the longer term—some degree of internal coherence that can help elucidate rather than obfuscate the very nature of the concept of constitutionalism. It is our hope that the contributions collected in this edition of the *Yearbook* may be a valuable resource in this regard.

[16] Ginsburg and Simpser 2013, p. 7.

References

Alviar García H, Frankenberg G (2019) Authoritarian Constitutionalism—Comparative Analysis and Critique. Edward Elgar, Cheltenham.
Bellamy R (2009) Political Constitutionalism—A Republican Defence of the Constitutionality of Democracy. Cambridge University Press, Cambridge.
Bui N S (2024) Confucian Constitutional Identity. In: Hirschl R (ed) Deciphering the Genome of Constitutionalism. Cambridge University Press, Cambridge, pp. 101–112.
Chen A (2010) Pathways of Western Liberal Constitutional Development in Asia: A Comparative Study of Five Major Nations. International Journal of Constitutional Law 8(4):849–884.
Chen A (2022) Constitutions and Constitutionalism: China. In: Law D S (ed) Constitutionalism in Context. Cambridge University Press, Cambridge, pp. 61–86.
Donnelly T (2012) Making Popular Constitutionalism Work. Wisconsin Law Review: 159–194.
Dupré C, Yeh J R (2013) Constitutions and Legitimacy Over Time. In: Tushnet M, Fleiner T, Saunders C (eds) Routledge Handbook of Constitutional Law. Routledge, Abingdon, pp. 45–56.
Fallon RH (2005) Legitimacy and the Constitution. Harvard Law Review 118(6):1787–1853.
Ginsburg T (2006) Confucian Constitutionalism? The Emergence of Constitutional Review in Korea and Taiwan. Law & Social Inquiry 27(4):763–799.
Ginsburg T, Simpser A (2013) Introduction: Constitutions in Authoritarian Regimes. In: Constitutions in Authoritarian Regimes. Cambridge University Press, Cambridge.
Greally R (2024) Ideologies of Political Constitutionalism. Oxford Journal of Legal Studies 44(4):949–978.
Hahm C (2003) Law, Culture, and the Politics of Confucianism. Columbia Journal of Asian Law 16(2):254–297.
Harel A, Shinar A (2022) Two Concepts of Constitutional Legitimacy. Global Constitutionalism 12(1):80–105.
Hirschl R (2007) Towards Juristocracy: The Origins and Consequences of New Constitutionalism. Harvard University Press, Cambridge.
Kapiszewski D, Groen D, Newman K (2023) Constitutionalism with Adjectives: Conceptual Innovation in the Comparative Study of Law. Law & Social Inquiry 49(1):178–208.
Kim S (2023) Confucian Constitutionalism—Dignity, Rights, and Democracy. Oxford University Press, Oxford.
Kramer L (2004) The People Themselves: Popular Constitutionalism and Judicial Review. Oxford University Press, Oxford / New York.
Lang A, Wiener A (2023) Handbook on Global Constitutionalism. Edward Elgar, Cheltenham.
Peters A (2015) Global Constitutionalism. In: Gibbons M, Coole D, Ellis E (eds) The Encyclopedia of Political Thought. John Wily & Sons, Oxford.
Pozas-Loyo A, Ríos-Figueroa J (2022) Authoritarian Constitutionalism. In: Mendes C H, Gargarella R, Guidi S (eds) The Oxford Handbook of Constitutional Law in Latin America. Oxford University Press, Oxford, pp. 340–353.
Stone Sweet A (2000) Governing with Judges: Constitutional Politics in Europe. Oxford University Press, Oxford.
Thio L A (2021) Varieties of Constitutionalism in Asia. Asian Journal of Comparative Law 16(2):285–310.
Tushnet M (1999) Taking the Constitution Away from the Courts. Princeton University Press, New Jersey.
Tushnet M (2015) Authoritarian Constitutionalism. Cornell Law Review 100:391–461.
Tushnet M (2016) Editorial—Varieties of Constitutionalism. International Journal of Constitutional Law 14(1):1–5.
Voermans W (2023) The Story of Constitutions—Discovering the We in Us. Cambridge University Press, Cambridge.

Chapter 2
Classifying Varieties of Constitutionalism

Mark Tushnet

Contents

Abstract This chapter offers some reflections that aim to help us arrive at a more analytic understanding or classificatory system of constitutionalism's varieties. It explores different avenues to arrive at such an understanding, suggesting that it may be instructive to consider differences in what is constitutionally entrenched and how strong such entrenchment is as well as the role of courts. The chapter also considers regional constitutionalism and argues that it is difficult to identify distinct regional institutions, rights and ideas that cannot also be found, in some form, outside the region in question. It concludes that scholars attach adjectives to the word "constitutionalism" because they believe that doing so illuminates the specific topic with which they are concerned. The adjective ties that form of constitutionalism to other nouns to which the adjective is attached, such as values, politics and culture. Seen in this way, we can classify varieties of constitutionalism no better than we can classify those other nouns.

Keywords Varieties of constitutionalism · Classification · Entrenchment · Role of courts · Regional constitutionalism · Diffusion studies

democratic constitutionalism, political constitutionalism, judicial constitutionalism, illiberal constitutionalism (oxymoron no more!), new constitutionalism, contemporary constitutionalism, popular constitutionalism, corporatist constitutionalism, negative constitutionalism, Russian constitutionalism, Confucian constitutionalism, African constitutionalism,

M. Tushnet (✉)
Harvard University, Cambridge, MA, USA
e-mail: tushnet@law.harvard.edu

M. De Visser et al. (eds.), *European Yearbook of Constitutional Law 2024*, European Yearbook of Constitutional Law 6, https://doi.org/10.1007/978-94-6265-699-4_2

> transformative constitutionalism, plurinational constitutionalism, feminist constitutionalism, secular constitutionalism, modern constitutionalism, aggregative constitutionalism, Sinicized Marxist constitutionalism, ... world constitutionalism.
>
> Ghai 2016, 143, 158

> (1) those that belong to the Emperor; (2) embalmed ones; (3) those that are trained: (4) suckling pigs; (5) mermaids; (6) fabulous ones; (7) stray dogs; (8) those included in the present classification; (9) those that tremble as if they were made; (10) innumerable ones; (11) those drawn with a very fine camelhair brush; (12) others; (13) those that have just broken a flower vase; (14) those that from a long way off look like this
>
> Borges 1964

As this Yearbook shows the interest in varieties of constitutionalism that Yash Ghai identified in 2016 continues. Yet, as his list suggests, our understanding of those varieties might resemble that of the list of subcategories of animals Borges provides—a hodge-podge unified only because we attach a more-or-less random adjective to the word "constitutionalism." Here I hope to make a bit of progress toward a more analytic understanding or classificatory system of constitutionalism's varieties.

2.1 Creating a Catalogue of Constitutionalism's Varieties

We need a preliminary distinction between varieties of *constitutions* and varieties of constitutional*ism*. Classifying the former is a well-established practice in comparative political science: we have absolute and constitutional monarchies, representative and plebiscitarian democracies, unitary and federal nations. Here the exercise is purely descriptive.

Classifying varieties of constitutionalism is a bit different because constitutionalism has some normative content. One aspect of variety is precisely variation in that normative content, though that is not the only source of variation. The classification effort is made more complicated by the risk that our classifying effort will privilege one variety of constitutionalism—typically, Western (or Northern) liberal democracy—in a way that interferes with our ability to think clearly about other varieties.[1]

How can we go about classifying varieties of constitutionalism? One possibility is a nominalistic catalogue like Borges's (or Ghai's, were it intended as a catalogue). Another possibility is something like a genealogical catalogue.[2] Here we identify a variety of constitutionalism and isolate its distinctive characteristics, then come up with a story about why this variety has those characteristics. This is inevitably an

[1] For a good statement of this risk, see Thio 2021, p. 285. See also the discussion below on the "Asian values" controversy.

[2] I draw this possibility from reflecting on the analysis offered by Larsen 2021, p. 477.

exercise in comparing this variety with others and so our story will be about why this particular variety emerged.[3]

I think there are a couple of difficulties with a genealogical catalogue. One raises deep questions about social-science methodology. I've referred to genealogical "stories", These stories *never* capture the actual historical development of the varieties of constitutionalism. They are, instead, given the fancy name "ideal types" or the pejorative name "just so" stories.[4] Ideal-type methodology is so prevalent in social science that it has to be telling us *something* about the real world. Exactly what it tells us, though, is quite unclear. Perhaps ideal types give us mental tools to help us think about particulars, which is to say that they don't tell us much about the substance of what we're looking at.

The second difficulty is more mundane: how do we go about organizing the genealogical catalogue? The label I've given it suggests that we might want to try something like a historical organization: first this type emerged, then that one, then ... (liberal constitutionalism, then social welfare constitutionalism, then transformational constitutionalism, ...).[5] Yet, this seems quite arbitrary. We can trace every nation's constitution, and therefore every variety of constitutionalism, back as far as we want. Put another way, history doesn't have a "first" and a "second" across the development of constitutions.

I suggest a different approach. Begin by asking, Would we think about things differently if we replaced "constitutionalism" with another word, for example, "governance"? How might environmental governance differ from environmental constitutionalism? The former is, I think, broader than the latter. "Governance" encompasses all the modes of regulating the environment, including private agreements, nuisance law, regulatory statutes, and administrative regulations whereas, as a general matter, "constitutionalism" does not unless we do quite a bit of analytic work associated with doctrines of direct and indirect horizontal effect.[6]

Constitutionalism is narrower than governance, then. I believe that one obvious path forward is unpromising. Many works about constitutionalism begin by asking, "What is constitutionalism for?" The answer, given in various ways and often after a fair amount of to-ing and fro-ing, is that constitutionalism is a way of simultaneously enabling and constraining the power of a nation's people to govern themselves. One might think that we could classify varieties of constitutionalism according to the ways in which they strike the balance between empowerment and constraint. I

---

[3] Larsen 2021 is a good example of this sort of exercise.

[4] Practitioners of some other disciplines sometimes try to replace the ideal types or just-so stories by identifying mechanisms, typically evolutionary, that actually explain why the variety takes the form it does. Ackerman 2019 gestures in the direction of identifying some relevant mechanisms but, in my view, it fails in the effort. I note that Ackerman explicitly refers to ideal-type methodology. Ackerman 2019 at p. 4.

[5] The familiar categorization of first-, second-, and third-generation constitutions is an example of a historically organized catalogue.

[6] Those doctrines place private law—in the environmental governance setting, contract and nuisance law most prominently—within the scope of constitutional attention.

believe, though, that doing so would replicate the political scientists' lists of forms of constitutions without adding anything analytically interesting.

2.2 A Catalogue Based Upon Entrenchment and the Role of Courts

Another path would begin with a different way of defining constitutionalism's domain. Traditionally that domain is defined by two features. (1) Constitutional provisions are entrenched, and (2) courts have a special role in ensuring that constitutional provisions are followed. Our initial classification of adjectival constitutionalisms might then be "tied to" those features in some loose sense. Environmental constitutionalism, for example, is tied to entrenchment when a written constitution contains entrenched provisions adverting to the environment or tied to judicial review when a constitutional court holds that some provision not on its face directed to the environment nonetheless requires or prohibits some government actions with respect to the environment. In contrast, "regional" constitutionalisms such as African or Latin American constitutional do not seem tied to entrenchment or judicial review as a general matter unless, as might be the case, the analysis of a region's constitutionalism leads us to identify distinctive ways in which nations in that region deal with entrenchment or judicial review.

The two features I have identified are more complicated than this first pass-through indicates. First, entrenchment is a matter of degree and practical political reality. As a first cut, think of an axis running from a low to a high degree of entrenchment. At the upper end (for the moment) are constitutionalisms with many eternity clauses (some explicit as in the German Basic Law, others created by constitutional courts implementing a "basic structure" doctrine ruling out as unconstitutional some amendments adopted through authorized procedures, still others implicit as in provisions usefully identified by Rivka Weill defining the national territory).[7]

Less entrenched constitutions might have some or no eternity clauses but amendment rules that require quite high levels of agreement for formal adoption of constitutional amendment (as with the United States' requirement of approval by two-thirds of each legislative house and three-quarters of the states, or Australia's "double majority" requirement of approval by majorities in a majority of the states, or the upper tiers of Canada's tiered amendment procedures).[8]

Weaker amendment rules mean even less entrenchment. At the limit (again for the moment), constitutions are freely amendable by ordinary political majorities—a phenomenon generally described as political constitutionalism. Yet, political constitutionalism itself comes in several forms. When dealing with constitutional matters, for example, ordinary majorities might be constrained by conventions that all major participants regard as normatively binding. Or ordinary majorities might be more

---

[7] Roznai 2017; Weill 2018, p. 905.

[8] Albert 2019.

weakly constrained by a general sense of fairness or other "guardrails" against precipitate constitutional change.[9] Simple first-order political calculations might lead politicians to refrain from altering the constitution if they fear that their adversaries might soon take control and not only undo such changes but—emboldened by what had already been done—adopt constitutional changes to entrench themselves (not any specific policies) in power. These constraints might be thought of as second-order limits on first-order change.

Having the image of this axis in mind we might think of transformative constitutionalism as "negative" entrenchment. That is, transformative constitutionalism aims at undoing the arrangements sustained by the ordinary politics of the status quo. It can empower the courts to undo congealed power arrangements, as in Roberto Unger's early formulation,[10] or give constitutional status to reformist political programs, as was the thought behind the 1937 Irish Constitution's creation of directive principles of public policy.

The political valence of these versions is clear: transformational reform is to be progressive. Perhaps predictably, though, we have seen the emergence of reactionary versions of transformative constitutionalism, most notably in in Hungary. There the governing party has built into its program a commitment to "restoring" Hungary's "historic" constitution. This does not mean (merely) stripping a liberal constitution of socialist or social democratic elements that the party takes to be legacies of Communism. It means reverting to some imagined past (hence the scare quotes around "restoring") of a harmonious, hierarchical, and ethnically homogenous nation. Narendra Moti has not articulated a comprehensive constitutional vision for India but the culturally reactionary Rashtriya Swayamsevak Sangh that was the foundation for Modi's later political career could easily be described as offering a reactionary transformative constitutional vision.

Thinking of transformative constitutionalism as negative entrenchment leads to another thought—what Duncan Kennedy once called "loopification".[11] Advocates for transformative constitutionalism typically believe that once uncongealed power relations will produce a permanent—entrenched—improvement of the constitutional system. The constitution is to be transformed into *something*, after all. True, that new thing can itself become congealed and Unger's destabilization branch is designed as a permanent (entrenched?) institution ever ready to go after new forms of congealed power. But, "after" the transformation, at least for a while, a new constitutionalism will be entrenched. Negative entrenchment, that is, becomes strong positive entrenchment—the loop is closed.[12]

The axis of entrenchment gives some structure to the varieties of constitutionalism. What, though, is entrenched? Here I believe a relatively simple dichotomy rather than an axis is helpful. Procedures can be entrenched; so can substance.

---

[9] On guardrails, see Levitsky and Ziblatt 2018.

[10] Unger 1987.

[11] Kennedy 1982.

[12] See Chap. 6 by Bakshi in this Yearbook for an illustration of loopification.

Consider first entrenchment (somewhere along the axis) of procedures for enacting policy into law accompanied by the entrenchment of a relatively thin set of basic human rights. This yields classically liberal constitutionalism. The entrenched procedures allow the polity to adopt whatever substantive policies it chooses through use of the entrenched procedures: the nightwatchman state, a social welfare state, an environmentally conscious state, and anything else. This must be qualified by noting that entrenched procedures might make it difficult to depart substantially from the status quo, as when the procedures require supermajority agreement for the adoption of some or even all policies. A related qualification is that even a thin set of fundamental human rights might in practice protect the status quo, with protections of private property and some aspects of freedom of expression (most notably those associated with the exercise of protected property rights) the most obvious examples.

Substantive policies can be entrenched as well. A constitution might entrench social welfare rights, environmental rights, or fiscal policies, for example. We can label these kinds of substantive constitutions *programmatic*. And programmatic constitutions can themselves be categorized. Some such constitutions are identitarian—that is, they entrench (again at varying points along the axis of entrenchment) distinctive characterizations of national identity ("Jewish and democratic" or "the crown of St. Stephen"). Others, as already suggested, involve the entrenchment of specific substantive policies (*Sozialstaat* or neoliberal policies).[13] Quite a few of Ghai's varieties of constitutionalism slot different substantive policies into the genus *programmatic constitutionalism*.

Another axis providing structure to the varieties of constitutionalism involves the role of courts. Here I can be relatively brief because the distinctions are quite well-known. I have treated political constitutionalism as occupying a bounded segment, so to speak, on the axis of entrenchment. It is also located on the axis of the courts' role because to the degree that political constitutionalism has entrenched elements, those elements are not enforced by the courts. Here too, though, political constitutionalism is less a single point than a bounded segment because some entrenched elements might be addressed by the courts through subconstitutional doctrines. Courts can deploy the ultra vires doctrine, that executive actions must be authorized by statute, with differential vigor depending upon whether the courts regard the executive action as constitutionally problematic. They can use "clear statement" rules in assessing whether a statute does indeed authorize the executive action.

Subconstitutional doctrines move in the direction of "weak form" judicial review.[14] Weak-form judicial review allows legislative responses short of formal constitutional amendment to judicial decisions invalidating primary legislation. These responses can be, as they have been labeled, "in your face" direct rejections of the judicial decision.[15] Or they can be dialogic, with the possibility of several iterations in which legislatures offer their constitutional interpretation, initially implicit in

[13] See Chap. 7 by Vasudev in this Yearbook.

[14] For an introduction, see Tushnet 2007.

[15] For the label, see Roach 2001.

the very act of adopting a statute, courts respond with their own interpretation, legislatures rethink their constitutional position and tinker with the invalidated legislation, and so on through additional iterations.

Strong-form judicial review lies at the end of this axis. Here the courts have the final word on constitutional interpretation subject only to the possibility of being overridden by constitutional amendment or being repudiated by the court itself (ordinarily with new members appointed through constitutionally authorized procedures). And, again, there is the possibility of "superstrong" judicial review, one variant of which involves judicial enforcement of (typically) constitutional rights not specified in relevant constitutional texts, another more important variant of which involves judicial invalidation of constitutional amendments adopted through authorized procedures because the amendments are inconsistent with judicially identified aspects of the constitution's basic structure.

Just as political constitutionalism lies at the intersection of "low" entrenchment and "no role for courts", so we might think of a variety of "superstrong" constitutionalism lying at the intersection of deep entrenchment through eternity clauses and a superstrong role for courts.

Combining the two axes of entrenchment and the judicial role with the dichotomy between procedural and programmatic constitutionalism does give some analytic structure to the general idea that there are varieties of constitutionalism. My technical skills are insufficient to allow me to create a clear diagram showing this structure but I think it clear that quite a few of Ghai's varieties would find a home in any such diagram (see Fig. 2.1 below).

2.3 The Problem of Regional Constitutionalisms

What is left out of the foregoing analysis is important, though. We need only look at the titles in various research handbook series to see a category of "regional" constitutionalism.[16] Perhaps there is a sociological rather an analytic explanation for that category's existence. The thought is that there are networks of scholars and judges co-located in a region who find it convenient to meet within the region (for reasons of expense and institutional support). The "regional constitutionalism" label can then be attached as a description of the networks rather than as a description of some coherent intellectual program.[17]

There is at least one candidate for thinking of regional constitutionalisms as distinctive varieties of constitutionalism, though. That candidate is the idea that regional constitutionalisms arise from the diffusion of constitutional "policies", and the structure of studies of such diffusion is reasonably clear. For present purposes we

[16] That category is illustrated in this Yearbook in Chap. 9 by Verdugo.

[17] I am quite confident that there are studies of such networks, for example in studies of the rise and fall of "area studies" programs, though I am unaware of any dealing with regional constitutionalism.

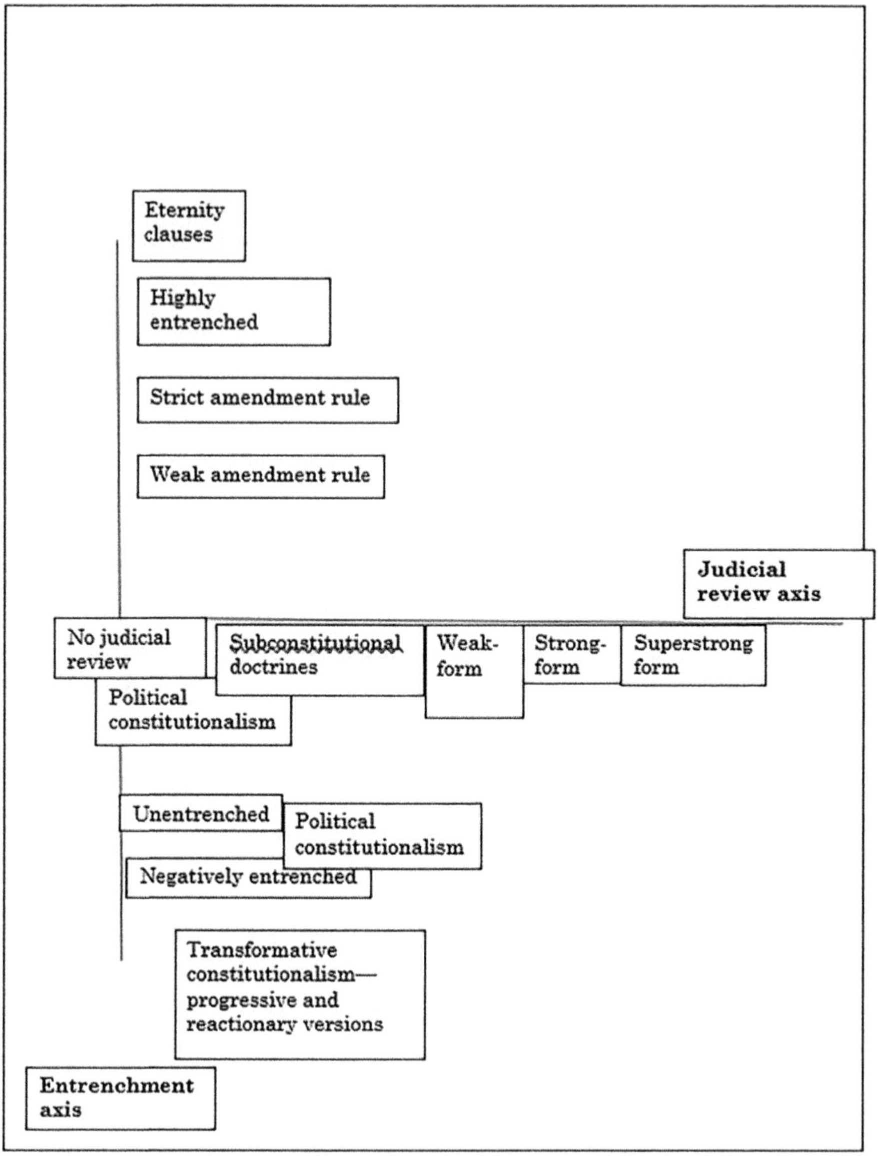

Fig. 2.1 Varieties of constitutionalism. *Source* The author

can identify two types of diffusion studies. The first would deal with regional constitutionalism as a whole, that is, whether constitutionalism within a defined region is different from constitutionalism in other regions. The second would deal with specific institutions such as electoral management bodies or legislatures, or specific rights such as the protection of human dignity or the environment, and would ask whether the structure of those institutions or rights within a region is distinctive from the structure of equivalent institutions or rights in other regions.

Multivariable regression studies of policy diffusion of regional constitutionalism as a whole would start with some sort of measure capturing constitutionalism as a whole.[18] The studies would try to explain variation in that measure by identifying the causal effects of the following (and probably more) relevant variables: national demographic and economic characteristics, membership in the traditional "families" of comparative law (measuring in part the legacy of colonialism, in part the kind of legal education a constitution's drafters have), and the existence of identical or similar constitutional provisions in "neighboring" nations. A region's constitutionalism would be distinctive if that final variable accounted for a fair amount of the variance among constitutions. My sense, unfortunately, is that well-designed diffusion studies are not going to make that showing.

Turning to the second type of diffusion studies, of specific institutions and rights, I have no doubt that we can find some distinctively regional specific institutions. My current favorite example is the prevalence in the constitutions of nations in the Caribbean region of institutions designed to oversee the executive's exercise of its prerogative power to pardon. And there are undoubtedly anecdotal accounts of diffusion when a constitutional drafting body—or an individual drafter—points to an institution in a nearby country as a model for a proposed institution.

Systematic diffusion, though, is another matter. One difficulty is something like selecting on the dependent variable, which in this context means choosing the institutions to study based upon some antecedent sense that they are particularly good candidates for finding regional distinctiveness (the pardon power example above). This risk can be avoided if we could figure out some way of randomly choosing the institutions (or rights) to study.

My skepticism about the possibility of showing regional distinctiveness with respect to specific institutions or rights is that there is too much commonality among constitutional ideas and the functions of constitutional institutions. As to the latter, consider electoral management bodies or anti-corruption agencies. The tasks they are charged with performing drive a great deal of their design—combining certain kinds of expertise with appropriate levels of independence and accountability. One nation's electoral management body might well look a great deal like the electoral management body of a nation with which it shares a border or a common colonial heritage—but there is more than a small chance that it would like just as much like the electoral management body of a nation on another continent because the range of choices is restricted.

[18] One candidate might be the "constitutional archetypes" David Law has identified. Law 2016, p. 153 (describing liberal, statist, and Universalist archetypes).

The case against the idea that there are regionally distinct constitutional ideas is similar. Two examples are, I think, prominent in the literature. The first is the so-called "Asian values" debate of the late twentieth century. Quasi-authoritarian leaders in Malaysia and Singapore defended illiberal aspects of their constitutional systems as reflecting distinctive Asian values. The debate ended when it became apparent that those values were not distinctively Asian but were found as well in European political philosophy, where they were typically offered as republican or traditionalist alternatives to liberal values.[19] Liberal or republican ideas wax and wane over time, and the Asian-values debate reflected the fact that in the late twentieth century the republican alternatives were only weakly represented in constitutional thinking in the global North—but not, again, that there were distinctively Asian (or global South) values.

Consider here Thio Li-Ann's careful description of three varieties of constitutionalism she finds in Asia: religious, socialist, and "communitarian",[20] I think it clear that these varieties are found outside Asia as well. Or, at least, we can find Western liberal constitutionalism alloyed with some religious elements, with some socialist elements, and with some communitarian elements. For the former, the Irish Constitution of 1937 explicit privileges Roman Catholicism and as interpreted and implemented the U.S. Constitution informally "establishes" Christianity as the nation's predominant religion.[21] It would not be inaccurate to describe the German Basic Law, with its commitment to a *Sozialstaat*, as liberal constitutionalism with socialist characteristics. For Thio, communitarian constitutions "evince a strong national identity and communal culture, promote moral solidarity, responsible citizenship and social harmony, anchoring a strong, interventionist state."[22] A recent overview of the idea that citizens have a right to effective governance shows that—subject to some quibbles about the word "strong"—these themes can be found in many of the world's constitutional systems.[23]

The second example involves the list of "African" values, especially *ubuntu*, in the South African Constitution. The list, it is often asserted, identifies values that African constitutionalism particularly emphasizes and that, it is said or implied, are lacking in Western or Northern constitutionalism. I believe, in contrast, that the list, when translated into English, French, or German, includes values that Northern constitutionalists regard as important and as built into *their* constitutions. Berihun Adugna

[19] See Acharya 2010, p. 1011 ("Critics argued that what passed as Asian values were in no way special or unique to Asian societies…."). I thank David Law for this reference.

[20] Thio 2021.

[21] On the latter, see Green 2010, 2018; Feldman 1996.

[22] Thio 2021, p. 288.

[23] Jackson and Dawood 2022.

Gebeye's recent book on African constitutionalism emphasizes legal syncretism—the merger of influences from above and below in specific constitutions.[24] It seems to me clear, though, that similar syncretism can be found well beyond Africa.[25]

The point here is not to disparage claims about values that can be found in Asian or African constitutionalism. Those values can indeed be found there and often feature more prominently in these regions' constitutions than they do in Northern constitutions today. So, for example, to signal the different ways of balancing religious and liberal constitutionalism we might describe Sri Lanka's constitution as Buddhist with liberal characteristics, Malaysia's as Islamic with liberal characteristics, and Ireland's as liberal with Roman Catholic characteristics.[26] Obviously I use this formulation to anticipate the more prominent one, the rule of law with Chinese characteristics, which perhaps might better be put as socialist with rule of law characteristics. Indeed, Thio's detailed discussion of Chinese constitutionalism contains a fair amount of material from which one could conclude that Chinese constitutionalism does have some liberal elements embedded in it (particularly in the role that what she calls popular constitutionalism plays in it).[27]

The key point here is historicist. Asian values and the varieties of constitutionalism Thio identifies are found in Northern constitutional thinking from its origins to today. Their instantiation in Northern (and Southern) constitutions varies over time. It may well be, for example, that as of the late twentieth century "Asian" constitutions gave more emphasis to citizens' and governments' duties and less to individual autonomy than did Northern constitutions at that time. It is an analytic mistake to take such differences in emphasis as capturing something essential about Northern and Southern constitutionalism—and therefore an analytic mistake to contend that there are distinctive regional constitutionalisms reflecting distinctively regional values.

To be clear: my argument is not that global South *perspectives* on constitutionalism are not different from global North perspectives. In my understanding global South perspectives ask the "subordination" question: how are domination and subordination manifested in the objects of our inquiry? Those objects can and should include constitutional systems of the global North. Rather my argument is that global South *constitutions* are not categorically different from global North ones.

---

[24] See Gebeye 2021.

[25] The literature on "imposed" constitutions, for example, could readily be recast as dealing with constitutional syncretism. For a recent introduction, see Albert et al. 2019.

[26] Thio 2021 offers the example of Iran as a thoroughly religious constitution with no liberal characteristics. For purposes of the present discussion of regional constitutionalisms I think it sufficient to note that that example might illustrate theocratic constitutionalism but not Asian constitutionalism.

[27] See Thio 2021, pp. 302–03.

2.4 A Skeptical Conclusion

The burden of this chapter has been to develop a structure for classifying varieties of constitutionalism by taking constitutionalism as the object of concern, identifying defining features of constitutionalism (entrenchment and judicial review), and allocating adjectives to those features.

That, though, might have things backwards. Scholars attach adjectives to the word "constitutionalism" because they believe that doing so illuminates the specific topic with which they are concerned. The adjective ties that form of constitutionalism to other nouns to which the adjective is attached. So, for example, Asian constitutionalism is part of a conceptual domain that includes Asian art, Asian literature, and Asian values; democratic constitutionalism is part of a conceptual domain that includes democratic politics and democratic culture. Seen in this way, we can classify varieties of constitutionalism no better than we can classify those other nouns—which is to say, perhaps, that Borges's system of classifying animals might provide a better model than mine.

References

Acharya A (2010) Asia is Not One. Journal of Asian Studies 69:1001–1013.
Ackerman B (2019) Revolutionary Constitutions: Charismatic Leadership and the Rule of Law. Harvard University Press, Cambridge.
Albert R (2019) Constitutional Amendments: Making, Breaking, and Changing Constitutions. Oxford University Press, Oxford.
Albert R, Contiades X, Fotiadou A (2019) The Law and Legitimacy of Imposed Constitutions. Routledge, Oxfordshire.
Borges JL (1964) The Analytical Language of John Wilkins. In: Other Inquisitions (Simms RLC (transl.)). University of Texas Press.
Feldman S (1996) Please Don't Wish Me a Merry Christmas: A Critical History of the Separation of Church and State. NYU Press, New York.
Gebeye BA (2021) A Theory of African Constitutionalism. Oxford University Press, Oxford.
Ghai Y (2016) Constitutionalism: African Perspectives. In: Singh MP (ed) The Indian Yearbook of Comparative Law 2016. Oxford University Press, Oxford.
Green SK (2010) The Second Disestablishment: Church and State in Nineteenth Century America. Oxford University Press, Oxford.
Green SK (2018) The Third Disestablishment: Church, State, and American Culture, 1940–1975. Oxford University Press, Oxford.
Jackson VC, Dawood Y (2022) Constitutionalism and a Right to Effective Government? Cambridge University Press, Toronto.
Kennedy D (1982) The Stages of the Decline of the Public/Private Distinction. University of Pennsylvania Law Review 130:1349–1357.
Larsen SR (2021) Varieties of Constitutionalism in the European Union. Modern Law Review 84:477–502.
Law DS (2016) Constitutional Archetypes. Texas Law Review 95:153–253.
Levitsky S, Ziblatt D (2018) How Democracies Die. Crown Publishing, New York City.
Roach K (2001) The Supreme Court on Trial: Judicial Activism or Democratic Dialogue? Irwin Law, Toronto.

Roznai Y (2017) Unconstitutional Constitutional Amendments: The Limits of Amendment Powers. Oxford University Press, Oxford.
Thio L (2021) Varieties of Constitutionalism in Asia. Asian Journal of Comparative Law 16:285–310.
Tushnet M (2007) Weak Courts, Strong Rights: Judicial Review and Social Welfare Rights in Comparative Perspective. Princeton University Press, Princeton.
Unger R (1987) False Necessity. Cambridge University Press, Cambridge.
Weill R (2018) Secession and the Prevalence of Both Militant Democracy and Eternity Clauses Worldwide. Cardozo Law Review 40:905–990.

Chapter 3
Republican Constitutionalism: Freedom as Non-domination and the Democratic Challenge to Liberalism

Thibault Carrère

Contents

Abstract Is constitutionalism irredeemably liberal? Constitutionalism is often defined as the limitation of power by the Constitution in order to preserve freedom. As such, it is often associated with liberalism, insofar as the latter places freedom at the foundation of all good government. The emergence of constitutionalism is therefore part of a broader history: that of the advent of liberalism. As such, liberal constitutionalism is based on two fundamental elements: natural rights and the existence of an alleged neutral and impartial power—constitutional judges—capable of protecting them. This contribution seeks to qualify this observation. It will show that another philosophy—republicanism—allows us to think constitutionalism differently. Based on a renewed definition of freedom (freedom as non-domination) and a renewed history of legal modernity, republicanism aims to demonstrate that constitutionalism can only protect freedom if it is part of a broader democratic and argumentative logic. This is why republicanism emphasises the ability of elected institutions and the people to protect the Constitution.

Keywords Constitution · Constitutional interpretation · Democracy · Disagreement · Freedom · Liberalism · Republicanism

---

T. Carrère (✉)
Department of Law, Avignon University, Avignon, France
e-mail: thibault.carrere@univ-avignon.fr

M. De Visser et al. (eds.), *European Yearbook of Constitutional Law 2024*, European Yearbook of Constitutional Law 6, https://doi.org/10.1007/978-94-6265-699-4_3

3.1 Introduction

> Here then is one moral implicit in the story I have told: it is remarkably difficult to avoid falling under the spell of our own intellectual heritage. As we analyse and reflect on our normative concepts, it is easy to become bewitched into believing that the ways of thinking about them bequeathed to us by the mainstream of our intellectual traditions must be *the* ways of thinking about them.
>
> Quentin Skinner[1]

Constitutionalism can be defined as the protection of individual freedom by the Constitution. From this perspective, constitutionalism is often viewed through a liberal and Lockean prism: liberty comes first and government is limited in the sense that it must respect the private sphere of each individual. This private sphere consists of natural rights, which every organ of the State must respect. Thus, the logical outcome of constitutionalism is the advent of constitutional justice and judicial review. Fortunately, nothing obliges us to think of constitutionalism within this liberal framework. While it is undeniable that constitutionalism has something to do with liberty, this does not mean that it is necessarily liberal. To put it another way, if when we talk about constitutionalism, we are talking about the ways in which the constitution can help to protect liberty, then we have to consider the different conceptions of liberty that exist. More specifically, this study aims to show that alongside the liberal definition of liberty, there is also a republican definition, outlining a renewed approach to constitutionalism. It will therefore be necessary to study the characteristics of liberal constitutionalism (Sect. 3.1.1) and then to analyse how republicanism has emerged as a critical discourse to this dominant paradigm (Sect. 3.1.2).

3.1.1 The Characteristics of Liberal Constitutionalism

Liberal constitutionalism is based on several ideas and arguments that can be grouped around two themes. Firstly, liberalism is based on the existence of pre-political or natural rights. Liberalism considers that certain legal rules exist independently of any specific legal order. These rights protect a private sphere that the State cannot reach. Consequently, all organs of the State must respect these rights, which pre-exist any political deliberation. From this point of view, rights are not the result of a particular political deliberation but, on the contrary, a way to "trump"[2] it. Moreover, this liberal approach has several consequences. The first is that rights are seen by liberals solely as norms, and their consequences are deemed to be the result of strict legal work. This means that liberal authors often regard rights as principles of justice, independent of any idea of the good.[3] In so doing, liberalism tends to deny the moral

---

[1] Skinner 1998, p. 116.

[2] Dworkin 1984, p. 153.

[3] Rawls 1988.

and political dimension of rights in favour of an alleged legal neutrality. The second consequence is that, within liberal philosophy, there is no necessary link between freedom and democracy.[4] Classical liberal writers rejected democracy in the name of representative government. Moreover, many of them defended forms of enlightened despotism.[5]

Secondly, this liberal approach of rights leads to the attribution of a fundamental role to courts. Since rights are simply legal instruments and individuals must be protected from interference by political bodies, it is up to the judge to guarantee these rights against all powers, including the legislature.[6] Moreover, since rights are considered to be conditions for good political deliberation, their implementation by constitutional courts would be a guarantee of democracy rather than an attack on it.[7] From this point of view, constitutional courts would therefore be both the final stage in the evolution of constitutionalism and the ultimate guarantee of a democracy that fully complies with the requirements of liberalism.

3.1.2 The Emergence of Republican Constitutionalism

From the 1960s onwards, a major epistemological development in the history of political ideas—*the linguistic turn*[8]—led to the questioning of the liberal hegemony in the understanding of modernity. In constitutional history, this challenge led to a relativisation of the liberal origins of modern constitution (particularly the Constitution of the United States). Until then, the reference work was that of Louis Hartz,[9] who presented a "naturally liberal"[10] America largely imbued with the liberal philosophy of John Locke.[11] The Machiavellian Moment[12] remains the standard work for understanding republicanism in the modern era. It shows that at the origin of modernity, alongside the liberal language largely based on a legal vocabulary, another language emerged. This second language described as republican and based on the concept of virtue would have had a decisive influence on the English and American revolutions.

---

[4] "It is that liberty in this sense is not incompatible with some kinds of autocracy, or at any rate with the absence of self-government. Liberty in this sense is principally concerned with the area of control, not with its source. Just as a democracy may, in fact, deprive the individual citizen of a great many liberties which he might have in some other form of society, so it is perfectly conceivable that a liberal-minded despot would allow his subjects a large measure of personal freedom [...] Freedom in this sense is not, at any rate logically, connected with democracy or self-government." Berlin 1958, pp. 21–22.

[5] Nowadays, this liberal trend is based on the theme of epistocracy. See Brennan 2016.

[6] See, for example, Dworkin 1977.

[7] See Dworkin 1981; Rousseau 1995; Pasquino 2014.

[8] Rorty 1992, p. 1.

[9] Hartz 1955.

[10] Michaut and Michelman 2010, p. 3.

[11] Sunstein 1988, p. 1540.

[12] Pocock 1975. See also Pocock 1985.

This discourse does not focus on the legal dimension of freedom but on its ethical and political dimensions. From this perspective, it is no longer clear that constitutionalism is intrinsically and exclusively liberal. As far as the American Revolution is concerned, historians such as Bernard Bailyn[13] and Gordon Stewart Wood[14]—as well as philosophers such as Hannah Arendt[15]—have been pointing to the republican origins of the American Constitution. This rediscovery of the modern heritage of republicanism was extended in the work of historian and philosopher Quentin Skinner.[16] Contemporary republicanism is now seen both as the reconstruction of a lost heritage and as a contemporary normative proposition.

This "republican revival"[17] has led to a renewal of republicanism philosophy.[18] Like liberalism, republican normative philosophy aims to be centred on liberty.[19] However, republican authors consider the liberal definition of "freedom as non-interference" to be insufficient.[20] Republicanism defines freedom as the absence of domination, which refers to the idea of *arbitrary* interference.[21] This concept differs from freedom as non-interference in two respects. Firstly, there are cases where there can be domination without interference, *i.e.,* cases where we are not free, even though we are not hindered.[22] This is the case whenever we are subject to the arbitrary will of a person without that person interfering with our actions. This enabled republican philosophers to take social domination into account.[23] The most enlightening example is the republican defence of political funding regulation. The argument is that regulating political funding ensures that no individual has a disproportionate influence on political life compared to another. Secondly, there are cases where there is interference without domination, all cases where the intervention of the public authorities is legitimate, *i.e.*, is not arbitrary.[24] Thus, a law will not be considered infringing freedom if citizens can participate in its drafting and control its application. Contrary to liberal philosophy, this implies a necessary link between freedom and democracy.[25] Therefore, from a republican perspective, the law is not inherently prejudicial to freedom. State intervention is even necessary to prevent any situation of domination, even if this reduces individuals' capacity for choice. The aim of republicanism is to protect the social dimension of citizenship against unwanted

---

[13] Bailyn 1967.

[14] Wood 1969.

[15] Arendt 1963.

[16] Skinner 1978a; Skinner 1978b; Skinner 1981; Skinner 1998, Skinner 2008b.

[17] Sunstein 1988.

[18] Spitz 1995, p. 9; Spitz 2005

[19] Pettit 1997.

[20] Skinner 1984; Pettit 2011.

[21] Pettit 1997, pp. 51–79; Spitz 1995, p. 180; Pettit 2008, p. 102.

[22] Pettit 2009, pp. 44–45.

[23] "It is of great importance in a republic not only to guard the society against the oppression of its rulers, but to guard one part of the society against the injustice of the other part." Madison 1788.

[24] Pettit 1997, p. 57; Skinner 2008b.

[25] Pettit 2012.

or barely perceptible forms of power, such as the power of the market. This is why, from a republican point of view, the concepts of equality and freedom cannot be contradictory; they are complementary.[26]

The republican revival has had a considerable influence on legal scholars. Once the republican origin of the 1787 Constitution had been revealed, it enabled certain American constitutionalists to propose new interpretations of the American Constitution and new representations of the legal order. In short, a new legal theory emerged. Taking republican philosophy into account has enabled legal scholars to update their reflections on the importance of rights, on the justification of judicial review, and on the relationship between the individual and the collective, between liberty and equality. In the same way, British legal scholars, on the occasion of the adoption of the Human Rights Act, have taken over this reflection on republicanism. They questioned the risks posed by the possible implementation of judicial review on their model of constitutionalism traditionally based on political accountability and parliamentary sovereignty.[27] The many international and collective works on the relationship between law and republicanism are convincing evidence of the existence of a republican legal theory[28] which has led to a renewed conception of constitutionalism.

Contemporary republicanism began as a critical discourse. Republican authors question the two main attributes of liberal constitutionalism that we have identified: rights and constitutional justice. This liberal constitutionalism would not make it possible to protect individual freedom, in particular because it would tend to remove them from the democratic exercise of power, in favour of a glorified role for judges. This judicial supremacy would also have an effect on legal doctrine itself, which no longer produces a philosophy of law that genuinely asks the question of autonomy.[29] Roberto Unger even goes so far as to suggest, in a famous phrase, that this "discomfort with democracy" is one of the "dirty little secrets of contemporary jurisprudence".[30] Republican writers have taken up this challenge head-on by placing the question of democracy at the heart of their constitutionalism. They intend to propose a new link between democracy and constitutionalism by excluding any recourse to pre-political rights and by denying the constitutional judge the role of regent.[31] From then on, republicanism is not just a critique of liberal hegemony, it is a proposal for a refoundation of the ideal of constitutional democracy.

Firstly, the liberal conception of constitutionalism tends to separate irremediably the field of law from that of politics. The law is idealised, as if it were not the result of a political exercise. Thus, rights are assumed to be capable, in a neutral way, of limiting political power. Republicanism is opposed to such a drastic distinction. It starts from the principle that what characterises our democratic societies is *disagreement*. Far

---

26 Spitz 1995, p. 194; Spitz 2000.

27 Tomkins 2005; Bellamy 2007.

28 For example, Besson and Marti 2009; Niederberger and Schink 2013. For a general overview, see Carrère 2025.

29 Waldron 2009b, pp. 170–171.

30 Unger 1996, pp. 72–73.

31 Habermas 1997, p. 304.

from subjecting the exercise of politics to substantial control, exercised by a judge and based on pre-political rights, republicanism defends the idea that it is the exercise of power by the greatest number that enables individuals to be free. Republican democratic theory will therefore be based on a procedural conception of democracy, leaving as much room as possible for the expression of democratic disagreement in deliberation (2). Secondly, liberal constitutionalism tends to neglect the role of individuals in the development of constitutional law. This role is often reduced to their ability to appeal to the constitutional court to protect their rights. From a republican point of view, the individual is only free if he or she lives in a free state. As a result, republicanism embarks on the path of popular constitutionalism, because it makes all individuals the ultimate guardians of freedom as non-domination (3).

3.2 The Political Nature of Republican Constitutionalism

Far from accepting a strictly legal definition of constitutionalism, republicans rely on its resolutely political dimension. They also stress the need to take account of the "circumstances of politics",[32] *i.e.,* disagreement and joint action, in the context of interpreting the Constitution. This goes against liberal constitutionalism that reserves to the courts the task of protecting the Constitution (Sect. 3.2.1). This conception of constitutionalism is part of a broader reflection on democracy. From a republican perspective, individual freedom depends on the ability of individuals to deliberate together. However, this democratic deliberation must meet certain requirements if it is to be considered necessary for freedom as non-domination (Sect. 3.2.2).

3.2.1 Republicanism and Political Constitutionalism

As we have seen, liberal constitutionalism refers to the essential idea of limiting power, in particular by subjecting all state powers to the Constitution. This definition is influenced by a liberal conception of the relationship between individuals and the state, according to which the rights and freedoms of individuals must be preserved from interference through a judge.[33] Proponents of political constitutionalism have attempted to define constitutionalism differently. For Jeremy Waldron, constitutionalism should refer less to the idea of limiting power than to a constitution's ability to establish powers.[34] For Richard Bellamy, political constitutionalism is characterised by its ability to constitutionalise the democratic process. In his words, "It is both constitutional, offering a due process, and constitutive, able to

---

[32] Waldron 1999b, pp. 101–106.

[33] Raynaud 2003, p. 266.

[34] Waldron 2009a, pp. 267–282.

reform itself".[35] Republican constitutionalism is therefore political in two senses: on the one hand, it insists on the establishment of a political system enabling democracy to be organised institutionally (Sect. 3.2.1.1). On the other hand, it leaves it to the democratic debate, to determine the meaning of the Constitution (Sect. 3.2.1.2). Republicanism provides a normative basis for this political constitutionalism, notably by placing particular emphasis on freedom as non-domination, as opposed to freedom as non-interference.[36]

3.2.1.1 The Political Foundation of the Constitution

Liberal authors develop a singular conception of the Constitution, which unfolds in two fundamental propositions: firstly, the Constitution is a limit on political power; secondly, the Constitution is a charter of rights protected by the judge. The republican authors have an opposite vision.

First, the Constitution is not just a limit on political power; it is also an enabling legal act. The Constitution is seen as the organisation of the deliberative structure of society. It is about empowering political bodies, but also directly or indirectly, the people. The distinction between the Constitution as a limit and the Constitution as empowerment seems to overlap with the distinction between liberal and republican conceptions of freedom. The Constitution as limit corresponds to freedom as non-interference or negative freedom.[37] In this sense, the individual is free as long as he is independent of the authorities and the latter do not impose on him any specific "idea of the good".[38] From this perspective, the Constitution exists to limit possible interference by the State. Conversely, freedom as non-domination, which is not an exclusively positive freedom, corresponds to the constitution as empowerment. In this republican perspective, public power, through the law, does not interfere with individual freedom, but rather guarantees it. In this sense, individuals are free because the Constitution gives them "legal status"[39] and empowers them to exercise power. The Constitution thus enables individuals to exercise their autonomy, and not simply to be independent. The proponents of political constitutionalism thus refer directly to this definition of freedom as non-domination.[40] Viewing the constitution primarily as an empowerment act leads to an intrinsic link between constitutionalism and democracy.

Secondly, and as a corollary, republicanism puts institutional issues back at the centre of constitutional thinking. It therefore calls into question the strictly judicial nature of the Constitution. This is innovative, particularly in France, where institutional issues have been largely neglected by legal scholars, who have defended

---

[35] Bellamy 2007, p. 5.

[36] Bellamy 2013, p. 1017.

[37] Berlin 1958.

[38] Rawls 1988.

[39] Spitz 2009, p. 21.

[40] Tomkins 2005, p. 61; Bellamy 2007, p. 145; Bellamy 2013, p. 1017.

the idea of a "new constitutional law" based essentially on case law.[41] For these scholars, institutional considerations would be known and would no longer require the enlightenment of constitutionalists. The latter should focus on constitutional litigation. Republicanism takes issue with this renewed conception of constitutional law, not because it denies the growing role of the constitutional court, but because it makes its study part of the overall "political system"[42] established by the Constitution. In so doing, republicanism opposes "judicial supremacy",[43] which in their view is based on a form of legal epistocracy, a "juristocracy".[44] This juristocracy covers two propositions: any constitutional problem can be solved by a constitutional judge, and no constitutional problem is really solved until it has been solved by a judge.[45] Ultimately, judicial supremacy is the idea that the meaning of the Constitution must be determined by judges. This proposition is rejected by republicanism. Thus, even if differences are perceptible, republican legal scholars all have in common an interest in constitutional interpretation outside the courts.[46] In that perspective, the concept of Constitution is broadened beyond its written form and constitutional court decisions. In this way, it includes the study of institutions and procedures, and non-written constitutional law.

3.2.1.2 The Political Implementation of the Constitution

For republican authors, constitutionalism can only be understood within a "philosophical and political doctrine of democracy".[47] This requirement is difficult to meet by liberal constitutionalism, which tends to consider that judicial protection of rights resolves the democratic question. In order to meet this requirement, republican authors consider that, by virtue of the political nature of the Constitution, the guarantee of constitutional principles should also be political. Indeed, if constitutionalism is to be part of a more general theory of democracy, it is inconsistent to leave the implementation of the Constitution to a judge. If the Constitution is open to different interpretations, it is necessary to give a body capable of representing and resolving disagreement the task of interpreting the Constitution as a last resort. Therefore, republican authors place their trust in political institutions rather than judges. Inversely, liberal doctrine tends to devalue the role of Parliament in protecting the Constitution. The main reason for this liberal criticism was the need to protect the Constitution against the encroachment of all powers, including the legislature. In

[41] See Favoreu 1990; Rousseau 1990. For an historical analysis, see Viala 2008; Pinon 2010; Manouguian 2022.

[42] Bellamy 2007, p. 5.

[43] Kramer 2004, p. 221.

[44] Hirschl 2007.

[45] Tomkins 2010, p. 3.

[46] Ackerman 1993. On Ackerman's link with republicanism, see his concept of "liberal republicanism", pp. 29–33.

[47] Raynaud 2003, p. 271.

response to this liberal criticism, republican authors renewed their attachment to the political implementation of the Constitution. This renewal involved the "deliberative path"[48] taken by contemporary republican writers.[49] In this respect, the republican demonstration is also based on theoretical and empirical arguments.

From a theoretical point of view, while liberals see an independent and impartial body as the ideal place for constitutional interpretation, republicans believe that Parliament is best placed to represent and resolve the democratic disagreement of our pluralist societies. If pluralism is to be taken seriously, the possibility of reasonable (*i.e.*, fair and not artificial) disagreement on constitutional provisions. This disagreement must first be embodied in an institution. In this respect, Parliament has a numerical advantage,[50] enabling it to take many different points of view into account, and an advantage in terms of political equality, enabling it to take all possible positions into account fairly.[51] This disagreement must then be resolved. For republican authors, under the influence of theories of deliberative democracy,[52] the most appropriate place to settle conflicts of interpretation of the Constitution is a deliberative forum. For republicans, the ideal place for deliberation is Parliament rather than the constitutional courts.[53]

From an empirical point of view, they find that, in practice, Parliaments take constitutional argument into account in their deliberations, and that they satisfactorily defend rights in countries without constitutional justice.[54] For Mark Tushnet, the quality of discussions is better in Parliament, and the presence of a constitutional judge only disrupts deliberation.[55] Indeed, either parliamentarians decide to pass the buck to the judge, and not take responsibility for their deliberations;[56] or, all the arguments have already been taken into account during the parliamentary deliberation, in which case the judge's review is redundant, superfluous and even dangerous, since it merely reopens the democratic rift. In that perspective, Bellamy and Waldron compare debates on abortion in the UK and the USA. They consider that the debates in the British Parliament were of a very high standard, both legal and political, and that everyone's arguments were taken into account, including those of a constitutional nature, particularly those relating to rights.[57] This deliberation would have nothing to envy the various deliberations of the Supreme Court of the United

---

[48] Audier 2015, pp. 99–101.

[49] Marti 2006, pp. 244–267.

[50] Bellamy 2007, p. 31; Waldron 2009c, pp. 340–345.

[51] Waldron 1999a, pp. 147–148; Waldron 1999b, pp. 108–114; Bellamy 2007, pp. 212–221.

[52] Habermas 1997, p. 311; Bohman 2008.

[53] Liberal writers have tried to justify the superiority of constitutional courts over parliaments in the name of the deliberative ideal. See Dworkin 1981; Rousseau 1995; Pasquino 2014.

[54] Bellamy 2007, pp. 26–48; Tushnet 2009, pp. 80–82.

[55] Tushnet 2000, p. 57.

[56] Tushnet 2009, pp. 81–82.

[57] Waldron 2003, p. 388; Bellamy 2007, p. 253.

States on this subject. Moreover, judicial deliberation has its disadvantages, since not every type of argument can be raised before it.[58]

3.2.2 Republicanism and Procedural Democracy

From a liberal perspective, the essential guarantee associated with constitutionalism is the protection of rights by the courts. This has the consequence of limiting the scope of deliberation, since certain issues should no longer be subject to democratic discussion. The political exercise is then confined to certain matters, and subjected to the control of a judge. In this context, constitutional courts would compensate for the errors of representative democracy: the risk of confiscation of public power by a grouped majority, the risk of violation of the rights of insular minorities, etc. Constitutional courts would therefore substantially guarantee certain values considered compatible, if not necessary, for the exercise of democracy. The guarantees offered by republicanism are quite different. Unlike liberalism, republicanism insists essentially on procedural guarantees. These guarantees can be described as procedural in that their purpose is not to resolve democratic disagreement. This is explained by the desire to preserve the autonomy of individuals, by leaving the choice of fundamental political solutions open. Nevertheless, the political guarantee of the Constitution, particularly through the institution of parliament, is only conceivable on condition that this institution meets certain requirements. Two requirements are central to the republican defence of political constitutionalism. The first is the legitimacy of political deliberation. This implies that the debate on constitutional provisions must be given within an elected and politically accountable institution (Sect. 3.2.2.1). Also, it must be made within an institution that is inclined to seek a genuine common good and not to give precedence to particular interests (Sect. 3.2.2.2).

3.2.2.1 The Procedural Guarantee of the Legitimacy of the Deliberation

The legitimacy of democratic deliberation rests on two guarantees: voting and accountability. Voting affects the legitimacy of appointments and decision-making, and accountability the legitimacy of the exercise of power. In this respect, it seems that elected institutions, such as a Parliament, because there are subjected to political and legal accountability mechanisms, are better able to conduct democratic deliberation.

With regard to the vote, this guarantee is twofold. Firstly, it lies, upstream of the decision, in the mechanism for appointing representatives likely to participate in interpreting the Constitution and resolving democratic disagreement. This is the elective principle that is best able to ensure that every citizen has an equal say in the composition of the deliberative bodies. Philip Pettit argues that republican democracy

[58] Bellamy 2007, p. 253.

must be "inclusive".[59] This is why he defends proportional representation in the name of freedom as non-domination. Indeed, proportional representation is consistent with the idea of justice, and it also provides protection for minorities by representing them politically and giving them weight in the political coalitions that necessarily result from such elections.[60] Secondly, it resides, at the moment of decision, in the mechanism for resolving the deliberation. This is the majority principle, which is both indispensable, because not all deliberations can end in consensus, and fair, because it is based on the principle of political equality. Republican authors have therefore rehabilitated the majority principle,[61] in particular by calling into question the all too often invoked but insufficiently justified argument of the "tyranny of the majority".[62] Moreover, the use of the majoritarian principle is a remedy for a fundamental evil identified by both classical and contemporary republican authors: the weight of factions.[63]

With regard to political accountability, this guarantee is fundamental. There is a strong link between republicanism and political responsibility, a link that is both historical and analytical. From a historical point of view, it is republicans who are at the origin of the first reflections on political accountability. From an analytical point of view, the principle of political accountability is both the condition of democratic exercise and the essential, if not the only, function of the Constitution.[64] Adam Tomkins, like the historians of the Cambridge School, pioneers of the republican revival, have endeavoured to show that the emergence of political responsibility in the United Kingdom was the work of thinkers using arguments derived from a republican conception of liberty.[65] The principle of responsibility also played a key role in the debates among the framers of the United States Constitution.[66] Originally, republicanism as opposition to the monarchical form of power is what led to the emergence of accountability.[67] If power becomes the "public affair", the *res-publica*, then rulers must be accountable to the public. Madison used the term republic in the sense of representative government. It is this representative regime, the Republic, that makes political accountability necessary if it is not to become tyranny. If the representative mandate means that voters cannot give instructions, or that members of parliament are legally irresponsible for expressing their political will, this does not mean that the representative is not accountable to the people.[68]

---

[59] Pettit 1997, p. 190; Pettit 2012, pp. 197–207.

[60] Pettit 1997, p. 192; Bellamy 2007, p. 237.

[61] Skinner 1998, p. 29; Bellamy 2007, pp. 5–11.

[62] For liberal arguments using the tyranny of the majority to legitimise constitutional justice, see Elster 2014, p. 159; Pasquino 2014, p. 219; Issacharoff 2014, p. 236.

[63] Madison 1787; Hamilton 1787; Skinner 1978b, pp. 60–65 and pp. 177–180.

[64] Tomkins 2005, pp. 1–3.

[65] Tomkins 2005, p. 87. See also Pocock 1975, pp. 477–486.

[66] Borowiak 2011, pp. 27–39.

[67] Waldron 2016, p. 176.

[68] Madison 1787.

3.2.2.2 The Procedural Guarantee of the Authenticity of the Deliberation

Once the legitimacy of democratic deliberation has been guaranteed, its authenticity, *i.e.*, its ability not to be hijacked for the benefit of a few, must also be. This is where a fundamental concept of republicanism—virtue[69] comes into play. The trust placed in elected representatives to discuss the law is only valid if they effectively represent the whole of society. More precisely, to preserve this principle of political equality, representatives must not allow private interests to take precedence over the general interest achieved through deliberation. Virtue is a political and civic principle. If virtue is really a civic commitment,[70] this can be understood in two ways. First, virtue is the need for individuals to participate in political life. But it is also, if not above all, the need for those who govern, as well as those who are governed, to be oriented towards the pursuit of the common good.[71] Virtue is therefore the ability of individuals to distinguish the general interest from their particular interests.[72] In this it is the exact opposite of corruption, which is the tendency to confuse the general interest with personal interests. Some liberal authors have seen fit to see in this concept of virtue a moral dimension that undermines individual freedom. In short, republican writers would replace the advantages of judicial protection of rights with a moral belief in a good and virtuous man.[73] This criticism is misguided. Acts of corruption, in the legal sense, are not just acts of personal enrichment. As Jean-Fabien Spitz points out, they are also a "manipulation of these [public] functions to place oneself more or less above the common law".[74] In this respect, the fight against corruption aims to protect political equality, which is the only way to ensure that power is exercised in common and that everyone is free. This is why corruption is not a problem of individual morality, but a political problem relating to the common good. This is also why Pocock argues that the Republic proceeds with an "institutionalization of virtù",[75] meaning that republican constitutionalism is based on institutional arrangements designed to limit the risks of corruption, even if this means restricting the choices of individuals. For republicans, freedom is not a faculty, a passion, or even a natural state, but a special legal status.[76] These institutional arrangements are therefore intrinsic elements of freedom as non-domination. From this perspective, republican constitutionalism relies on specific mechanisms to combat corruption.[77] These may be filtering or sanctioning mechanisms to prevent

[69] Viroli 2011, pp. 70–80.

[70] Pettit 2012, pp. 226–227.

[71] Machiavelli 1531, Book 2–II.

[72] Pocock 1975, pp. 183–218; Sunstein 1988, pp. 1547–1548 and pp. 1564–1566; Michelman 1988, pp. 1518–1519; Spitz 1995, p. 252; Pettit 1997, pp. 212–214.

[73] Hayek 1960.

[74] Spitz 1993, p. 167.

[75] Pocock 1975, p. 300.

[76] Spitz 1995, p. 208.

[77] Carrère 2025, pp. 630–673.

individuals defending special interests from participating in decision-making. These days, this includes the legal regimes governing conflicts of interest, incompatibilities and the financing of political life. It may also involve filtering or sanction mechanisms enabling individuals taking part in the decision to do so without being subject to external influence, whether intended or unintended. These days, this includes the legal regimes governing parliamentary incompatibilities and interest groups.

3.3 The Popular Nature of Republican Constitutionalism

Republicanism establishes a direct link between democracy and freedom as non-domination. However, being a thoroughly modern philosophy, republican authors do not defend the idea of a direct democracy. They accept the need for representation. On the other hand, the political representation defended by these authors is not a simple principle of imputation; it must always be exercised under the control of all citizens. This led the republican authors to propose a reflection on the "people". The people are seen as all the individuals living in the same territory.[78] The people are not mythologised, it is not simply a legal fiction, it is perceived in all its diversity. In this respect, republican writers from Machiavelli to Pettit have an almost sociological conception of the people, relying on the opposition of the diversity of opinions to achieve the common good. This has two consequences. Firstly, republican constitutionalism defends a plural conception of the people based on the concept of a mixed constitution rather than that of sovereignty (Sect. 3.3.1). Secondly, if the people are not a fictitious being, but a sociological reality, then they are capable of exercising power. Consequently, some republican authors defend the idea that "the people themselves"[79] should draw up the constitutional text and take part in putting it into practice (Sect. 3.3.2).

3.3.1 Republicanism and Mixed Constitution

At a time when State's sovereignty seems to be being called into question, it is undoubtedly relevant to take an interest in the republican conception of collective power. In this respect, the concept of a mixed constitution, which plays a fundamental role in republican doctrine, is a useful reinforcement, provided that it is updated (Sect. 3.3.1.1). This conception of power has a particular significance in France, where the Republic has often been equated with the unitary and centralised nation-state (Sect. 3.3.1.2).

---

[78] Skinner 1998, pp. 27–29.

[79] Kramer 2004.

3.3.1.1 A Republican Theory of Power

Republicanism must be distinguished from modern political law based on the idea of sovereignty, which is neither a reflection on democracy, even when its holder are the people, nor a defence of individual autonomy. It is therefore because republicanism has a different conception of freedom that it defends a singular theory of power that differs from the liberal diptych of human rights and sovereignty.[80] Linking legality and legitimacy in a specific way, republicanism will update the theory of the mixed constitution that preceded the emergence of sovereignty. This updating will involve taking into account the idea that the people have become the only principle of legitimacy that remains relevant; while at the same time trying to ensure dispersion and balance of powers.

The fundamental point of the theory of the mixed constitution is that it is both about the organisation of power and the legitimacy of power. It is therefore a politico-legal theory as well as a sociological theory. It tends to emphasise the necessary participation of different social groups in the exercise of power. These different forces are not socio-economic, but are determined by the law and the submission to certain statuses. This is particularly perceptible in Polybius' writings, who sees in each of the great institutions of the Roman Republic—the consuls, the Senate and the people—the respective monarchical, aristocratic and democratic manifestation of its organisation.[81] Machiavelli proposes a less pacified interpretation of the ancient ideal. He argues that the virtue of the Roman Republic lay less in the constitutional benefits of the three types of regimes mentioned above, than in the institutional organisation of conflicts of interest between the Great and the People.[82] Pocock have also highlighted the link between republican philosophy and the invocation of mixed government during the English Revolution of the seventeenth century.[83] For Montesquieu, the genius of the English constitution was not so much in separating the three powers, which were shared between three institutions, as in the fact that these three institutions represented three categories of individuals who were going to oppose each other because their interests diverged.[84]

The republican theory of the mixed constitution has taken various forms, but has been greatly weakened by the emergence of sovereignty, and by the democratisation of western societies. Contemporary republican writers have nonetheless attempted to reconcile this ancient ideal of a mixed constitution with theories of popular sovereignty. They are thus democratising the republican ideal. In this way, republicanism attempts to avoid the subjectivist pitfall of the existence of an idealised will

---

80 Viala 2010, pp. 44–68.

81 Polybe 2005, pp. 549–558; Machiavelli 1531, pp. 383–388.

82 Machiavelli distinguishes two groups of persons in every republic. "Great" (*Grandi*), synonymous with "nobles" or the "elite", refers to the holders of economic and political power, whereas "People" (*Popolo*) refers to those who are subjected to such power. Machiavelli 1531, pp. 390–391. For an analysis, see McCormick 2001.

83 Pocock 1975, pp. 381–400.

84 Montesquieu 1748, Book XI, Chapter VI.

of an untraceable people and the objectivist pitfall of the existence of an ideal law disconnected from any political will.[85] To do this, they will use Habermas' philosophy. For Habermas, popular sovereignty is above all a "procedure".[86] This means that it is neither substantial, *i.e.*, based on an *a priori* moral law, nor formal, *i.e.*, built on a decision. It resides in the deliberative procedure itself. Democratic theory is decoupled from the idea of popular sovereignty understood as the decision of the people. Instead, it is based on the ability of each individual to take part in democratic deliberation, whether formal, within public institutions, or informal, within the public sphere. Republican authors have drawn upon this philosophy, in order to update their theory of the mixed constitution. Their starting point is the ideal of freedom as non-domination. No individual or group of individuals can impose their will on others arbitrarily, *i.e.*, without their participation or control. Unlimited sovereignty on the part of a collective subject would then be an attack on freedom as non-domination.[87] The republican authors therefore sought a form of power that would allow everyone's opinion to be taken into account on an equal basis. This was the original goal of the theories of the mixed constitution. The idea of intersubjectivity is already present, insofar as power does not reside in a particular body, or in an idealised social group, but in the confrontation between different individuals, or groups of individuals. The challenge of democratic deliberation is then to transform these interests into arguments that are acceptable to all, and thus ultimately to transcend the sum of individual interests in order to achieve a genuine common good.[88] The democratisation of mixed constitution theories lies in the fact that there is no longer any status, and therefore only equal individuals who will participate in this deliberation.[89]

3.3.1.2 A Republican Theory of the State

In republicanism, there is not a unitary people exercising a will, but a plurality of individuals engaged in deliberative activity. Republicanism thus makes it possible to apprehend different *demoi* who, by engaging in deliberative practice, define themselves in a continuous manner.[90] From this perspective, an individual can belong to different spheres, *i.e.* possess several citizenships. Mixed constitution seems particularly relevant for thinking about different organisations of power, such as the Federation or the European Union. Therefore, if there is a republican theory of the State, it is, in effect, a theory of the trivialisation of the State phenomenon. This means two things.

---

[85] Bellamy 2003, p. 167.

[86] Habermas 1997, pp. 325–327.

[87] Pettit 2012, p. 22.

[88] Spitz 1997, p .267.

[89] Mongoin 2012, pp. 320–321.

[90] Bellamy 2003, p. 184.

Firstly, the nation-state is not the sole framework for deploying the republican ideal. This runs counter to certain nationalist discourses, particularly in France, which equate the Republic with the nation-state. These nationalist views are based on two arguments. On the one hand, there is the idea that the Republic can only be suitable for small states,[91] insofar as a large state would imply too great a diversity of interests, which could not lead to the emergence of a common good. This argument has long been undermined, particularly by the American revolutionaries, who took up the idea of the "extended republic" already present in Machiavelli's writings.[92] For Madison, for example, it was precisely the extension of the territory of the republic that enabled the defence of a common good, and therefore the protection of everyone's freedom. Why? Because the extension of the republic is accompanied by a multiplication of the interests involved, which ensures that no one interest can dominate.[93] The second argument is the idea that power can only be exercised within a nation-state. This argument has no value, especially historically, because the concept of the Republic emerged long before that of the State. The concept of a mixed constitution emerged before that of sovereignty, and is therefore particularly relevant for thinking about a phenomenon such as the European Union,[94] which seems to call into question this very concept of sovereignty.

Secondly, republicanism seems incompatible with unitary and centralised organisation. The federal system even seems to be particularly suited to the requirements of republicanism. Indeed, strengthening the local exercise of democracy seems particularly compatible with the ideal of freedom as non-domination, for at least two reasons. The first reason is that it makes the democratic system more complex, above all by reinforcing the republican requirement of the separation of powers; it then makes it possible to encourage the expression of disagreement, which reinforces the deliberative nature of democracy; it also makes it possible to represent the people by different means and in different places; finally, it makes it possible to preserve a sphere of autonomy for individuals, by encouraging proximity with the institutions and by multiplying the possibilities for the people to participate in the development of legal rules. The second reason why federalism is particularly compatible with freedom as non-domination is that virtue is more likely to emerge at local level. This is why Maurizio Viroli defends the idea of a federal organisation, making the communes the privileged place for civic commitment.[95] To do this, he draws on classic authors such as Alexis de Tocqueville.[96] De Tocqueville emphasised the communal duties that each citizen owed to the community, which were part of patriotism, in other words, virtue. Virtue is thus a bottom-up movement that starts with the closest government: the commune, and can then extend, in Viroli's

---

[91] Montesquieu 1748, Book VII—Chapter XVI.

[92] Mongoin 2012, p. 553.

[93] Madison 1788. Madison adopts an argument found in Harrington. See Harrington 1656, p. 244.

[94] For a republican reading of the institutional organisation of the European Union, see Johnson 2018.

[95] Viroli 2011, pp. 107–112.

[96] De Tocqueville 1835/1992, pp. 65–75.

thinking, to the emergence of a European patriotism. Tocqueville's associationism and his defence of freedom of assembly should also be understood in the context of this upward movement.[97] Federalism is a means of fostering local democracy and therefore, ultimately, freedom as non-domination.

3.3.2 Republicanism and Popular Constitutionalism

While freedom as non-domination is linked to the democratic ideal, republican authors vigorously reject any idea of direct democracy. However, republican authors never intended to reject the influence of the people. Since the people are the sole source of legitimacy for all powers, they must ultimately be the masters of their own destiny. This is why it is not surprising that republican writers were attracted to the concept of popular constitutionalism. Liberal constitutionalism limits citizen intervention in the name of liberal values to the advantage of courts. In reaction to this, republicanism defends Parliament's ability to guarantee respect for the Constitution. It also rehabilitates the role of the people in drafting and implementing the Constitution. In this respect, some republican authors refocused their criticism of liberal constitutionalism on the people's ability to take control of the Constitution. Therefore, the people should be at the origin of the constitutional text (Sect. 3.3.2.1), but also at the origin of constitutional interpretation (Sect. 3.3.2.2).

3.3.2.1 The Popular Foundation of the Constitution

Liberal constitutionalism is based on a paradox.[98] Even though it is particularly suspicious of interventions by the people, it must, in some of its manifestations, presuppose that the Constitution stems from the will of the people. This allows liberal authors to justify the intervention of a constitutional judge who is supposed to oppose the will of the representatives residing in the law with the will of the people residing in the Constitution. However, the people are very rarely at the origin of the constitutional text or its revisions. Liberalism therefore reduces the role of the people to a minimum, notably because of the risk of the tyranny of the majority, which is why, for example, a large part of the legal scholars rejects referendums. Conversely, both republicanism defends the possibility for citizens to participate in the drafting of the constitution.

By trivialising constituent power, republicanism intends to reduce the distance that might exist between the individuals behind the constitutional text and those subject to it. Thus, republican authors have criticised excessive constitutional rigidity insofar as it constitutes a limit to the appropriation by the people of the most important norms of the legal system. This is notably the case of the United States and the excessive

[97] De Tocqueville 1835/1992, p. 212.

[98] Waldron 2016, pp. 38–41.

rigidity of the Constitution of 1787.[99] It is also the case with British authors, who, in a much more radical approach, deny any distinction between constituent and constituted power, in the name of the sovereignty of Parliament and indirectly that of the people.[100] If there is no constituent power, republican authors justify this by the need for a continuous link between representatives and the represented, legally embodied in the principle of political accountability.[101] This trivialisation can also be understood from a temporal point of view, as the need for contemporary citizens to submit to rules that they themselves have chosen. By rejecting the very idea of tradition, republican authors reveal an anti-metaphysical conception of the people. This argument can be found in the writings of classical republicans such as Jefferson, Paine and De Condorcet.[102]

As Franck Michelman points out, the "impermanence" of the constitution among republicanism is linked to its deliberative conception of democracy.[103] Unlike in liberalism, the validity of the constitution does not depend on its conformity to natural law, but on effective deliberation between the members of the political community.[104] Thus, republicanism is based on a civic commitment on the part of citizens. In order to move towards freedom as non-domination, political participation must have deliberative qualities, which is why Pettit rejects what he calls populist democracy. From then on, republican authors developed mechanisms enabling the people to participate in the constituent power while respecting this deliberative ideal. In the name of freedom as non-domination, they will defend the popular initiative in constitutional matters[105] and the creation of independent deliberative bodies.[106] In this respect, the influence of digital technologies can promote the exercise of republican citizenship.[107] They will also dwell on more informal deliberative mechanisms, again drawing upon the philosophy of Habermas, stressing the need for a dynamic civil society that they see as a contemporary manifestation of the concept of virtue.[108]

---

[99] Michelman 1988; Sunstein 1988, p. 20; Tushnet 2000, p. 175.

[100] Bellamy 2007, p. 113.

[101] Tomkins 2005, pp. 1–5; Bellamy 2007, pp. 10–11 and p. 239.

[102] Jefferson 1789; De Condorcet 1791, pp. 3–4; Paine 1791–1792, p. 298.

[103] Michelman 1988, pp. 1516–1517.

[104] Marti 2006, p. 286.

[105] Marti 2006, p. 308.

[106] Marti 2006, pp. 310–312; Ackerman and Fishkin 2002.

[107] Marti 2006, p. 301.

[108] In this sense, institutions must develop the virtue of citizens, enabling them to engage in this informal deliberation. See Spitz 1995, pp. 252–254; Pettit 1997, p. 329; Pettit 2012, pp. 163–164; Marti 2006, pp. 297–300; Ovejero 2008, pp. 236–238.

3.3.2.2 The Popular Implementation of the Constitution

However, republicanism does not stop with the drafting of the constitutional text by the people. No doubt influenced by legal realism,[109] republicanism clearly understand that adopting a text does not resolve disagreement. In this perspective, republicanism identifies two ways in which the people can produce interpretations of the Constitution.[110]

On the one hand, citizens would produce interpretations of the Constitution by settling conflicts between institutions, through the exercise of their political rights. In short, the people would produce an interpretation of the Constitution even when this is not the purpose of their intervention. As such, it rejects the liberal perspective of judicial supremacy in matters of constitutional interpretation. From this perspective, republican authors insist on the plurality of interpreters of the Constitution and on the fact that few constitutions establish a hierarchy between these different interpreters.[111] Moreover, this judicial supremacy would constitute an oligarchic drift because it would confiscate the interpretation of the constitution from democratic deliberation for the benefit of the judge.[112] Also, judicial supremacy would lead to a decline in the political virtue of citizens, who would be driven to defer to the constitutional judge and no longer take an interest in the common good, in favour of their own particular interests.[113] Constitutions should therefore have a plurality of interpreters and, as a last resort, conflicts of interpretation should be settled by the people themselves. This settlement can be made in various ways: by a president remaining in power, thus sanctioning his interpretation of the Constitution, by a change of parliamentary majority, etc.[114] The limit to this conception of constitutionalism is the following: how can we identify the moments when the people settle conflicts of interpretation, especially if they do so by performing an act that can have several meanings? The problem with this theory is that this so-called will of the people is often reconstructed *a posteriori*, by representatives, as an argument for legitimising an action that is often contrary to certain legal norms, or may be considered as such. More attractive solutions therefore need to be found, which would make it easier to identify a popular interpretation of the Constitution. In that perspective, Roosevelt defended the possibility of a direct vote by the people to override a Supreme Court decision.[115]

On the other hand, the people would produce interpretations of the Constitution by challenging institutional decisions. Popular constitutionalism, in its concern to guarantee the people an influence on the evolution of the meaning of the Constitution, seems to meet certain republican requirements. It revives the concept of *contestation*

---

[109] Michaut and Michelman 2010.

[110] Pettit 2012, pp. 268–273.

[111] Kramer 2001, p. 130; Kramer 2004, p. 227.

[112] Kramer 2004, p. 242; Tushnet 2000, p. 177.

[113] Kramer 2004, p. 228.

[114] Ackerman 1998; Kramer 2004.

[115] Kramer 2004, pp. 216–217.

that is central to contemporary republican philosophy.[116] The contestation[117] theorised by Philip Pettit aims not only to control those in power but also to influence them. It revives Machiavelli's conflictualist tradition of the republic and the principle of a mixed constitution.[118] It also illustrates the fact that, in the end, all political systems are based on the existence of virtuous citizens who participate in public deliberation. This is what Philip Pettit calls "contestatory citizenry".[119] Through informal protest and the organisation of civil society around social movements and demonstrations, people fight for the recognition of new rights. In this way, they played a key role in shaping the interpretation of the Constitution.[120] However, this contestatory citizenry does raise a number of questions. Are all claims legitimate? Are all protests likely to signify the will of the people? Moreover, how can we distinguish between a republican protest and a populist drift in our democracies? Republican authors have not yet cleared up all the ambiguities associated with their attempt to take the people seriously.

Nevertheless, considering the conservative shifts in the composition of constitutional and supreme courts, such as the United States Supreme Court, republicanism provides a compelling basis to for criticising courts' decisions from a democratic perspective. Moreover, republicanism requires us to consider the democratic realisation of our rights. Therefore, republican authors advocate the development of participatory mechanisms.[121] In this respect, citizens' conventions held to discuss complex matters of principle, such as environmental issues or medical aid in dying, can be seen as republican means of deliberating about our rights. Reforming constituent power, creating new deliberative forums, and distancing ourselves from the alleged virtues of constitutional courts: these are all avenues explored by republican constitutionalism.

3.4 Conclusion

While liberalism neglects democracy in order to defend rights, and populism neglects individual freedom in favour of democracy, republicanism attempts to find a third way in which the meaning of the Constitution is always under constant discussion. This discussion is not solely dominated by courts, but extends to political bodies and even the people. As such, disagreement and conflict are central to republican theory. Far from being a theory of political consensus, republicanism seeks the common good through opposition between the different interests and arguments present in society. It is because we are always in disagreement that we cannot leave it to the judge to settle conflicts of interpretation, but must find a democratic resolution to

[116] Pettit 1997, pp. 206–240.
[117] Pettit 2012, pp. 218–220.
[118] Pettit 2012, pp. 220–225.
[119] Pettit 2012, pp. 225–229.
[120] Ackerman 1984; Michelman 1988, p. 1531; Sunstein 1988, p. 40; Ackerman 1998, p. 281.
[121] For example, see Marti 2006, pp. 310–312.

them. Thus, the heart of republican thinking lies in an attempt to reconcile law and politics. This original conception of constitutionalism is based on the definition of freedom as non-domination. It establishes a close link between the political activity of citizens and the preservation of their freedom. From then on, individuals can only be free on condition that they participate actively, directly or indirectly, in public affairs, to ensure that political deliberation is always aimed at the common good. The Constitution therefore preserves freedom insofar as it organises the collective autonomy of the people. Unlike the liberals, the republican authors do not believe that, for everyone to be free, it is sufficient for individuals to be content to protect their rights. In the course of deliberation, individuals must aim for common good that is not reducible to the sum of their particular interests, and this is what is known as virtue. Some liberals will argue that this is asking too much of individuals in a postmodern market society, while republicans will retort that it is the condition of their freedom.

References

Ackerman B (1984) The Storrs Lectures: Discovering the Constitution. Yale Law Journal 93:1013–1072.

Ackerman B (1993) We the People, Volume 1: Foundations. Belknap Press, Cambridge.

Ackerman B (1998) We the people, Volume 2: Transformations. Belknap Press, Cambridge/London.

Ackerman B, Fishkin J S (2002) Deliberation Day. The Journal of Political Philosophy 10(2):129–152.

Arendt H (1963) On Revolution. The Viking Press, New York.

Audier S (2015) Les théories de la république [Theories of the Republic]. La Découverte, Paris.

Bailyn B (1967) The Ideological Origins of the American Revolution. Harvard University Press, Cambridge.

Bellamy R (2003) Sovereignty, Post-Sovereignty and Pre-Sovereignty: Three Models of the State, Democracy and Rights within the EU. In: Walker N (ed) Sovereignty in Transition. Bloomsbury Publishing PLC, pp. 167–190.

Bellamy R (2007) Political Constitutionalism: A Republican Defence of the Constitutionality of Democracy. Cambridge University Press, Cambridge.

Bellamy R (2013) Democracy as Public Law: The Case of Constitutional Rights. German Law Journal, 14(8):1017–1037.

Berlin I (1958) Two concepts of liberty. Clarendon Press, Oxford.

Besson S, Marti JL (eds) (2009) Legal Republicanism. National and International Perspectives. Oxford University Press, Oxford.

Bohman J (2008) Réaliser la démocratie délibérative comme mode d'enquête: le pragmatisme, les faits sociaux et la théorie normative [Realizing deliberative democracy as a mode of inquiry: pragmatism, social facts and normative theory]. Tracés: Revue de Sciences humaines 1–29.

Borowiak CT (2011) Accountability and Democracy. The Pitfalls and Promise of Popular Control. Oxford University Press, Oxford.

Brennan J (2016) Against Democracy. Princeton University Press, Princeton.

Carrère T (2025) La démocratie constitutionnelle à l'épreuve du Républicanisme. Sur la dualité philosophique du constitutionnalisme moderne [Constitutional democracy put to the test by Republicanism. On the philosophical duality of modern constitutionalism]. Mare&Martin, Paris.

De Condorcet N (1791) Des conventions nationales [National conventions]. Cercle social, Paris.

De Tocqueville A (1835/1992) De la démocratie en Amérique [On Democracy in America]. Gallimard, Paris.
Dworkin R (1977) Taking Rights Seriously. Harvard University Press, Cambridge.
Dworkin R (1981) The Forum of Principle. New York University Law Review, 56:469–518.
Dworkin R (1984) Rights as trumps. In: Waldron J (ed) Theories of Rights. Oxford University Press, Oxford, pp. 153–167.
Elster J (2014) Tyranny and brutality of the majority. In: Novak S, Elster J (eds) Majority Decisions. Principles and Practices. Cambridge University Press, New York, pp. 159–176.
Favoreu L (1990) Le droit constitutionnel, droit de la Constitution et constitution du droit. Revue française de droit constitutionnel [Constitutional law, constitutional law and constitution of law]. French Review of Constitutional Law 1:71–89.
Habermas J (1997) Droit et démocratie : Entre faits et normes [Law and democracy: Between facts and norms]. Gallimard, Paris.
Hamilton A (1787) The Union as a Safeguard against Domestic Faction and Insurrection. The Federalist, n° IX.
Harrington J (1656) Océana, edn. 1995. Belin, Paris.
Hartz L (1955) The Liberal Tradition, in America: An Interpretation of American Political Thought since the Revolution. Harcourt, New York.
Hayek F (1960) The Constitution of Liberty. Routledge/Kegan Paul, London.
Hirschl R (2007) Towards Juristocracy. Harvard University Press, Cambridge.
Issacharoff S (2014) The majoritarian threat to democracy. Constitutional courts and the democratic past. In: Novak S, Elster J (eds) Majority Decisions. Principles and Practices. Cambridge University Press, New York, pp. 236–256.
Jefferson T (1789) Letter to James Madison.
Johnson D (2018) Institutional Balance, Civic Virtue and Dialogue: A Republican Balancing Act for the EU Constitutional Order. UCL Journal of Law and Jurisprudence 1(1):11–39.
Kramer L (2001) The Supreme Court 2000 Terme Foreword: We the Court. Harvard Law Review 115:4–169.
Kramer LD (2004) The People Themselves: Popular Constitutionalism and Judicial Review. Oxford University Press, New York.
Machiavelli N (1531) Discours sur la première décade de Tite-Live [Discourse on the first decade of Titus Livius], edn. 1952. In: Œuvres complètes. Gallimard, Paris.
Madison J (1787) The Same Subject Continued. The Union as a Safeguard Against Domestic Faction and Insurrection. The Federalist, n° X.
Madison J (1788) The Structure of the Government Must Furnish the Proper Checks and Balances Between the Different Departments. The Federalist, n° LI.
Manouguian A (2022) La juridictionnalisation du droit constitutionnel français. Étude d'un phénomène doctrinal [The jurisdictionalization of French constitutional law. Study of a doctrinal phenomenon]. Dalloz, Paris.
Marti JL (2006) La Republica deliberativa: una teoria de la democracia [The deliberative Republic: a theory of democracy]. Marcial Pons, Madrid.
McCormick JP (2001) Machiavellian Democracy: Controlling Elites with Ferocious Populism. The American Political Science Review 95(2):297–313.
Michaut F, Michelman FI (2010) Le mouvement des Critical Legal Studies entre républicanisme et libéralisme. Traces de gouvernement de soi par soi : préface à la session 1985 de la Cour suprême [The Critical Legal Studies Movement Between Republicanism and Liberalism. Traces of Self-Government by Self: Preface to the 1985 Session of the Supreme Court]. Presses de l'Université Laval, Québec.
Michelman FI (1988) Law's Republic. Yale Law Journal 97:1493–1537.
Mongoin D (2012) Le Pari de la liberté. Étude sur le Fédéraliste [The Wager of Liberty. A Study of the Federalist]. Garnier, Paris.
Montesquieu (1748) De l'esprit des lois [On the spirit of the laws].

Niederberger A, Schink P (eds) (2013) Republican democracy. Liberty, Law and Politics. Edinburgh University Press, Edinburgh.
Ovejero F (2008) Incluso un pueblo de demonios: democracia, liberalismo, republicanismo [Even a village of demons: democracy, liberalism, republicanism.]. Katz Editores, Buenos Aires/Madrid.
Paine T (1791–1792) Les droits de l'homme [Human rights], edn. 1987. Belin, Paris.
Pasquino P (2014) Majority rule in constitutional democracies: Some remarks about theory and practice. Majority Decisions. Principles and Practices. Cambridge University Press, New York, pp. 219–235.
Pettit P (1997) Republicanism: A Theory of Freedom and Government. Oxford University Press, Oxford.
Pettit P (2008) Republican Freedom: Three Axioms, Four Theorems. In: Laborde C, Maynor J (eds) Republicanism and Political Theory. Blackwell Publishing, Malden, pp. 102–130.
Pettit P (2009) Law and Liberty. In: Besson S and Marti J L (eds) Legal Republicanism. National and International Perspectives. Oxford University Press, Oxford, pp. 39–59.
Pettit P (2011) The Instability of Freedom as Noninterference: The Case of Isaiah Berlin. Ethics 121(4):693–716.
Pettit P (2012) On the people's terms: a republican theory and model of democracy. Cambridge University Press, Cambridge/New York.
Pinon S (2010) Le nouveau droit constitutionnel à travers les âges [The new constitutional law through the ages]. In: Mavrias K, Melin-Soucramanien F (eds) Constitution, enseignement et doctrine [Constitution, teaching and doctrine]. Sakkoulas/Bruylant, Athens/ Brussels.
Pocock JGA (1975) The Machiavellian Moment. Florentine Political Thought and the Atlantic Republican Tradition. Princeton University Press, Princeton.
Pocock JGA (1985) Virtue, Commerce, and History. Cambridge University Press, Cambridge.
Polybe (167–149 BC) Histoires, edn. 2005. Gallimard, Paris.
Rawls J (1988) The Priority of Right and Ideas of the Good. Philosophy & Public Affairs 17(4):251–276.
Raynaud P (2003) Constitutionnalisme [Constitutionalism]. In: Alland D, Rials S (eds) Dictionnaire de la culture juridique [Dictionary of legal culture]. Presses Universitaires de France, Paris, pp. 266–271.
Rorty R (1992) Introduction. Metaphilosophical Difficulties of Linguistic Philosophy. In: Rorty R (eds) The Linguistic Turn: Essays in Philosophical Method. University of Chicago Press, Chicago, pp. 1–40.
Rousseau D (1990) Une résurrection: la notion de Constitution [A resurrection: the notion of Constitution]. Revue de droit public, 1:5–22.
Rousseau D (1995) La démocratie continue [Democracy continues]. L.G.D.J.-Bruylant, Paris.
Skinner Q (1978a) The Foundations of Modern Thought, Volume I: The Renaissance. Cambridge University Press, Cambridge.
Skinner Q (1978b) The Foundations of Modern Political Thought, Volume II: The Age of Reformation. Cambridge University Press, Cambridge.
Skinner Q (1981) Machiavelli. Oxford University Press, Oxford.
Skinner Q (1984) The Idea of Negative Liberty: Philosophical and Historical Perspective. In: Rorty R et al (eds) Philosophy of History: Essays on the Historiography of Philosophy. Cambridge University Press, Cambridge.
Skinner Q (1998) Liberty before Liberalism. Cambridge University Press, Cambridge.
Skinner Q (2008a) Hobbes and Republican Liberty. Cambridge University Press, Cambridge.
Skinner Q (2008b) Freedom as the Absence of Arbitrary Power. In: Laborde C and Maynor J (eds) Republicanism and Political Theory. Blackwell Publishing, Malden, pp. 83–101.
Spitz J-F (1993) Corruption, obligation et liberté civile [Corruption, Obligation and Civil Liberty]. Le Débat 74:167–172.
Spitz J-F (1995) La liberté politique [Political freedom]. Presses Universitaires de France, Paris.
Spitz J-F (1997) République et Démocratie de Montesquieu à Madison [Republic and Democracy from Montesquieu to Madison]. Revue de Synthèse, 118:259–283.

Spitz J-F (2000) L'amour de l'égalité. Essai sur la critique de l'égalitarisme républicain en France 1770–1830 [The Love of Equality. Essay on the Critique of Republican Egalitarianism in France 1770–1830]. Vrin, Paris.
Spitz J-F (2005) Le moment républicain en France [The Republican Moment in France]. Gallimard, Paris.
Spitz J-F (2009) Républicanisme et libéralisme dans le moment révolutionnaire [Republicanism and liberalism in the revolutionary moment]. Annales historiques de la révolution française 358:19–45.
Sunstein CR (1988) Beyond the Republican Revival. Yale Law Journal 97:1539–1589.
Sunstein CR (1993) The partial constitution. Harvard University Press, Cambridge.
Tomkins A (2005) Our Republican Constitution. Hart Publishing, Oxford.
Tomkins A (2010) The role of the courts in the political constitution. University of Toronto Law Journal 60(1):1–22.
Tushnet M (1988) Red, White, and Blue: A Critical Analysis of Constitutional Law. University Press of Kansas, Lawrence.
Tushnet M (2000) Taking the Constitution Away from the Courts. Princeton University Press, Princeton.
Tushnet M (2009) Weak Courts, Strong Rights: Judicial Review and Social Welfare Rights in Comparative Constitutional Law. Princeton University Press, Princeton.
Unger RM (1996) What Should Legal Analysis Become? Verso, New York.
Viala A (2008) De la promotion d'une règle à la normalisation d'une discipline [From the promotion of a rule to the standardization of a discipline]. In: Mathieu B (eds) 1958–2008 Cinquantième anniversaire de la Constitution française [1958–2008 Fiftieth anniversary of the French Constitution]. Dalloz, Paris, pp. 518–526.
Viala A (2010) Philosophie du droit [Philosophy of law]. Ellipses, Paris.
Viroli M (2011) Le Républicanisme [Republicanism]. Le Bord de l'eau, Paris.
Waldron J (1999a) The dignity of legislation. Cambridge University Press, Cambridge.
Waldron J (1999b) Law and Disagreement. Oxford University Press, Oxford.
Waldron J (2003) Legislating with Integrity. Fordham Law Review 72:373–394.
Waldron J (2009a) Constitutionalism: A Skeptical View. In: Christiano T, Christman J (eds) Contemporary Debates in Political Philosophy. Blackwell Publishing Ltd, Oxford, pp. 267–282.
Waldron J (2009b) Judicial Review and Republican Government. In: Wolfe C (eds) That Eminent Tribunal, Judicial Supremacy and the Constitution. Princeton University Press, Princeton, pp. 159–180.
Waldron J (2009c) Representative lawmaking. Boston University Law Review 89:335–355.
Waldron J (2016) Political Theory: Essays on Institutions. Harvard University Press, Cambridge.
Wood GS (1969) The Creation of the American Republic, 1776–1787. The University of North Carolina Press, Chapel Hill.

Chapter 4
Muddling-Through Constitutionalism in the United Kingdom: The Importance of the Relationship Between the Monarch and the Prime Minister

Chris Monaghan

Contents

Abstract The United Kingdom's constitution can be described as the muddling-through constitution. The constitution, which is highly flexible, evolutionary in nature and responsive to changing circumstances, has proved capable of surviving historical challenges by adapting or weathering countless constitutional crises. Unlike most other constitutions, the United Kingdom's is said to be unwritten (even if in reality many of its sources are written) and consequentially has been criticised as unfit for modern circumstances. Central to the concept of muddling through is the relationship between the monarch and the Prime Minister, who both must work effectively in order for the constitution to work. This key relationship has seen considerable change in terms of the allocation of political power. The premiership of Boris Johnson (2019–2022) pushed boundaries and witnessed a willingness by those in power to disregard the unwritten constitutional norms that underpin the operation of the constitution. Johnson's premiership in the twilight years of Elizabeth II's reign challenged conventional constitutional norms, showed a willingness to silence Parliament, and has been reported to have caused concern at Buckingham Palace. This chapter will argue that the muddling-through constitutionalism that exists in the United Kingdom has been proven to work, and the term 'muddling through' should not be seen as a criticism, or an acknowledgment of persistent incompetence or lacklustre performance, but rather an acknowledgment of the strength of the constitution and how it has responded to

C. Monaghan (✉)
School of Law, University of Worcester, Worcester, UK
e-mail: c.monaghan@worc.ac.uk

M. De Visser et al. (eds.), *European Yearbook of Constitutional Law 2024*, European Yearbook of Constitutional Law 6, https://doi.org/10.1007/978-94-6265-699-4_4

challenges. There is a caveat, and that is the need for those in power to respect constitutional norms. The Johnson premiership resulted in concern that Johnson had proved the constitution to be defective and in need of fixing. How would we fix the post-Johnson constitution? This chapter argues that the solution of drafting a new written constitution whilst attractive, is not needed and we should not be too quick to abandon our current arrangements. History offers lessons on how we should view the constitution, and these provide broader historic context and illustrates how the constitution has survived challenges (such as in the 1780s) which were more significant than that posed by the Johnson premiership.

Keywords Constitution · Constitutional reform · Monarch · Monarchy · Muddling-through · Prime Minister · United Kingdom · Unwritten constitution

4.1 Introduction

In this chapter I argue that the United Kingdom's (UK) constitution, despite being doubted in terms of its existence (such as by Lord Neuberger, the then President of the Supreme Court in 2015,[1] and the English radical Thomas Paine in 1791),[2] has demonstrated the historical ability of the English (and then the British) state to muddle through. In doing this it has successfully developed meaningful institutional compliance with the rule of law, the safeguarding of judicial independence through the enactment of the Act of Settlement 1701,[3] an executive accountable to Parliament, and a robust system of judicial review.[4] The focus of the chapter will be on the key relationship between monarch and Prime Minister, and how this relationship needs respect (both for the other and also for the constitution) in order for the constitution to effectively muddle through. The focus here will be on the nature of the constitution and the importance of muddling through, and will seek to demonstrate the centrality of the relationship between the monarch and the Prime minister to ensure the effective working of the UK's constitution.

This concept of 'muddling through' does not mean that the UK's constitution is afflicted by institutional incompetence, intellectual malaise, or indeed terminal decline, rather it is an acknowledgment of the realities of constitutionalism within the UK. Realities which could be described as evolutionarily, reactive, hierarchical,

---

[1] Neuberger 2015b. See also Neuberger 2015a. Here Lord Neuberger implicitly treats the UK as having an informal constitution (in contrast to the 'formal constitution' of the USA), with Neuberger arguing that the Magna Carta "can claim to be the Bible of our constitution", para 63.

[2] Paine 1791.

[3] The Act of Settlement 1701 guaranteed security of tenure for senior judges subject to their good behaviour. They could only be removed after a resolution of both Houses of Parliament to the monarch requesting the dismissal of the judge. Since 1701 just one judge has been dismissed under the mechanism established by the Act of Settlement, which was Sir Jonah Barrington in 1830.

[4] For the development of judicial review in the second part of the twentieth century see Arvind et al. 2021.

and opaque. This is a positive, as Brian Christopher Jones argues that the adaptability of the constitution since the 1950s "demonstrate the vitality and dynamic nature of constitutional change in Britain."[5] This chapter will argue that the threat posed by the premiership of Boris Johnson and a tide of anti-elite (or rather anti-expert) populism (driven from within the traditional elites, see for example the Home Secretary's criticism in May 2023),[6] reveals that the UK's constitution has demonstrated *inter alia* two things. The first is that it is clearly under considerable strain because of the readiness of those in power to disregard the accepted norms of the constitution. The second is that actors within the constitution are prepared to confront this challenge (such as the rumoured willingness of the late Queen Elizabeth II to avoid being available to hear any request by Johnson that she dissolve Parliament).[7]

Thus, the muddling-through constitution reveals that whilst it is under considerable stress, there is still a determination to ensure compliance. History demonstrates that the UK's constitution has shown resilience due to its ability to muddle through and adapt when needed.[8] An important question is to ask what this 'muddling through' indicates after the fall of Johnson and what may need to be 'fixed' to weather a future Johnson (and other future possible eventualities)? The answer lies with considering constitutional history and the broader political context. This chapter will consider key examples of how the constitution has muddled through and survived without the need for fundamental constitution reform.

4.2 Mapping the Constitution

What exactly is the British constitution? As a starting point the idea that the UK possesses a constitution is a contested point. If one likes plans and maps, then the cartographer's approach to the constitution would be to alight at St Pancras Station in central London and to walk to either the British Library or British Museum and seek to examine the constitution and read the original text. If one did not have the luxury of a ready commute into central London, then the website of the National Archives would suffice, and a quick internet search would reveal original text of the constitution. Alas, it is no surprise that this is not the case. If we view a constitution to

---

[5] Jones 2020, p. 160.

[6] Walker, "Suella Braverman rails against 'experts and elites' in partisan speech" The Guardian, 15 May 2023. Available at: https://www.theguardian.com/politics/2023/may/15/suella-braverman-rails-against-experts-and-elites-in-partisan-speech. Accessed on 2 November 2023. The Home Secretary would later critique the main domestic human rights framework in the UK, the Human Rights Act 1998, by saying that it should have been called the Criminal Rights Act. See Patrick, "Surprising that Human Rights Act wasn't called 'Criminal Rights Act,' says Suella Braverman" Independent, 3 October 2023. Available at: https://www.independent.co.uk/tv/news/suella-braverman-speech-human-rights-criminal-b2423252.html. Accessed on 2 November 2023.

[7] See Sect. 4.3.1 below.

[8] See for example Blick 2019.

mean the idea of a written document that has special legal status and is often revered, then we would be immediately disappointed by the UK's constitution.

The closest that one might come to being in the presence of the constitution was the British Library's excellent exhibition on Magna Carta in 2015. Visitors to the exhibit would have walked past various contemporary copies of Magna Carta, the law reports of Sir Edward Coke and other associated constitutional documents and curiosities. Given the recent fanfare of the 800th celebration of Magna Carta, it is perhaps telling that the pivotal role of the Great Charter in the evolution of the constitution and the triumph of the rule of law, is readily questioned, with the former Supreme Court Justice, Lord Sumption, regarding the document as somewhat conventional and no more worthy of celebration than any other similar document from the period.[9] Although the go-to feature in any eighteenth century and early nineteenth century pictorial depiction of the constitution,[10] the Magna Carta was hardly held in high regard by the great rebel Oliver Cromwell, who was recorded as dismissing the charter as 'Magna Farta'.[11]

This walk-through of constitutional history and the importance of symbolic milestones sums up the constitution. It is a product of the country's story. For good reason most countries (bar three)[12] have found that their national story requires a written constitution. For America it was independence from Great Britain and the challenges of deciding the future composition of an American State. Inherent to this was the problem of balancing the needs of the constituent independent states and those who favoured federalism. For France, whose recent history has seen revolution, republic, empire, monarchy and so forth– the series of written constitutions that France has possessed both responses to, and reflects, its national story.[13]

The closest that Britain came to a constitution was the short-lived Instrument of Government in 1653, which outlined how a single British and Irish state would function and the powers of Parliament and the Lord Protector.[14] It is not true that the UK has not gone through its own seminal moments, not least its creation which did not give rise to a constitution. In the case of the Union with Scotland, any notions of a federative union between the two nations was rejected, and the Scottish parliamentarians were obliged to join the new British Parliament in London (which was essentially the English Parliament).[15] This has consequences: not least now with disaffection with the Union in Scotland, but in how the constitution is

[9] Sumption 2015.

[10] See Dickinson 1986. An example is Thomas Rowlandson's "A Peep into Friar Bacon's Study" (William Humphrey, 3 March 1784) which offers an account of the changing nature of the constitution and the danger of George III increasing the power of the Crown.

[11] Breay and Harrison 2015. Conversely, see William Pitt's description of the Magna Carta as "the Bible of the English constitution".

[12] Including the UK, these are New Zealand and Israel.

[13] See, for example, Grzybowski 1959.

[14] See Gaunt 1989.

[15] Macinnes 2007, pp. 278–283. Macinnes is clear that "English views of parliamentary sovereignty, legislative precedent and the common law continued to take precedence over Scottish claims for a written constitution as an aspect of fundamental law...", p. 314.

construed through a English lens, rather than a British lens (i.e. with Scotland).[16] Symbolic of the muddling-through nature of the constitution, the Act of Settlement 1701 promised to create a separation of powers in England but these provisions were quickly repealed. The Act would have meant that "the present English system of Cabinet government would have been impossible... There would have resulted a practical separation of powers—separation of executive and legislative personnel. The king would have chosen his ministers from the Upper House, and the power of the Lower House would have materially diminished."[17] In typical form the British constitution muddled through the repeal of these provisions in 1707.

It is key to accept its evolutionary nature and not fixate on whether, or not, there is a constitution. As Lord Norton remarked, "Constitutions, as John Stuart Mill observed in 1861, did not emerge one morning fully formed. The British constitution in particular has developed over centuries, indeed a millennium."[18] Norton noted that the historical development had given "rise to ambiguities and uncertainties".[19] Despite these ambiguities, Norton observed that, "By the twentieth century, the UK had a constitution that was both stable and well regarded."[20] Hannah White provides a more colourful description to the constitution: "the UK constitution is an unusual beast: a centuries-old amalgam of precedent, convention and rules scattered across numerous texts, laws and institutions, unlike any other in the world in its longevity and lack of codification."[21] This was problematic, as "with such an amorphous object to describe, it is hardly surprising that constitutional reality flees before the commentator's pen."[22]

The existence of a British constitution is contested. In the late 1980s FF Ridley argued that:

> Not to be left out of the world of constitutional democracies, British writers define constitution in a way which appears to give us one too, even though there is no document to prove it. The argument is that a constitution need not be embodied in a single document or, indeed, wholly written. We say instead that a country's constitution is a body of rules – some laws, some conventions – which regulate its system of government. Such a definition does not, however, bridge the gap between Britain and the rest of the world by providing us with a

---

[16] An example of this is Parliamentary Sovereignty, which is a central feature of the constitution. However, this had been developed in England and had never applied in Scotland. Nonetheless, the English tradition was wholly incorporated into the constitutional arrangements of Great Britain. This point was articulated by Lord President Cooper in the Inner House of the Court of Sessions: *MacCormick v. Lord Advocate*, 1953, SC 396. See also Lord Walker in the House of Lords: United Kingdom House of Lords Decisions *R (on the application of Jackson) v. Attorney General* opinions of the lords of appeal for judgment in the cause 2005, 56, para 159.

[17] Tarkow 1943, p. 555.

[18] Norton 2020, p. vii.

[19] Ibid., p. vii.

[20] Ibid., p. 6.

[21] White (2022) What Boris Johnson taught us about the UK constitution. Prospect, August 17 2022. Available at: https://www.prospectmagazine.co.uk/politics/38876/what-boris-johnson-taught-us-about-the-uk-constitution.

[22] Marshall and Moodie 1967, p. 19.

substitute for a documentary constitution: it simply shifts the ground, by using the word in an entirely different way.

Ridley added, "It is to show that Britain does not really have a constitution at all, merely a system of government, even if some parts of it are more important to our democratic order than others or are treated... with greater veneration."[23] Ridley was clear that the traditional British approach created problems due to uncertainty and the broad approach taken in determining what was within the constitution. It was perhaps surprising that in 2015 Lord Neuberger, the then President of the Supreme Court observed, "the UK has no constitution. Some people like to say that we have constitutional conventions and some constitutional documents, and even that we have an unwritten constitution."[24] Neuberger rejected this approach and took umbrage with this attempt to magic a constitution out of thin air: "I find it hard to accept that a few random conventions and a few disparate statutes, all or any of which can be removed or varied by a simple majority in Parliament can amount to much of a constitution." However, Lord Neuberger was clear that the question depended on how one defined a constitution. A year later Neuberger observed that if you believed that the UK had a constitution, then "On that basis", the UK has, "I accept, a constitution, much of which is in the form of unwritten conventions....". Though Neuberger was clear that his own definition had not changed, "we have no Constitution in the sense in which I use the term." The central problem is that "At the risk of being accused of caricature, it seems to me that the UK can make up or abandon its constitutional conventions as the mood takes it". This is also the fear of those distrust or want to fetter the political constitution, through enhancing the role of the law and the possibility of restraints on Parliament.[25] Although Lord Neuberger had rejected the approach suggested by Lords Steyn and Hope in *obiter* in *R (on the application of Jackson) v. Attorney General*[26] which sought to justify a case for judicial strike-down of legislation.[27] Recently the Supreme Court in *R (on the application of Miller) v The Prime Minster (No. 2)*[28] offered a subtly different approach to Neuberger's: "Although the United Kingdom does not have a single document entitled 'The Constitution', it nevertheless possesses a Constitution, established over the course of our history by common law, statutes, conventions and practice." The judgment was written by Lady Hale (the new President of the Supreme Court) and her deputy Lord Reed. Hale had previously in 2016 taken the view that there was without question a constitution: "But the fact that we in the United Kingdom do not have a written Constitution does not mean that we do not have a constitution. We clearly do."[29]

---

[23] Ridley 1988, p. 349.

[24] Neuberger 2015a, para 32.

[25] See Scarman 1974, pp. 69–70; Hailsham 1976; Woolf 1995; Griffith 1979.

[26] United Kingdom House of Lords Decisions *R (on the application of Jackson) v. Attorney General* opinions of the lords of appeal for judgment in the cause 2005, 57.

[27] For commentary from a common law constitution perspective see Allan 2011.

[28] The Supreme Court of the United Kingdom, *R (on the application of Miller) v. The Prime Minster (No. 2)*, UKSC judgment of 2019, 41.

[29] Hale 2016.

Whilst there are grounds for doubting the existence of a constitution, this is ultimately a question of definition. The UK does have a constitution. It encompasses institutional practice, political norms, and law, but its vulnerability in its fluidity and disjointedness, is also its strength. Whilst Sir Frederic Maitland may have quipped that "There is hardly any department of law that does not, at one time or another, become of constitutional importance", this has arguably not hurt the development of a modern constitutional state.

In his critique Ridley had cited NH Brasher who had written that "[t]he constitution of Britain is unknowable, like the weather."[30] Is the constitution really that unknowable? As Norton remarked in the 1980s, "What distinguishes the British Constitution from others is that it is uncodified. This is of special importance. It makes it difficult to identify clearly and authoritatively what constitutes the provisions of the constitution."[31] Whilst there may be room for differing interpretations, it does not mean that the basic tenets are unknown. However, the potential benefit of a codified written constitution is it easy to locate and the ordinary citizen can read the text of the constitution, even if the text does not provide an account of how things operate in practice. However, those actors within the constitution can hardly claim that the constitution is unknowable.

A significant and regular criticism of Johnson was his approach to constitutional norms. These norms are unwritten and are open to abuse. There is no denying that this is a problem. The point though is that despite concerns that the constitution was imperilled by Johnson and was not capable to weather the storm, it did. There was broad consensus (albeit excluding the supporters of the government) that the Prime Minister and his government was acting unconstitutionally—thus the core expectations and norms were knowable. The Supreme Court in *R (on the application of Miller) v The Prime Minster (No. 2)*[32] knew what was expected and its judgment whilst controversial, is controversial because it sought to protect the constitution from being abused.[33]

A major critique though is that the constitutional arrangements of the United Kingdom risks being elitist, whereby the ordinary citizen will struggle to grapple with why X and Y breach constitutional norms, and indeed whether this is actually the case or the criticism of X and Y's political opponents. This whiff of presumed partisanship does stick to written constitutions, with the impeachments of Presidents Clinton and Trump viewed as politically motivated by their opponents and unprincipled opportunism.[34] However, Brian Christopher Jones rejects the view that the unwritten nature of the constitution results in difficulty in understanding what it is and he

---

[30] Ridley 1991, p. 114.

[31] Ibid., p. 102.

[32] The Supreme Court of the United Kingdom, *R (on the application of Miller) v. The Prime Minster (No. 2)*, UKSC judgment of 2019, 41.

[33] For commentary see Elliot 2020 and Monaghan and Welsh 2023. The decision in *R (on the application of Miller) v. The Prime Minster (No. 2)* will be explored below.

[34] For a general discussion on this concern, see Rakove 2024. Rakove observed that "The more urgent concern today rests elsewhere: on the potential 'weaponization' of impeachment, on the idea that it will soon become a tool that an opposition party can deploy opportunistically whenever it

notes that "UK citizens are not lost or confused on the mechanics of the unwritten constitution, and they perform just as well as, or sometimes better than, those citizens living under written constitutional arrangements."[35]

There have been a number of proposals for reforming the constitution, such as Robert Blackburn who drafted a comprehensive report for Parliament that offered three different approaches to constitutional reform.[36] These spanned a wide spectrum, as these were a descriptive Constitutional Code, a Constitutional Act (i.e., ordinary legislation), and a written constitution.[37] Richard Gordon observed that there is an urgent case for a written constitution as a consequence of a lack of accountability and failings of the political elite.[38] Gordon argued that a written constitution could improve "good and effective government". The central aim would to be empower the British people and improve accountability. Although Gordon notes that a written constitution would not be a magic panacea overnight, but its impact would be positive and give "people more power in terms of how they are governed". Dawn Oliver has offered a sceptical view on the benefits of adopting Gordon's proposal.[39] Two points stick out, the first Oliver's comment that "Would politicians behave better because they operate under this written Constitution? I very much doubt it", and the second, that "If a 'We the People' Constitution were adopted, would the government, the press and the public be content for a court to strike down the offending provision on the new ground that it was contrary to the Constitution? I very much doubt it."[40] Oliver does not dismiss the utility of Gordon's proposal but is conscious of the problems that such a constitution would face in reality. This assessment is fair, but it is telling: "This does not mean, of course, that a written Constitution would be negative, only that not too much should be expected of it. My own sense, however, it that it is not going

controls the House." See also the criticism of the former Associate White House Counsel for the Clinton administration Karen Popp, Popp 2000.

[35] Jones 2023.

[36] House of Commons (2014) Political and Constitutional Reform—Second Report. A new Magna Carta? Available at: https://publications.parliament.uk/pa/cm201415/cmselect/cmpolcon/463/46302.htm

[37] Ibid. Robert Blackburn (the report's author) was clear that "The work been prepared in an impartial way, adopting a pragmatic approach to the issues involved, and does not seek to advocate either codification or non-codification."

[38] Gordon 2010.

[39] Oliver 2010, p. 399.

[40] Oliver 2010, p. 402. Oliver took a similar position regarding Lord Hope's challenge to Parliamentary sovereignty in the House of Lords: House of Lords Judgments, *R (on the application of Jackson) v Attorney General*, Opinions of the Lords of Appeal for Judgment in the Cause, 2005, 56, and argued that "The practice of striking down legislation in our unwritten constitution and constitutional culture would not work". Oliver continued, "I suspect therefore that the dominant though unarticulated reason why courts in the UK accept parliamentary sovereignty is that it represents a way of avoiding a conflict between the courts and the executive which the courts could not win. It could well be different if the UK had a written Constitution which mandated the courts to refuse to give effect to 'unconstitutional' laws. But that is not the current position". See Oliver (2012) Parliamentary Sovereignty: A Pragmatic or Principled Doctrine? UK Constitutional Law Association Blog May 3 2012. Available at: https://ukconstitutionallaw.org/2012/05/03/dawn-oliver-parliamentary-sovereignty-a-pragmatic-or-principled-doctrine/.

to happen."[41] Oliver's solution is to focus *inter alia* on "incremental, opportunistic reforms to the electoral system and parliamentary procedures."[42]

Another critic is Iain McLean who argues that there is a real case for reform: "Well, what is wrong with the British Constitution? For a start, nobody knows what it is. That is not to say (as people often and lazily do) that it is unwritten. Parts of it are very written indeed"[43] This view is attractive in part, as he targets those who would dismiss the constitution as being merely unwritten, but arguably is really that unknowable? His charge that those who decide what exactly is within the constitution is controlled by a magic circle, is interesting, and attractive to those who might see the ownership of the constitution as being dominated by the elite: "The magic circle of those entitled to say what the constitution is includes judges, law professors, and a few journalists... However, the custodians of the magic circle have always been reluctant to allow political scientists into it."[44]

McLean's criticism is aimed at the muddling-through approach. An example of this is his argument that "The incoherence of the British constitution is not a new problem. It dates back to the union of 1707, when two constitutional traditions were awkwardly merged."[45] It is certainly a sound argument to criticise the Anglo centric nature of the British constitution and how it is presumes to simply be a continuation of the path of travel prior to 1707. As McLean remarks, "English commentators have assumed without hesitation that legal doctrines derived from English history apply throughout Great Britain, although Scots law remained distinct under the terms of the Treaty and Acts of Union."[46] This assumption is telling, as McLean gives the example of Dicey referring to English Constitution to mean the British Constitution.[47] Is this merely academic shorthand, or is it a product of English dominance and an acceptance of the pre-1707 path of travel by English academics? There is indeed a fuzziness regarding how we treat the development of the constitution. McLean is critical of how the gravity and significance of events such as the proposal for Irish Home Rule has been underplayed by academics. He points to the crisis of Irish Home Rule and how actors within the constitution, including the King George V, the leader of the official opposition, and military leaders were prepared to defeat government policy.[48] Thus, McLean is adamant that "...these events...show that at times of heightened partisanship—exactly the times when a constitution must be most robust—the British Constitution was at its most fragile."[49]

---

[41] Oliver 2010, p. 403.

[42] Ibid., p. 403.

[43] McLean 2009, p. vii.

[44] Ibid., p. viii.

[45] Ibid., p. 6.

[46] Ibid., p. 8.

[47] Ibid., p. 8.

[48] Ibid., pp. 9–10.

[49] Ibid., p. 10.

A key critic of the argument that the UK's constitution is deficient due to its unwritten nature is Brian Christopher Jones. Jones is adamant that the UK's arrangements result in positives, rather than the typical concern (amongst many commentators) that things would almost certainly be better but for a written constitution. It is hard to dispute Jones' assessment that "The UK constitution has undoubtedly been under pressure in recent years, but it is not broken or in disarray. It is working just as well as, or perhaps even better than, many written constitutions around the world."[50] To Jones the UK's current arrangements work well, permitting constitutional change and flexibility, the protection of human rights, and constitutional literacy amongst the population. The storms that have smashed against the citadel of British constitutionalism do not, according to Jones lead to the conclusion that the UK would have weathered these storms better, but for a written constitution. Jones' assessment of the recent challenges is compelling as he offers a broader perspective, "Brexit is arguably the most significant UK constitutional change in decades. It was never going to be smooth or easy; constitutional change rarely is.... The many and various calls during Brexit that the UK constitution was 'broken' or 'in turmoil' were overblown and inaccurate".[51] The bogeyman of the traditional constitution, the premiership of Johnson, is regarded by Jones as a "sustained constitutional crisis", however his "downfall demonstrated the UK constitution working well, perhaps even admirably."[52] Indeed, Jones is clear that "it is difficult to see how a written constitution would benefit the UK going forward."[53] This is the muddling-through constitution in action. The constitution does work, even if tested or treated with apparent disrespect (through the disregard of constitutional norms).

Jones has previously warned against the possible dangers of having a written constitution in the UK, arguing that "Presently, UK constitutional values are not worshipped by the citizenry, not overtly used as political weapons, and rarely used as legal tactics against ministers or others."[54] Jones argues that a written constitution could lead to "Individuals or groups... claiming to be guardians or protectors of such a document, and 'constitutional' could be used as an all-compassing truncheon for 'right or wrong'."[55]

It is telling to consider Nick Barber's observation as to why academics are interested in constitutional reform: "The project is attractive to academics for many reasons: there is the fun of debating abstruse constitutional issues, the chance of bringing certainty to areas long characterised by vagueness, and, perhaps, the opportunity to take a privileged role in the construction of the constitutional foundations of the state."[56] As an academic the freedom with the classroom to propose the case for a new written constitution and to have students sketch out how this might work is an

[50] Jones 2023, p. 2.

[51] Ibid., p. 6.

[52] Ibid., p. 8.

[53] Ibid., p. 2.

[54] Jones 2020, p. 26.

[55] Ibid.

[56] Barber 2008, p. 211.

exciting prospect. To Barber the unwritten nature of the constitution does not justify reform and the introduction of a written constitution. Barber is uncompromising in his view, "Britain's constitution has, by and large, been a success. It has produced stable government and—in terms of democracy, transparency, human rights and the provision of social welfare—it compares reasonably favourably with many other constitutions."[57] Barber does, quite rightly, admit that those who reform of "particular areas often make a strong case", but he questions whether these particular areas justify the need for a written constitution.[58]

In an insightful review of proposals for a written constitution, Jo Eric Khushal Murkens rejected the arguments put forward (as of yet) for codifying the constitution: "While I have expressed here my concerns about the desirability of codifying the existing UK constitution, I have at the same time offered no defence of the institutions, conventions and practices of the unwritten constitution. I am, therefore, not convinced by the attempts to convert the unwritten constitution into a written one. Nor am I against codification as a matter of principle."[59] Murkens considered the arguments that have been advanced to justify codification, noting that these argue that "The central benefit of codification would, therefore, be 'clarity and definiteness'".[60] Likewise, Murkens considers the arguments put forward that recent events necessitate a written constitution, "The process of withdrawal has left the unwritten constitution in 'crisis', in a 'molten' condition, and has highlighted the need for a written constitution."[61] He is clear that if there was to be a written constitution, then these would need to be more than a case of capturing the present state of the constitution and should be used as an opportunity to renew the UK's system of government.[62]

Despite the possible attraction of drafting a written constitution for the UK, the point is that the current UK arrangements work. They have proved capable of weathering so many storms over the past decade, and the constitution has muddled through, and will no doubt continue to do so as the UK will no doubt weather many a future storm. The constitution could benefit from further reforms and there is scope to buttress the existing accountability mechanism. However, it is not on its last legs.

The muddling-through constitution is not without its defenders, but how can it weather the challenges that it has faced both recently, and in the past.

[57] Ibid., p. 18.

[58] Ibid., p. 18.

[59] Murkens 2021, p. 985.

[60] Ibid., p. 965.

[61] Ibid., p. 966.

[62] Ibid., p. 967.

4.3 The Need for a Broader Perspective

It could be observed that many British commentators are proud of its unique constitution and relative stable domestic social and political history. The problem today is that UK has endured a series of constitutional challenges. These contemporary challenges could be categorised as populist and anti-elite (elites) who criticise the role of expertise, the universality of human rights, and the politically neutral institution that is the civil service (which is evidenced by the administrations of Johnson, Truss and Sunak); successional in terms of Brexit, Scotland, and Northern Ireland; and national 'decline', ebbing confidence and unease about the future. It is argued that the British state is under threat. The constitution has muddled through until now. The problem that we face is how the constitution, its institutions, current and future actors, can respond to the challenges ahead that may well see major territorial changes—such as a United Ireland, the secession of Scotland from the Union, and the tensions that may well boil over across parts of England when faced with the shock that will no doubt descend on England and its further reduced role in the world. This is not to delight in, or eagerly speculate over the break-up of the UK. A major event needs a robust constitution and actors strong enough to offer integrity and intellectual honesty in responding to the future. Does the UK constitution provide this? My answer is yes.

4.3.1 The Problem with Johnson

The particular problem that will be discussed here is when one party in the relationship between the Prime Minister and the monarch disregards the accepted norms of the constitution. Johnson is often presented as the constitution's bogeyman and fits within all three types of challenges discussed above. If the constitution muddles-through, then what are we to make of Johnson. Should his short premiership be seen as an acute threat to the constitution or just one more challenge that will blow over and for the most part be relegated to the pages of political history.

Johnson did however illustrate some long-standing problems within the constitution. Many within the UK (and beyond) are particularly interested in the relationship between the monarch and their Prime Minister. This relationship is key for the successful working of the constitution. The changing dynamics of the relationship has allowed the constitution to muddle-through, from George III to Charles III British monarchs have had to adapt the monarchy and the role of monarch to suit and survive changing political and social realities. This change in who exercises the core executive power is represented by the increased status of the Prime Minister, who not only commands the confidence of the House of Commons, but also through the electoral process enjoys the confidence of the public.

So what is the place of the modern monarch in the constitution and how should the relationship between the monarch and the Prime Minister work? As Walter Bagehot observed in the mid-nineteenth century observed, the monarch as "head of the dignified part of the constitution" has "three rights—the right to be consulted, the right to encourage, the right to warn."[63] The modern constitutional monarch may not wield real power, yet they hold regularly weekly audiences with their Prime Minister.[64] As Vernon Bogdanor noted regarding the late Queen Elizabeth II, "A fundamental condition for the success of her reign was that she made no attempt to intervene in politics, or even to express a political opinion."[65] These audiences conducted on a one-to-one basis are confidential, and allowed the Prime Minister in the case of the late Elizabeth II, to draw upon the counsel of someone whose institutional experience stretched back to 1952 and who had seen first-hand the struggles facing Prime Ministers from Churchill onwards. The dynamic of the relationship between the monarch and the Prime Minister offers potential for real or imagined conflict. Perhaps the closest that the United Kingdom has got to such conflict was the constitutional crisis caused by Edward VIII's wish to marry Wallace Simpson in 1936, which resulted in the king's abdication (but not before the king had contemplated bypassing his government and going to the people).[66] Stanley Baldwin, the Prime Minister, although not in favour of the marriage, would not oppose it, and simply informed the king that it "would not be approved by the country."[67] Bogdanor is clear that Edward VIII could have remained on the throne and married Wallace Simpson, but to do so he must be "prepared to reject the wishes of his ministers. This, contrary to what is generally suggested, was certainly a course that he contemplated, and it would have caused a constitutional crisis".[68]

[63] Bagehot 1963, p. 111. Bagehot's approach had considerable influence over George V, see Heffer 1998.

[64] Bagehot 1963, p. 66. As Bogdanor has quipped, "As a constitutional monarch, the Queen had no power. But this did not mean she had no influence." See Bogdanor (2022) How the Queen's constitutional role shifted over her reign'. The Guardian, 9 September 2022. Available at: https://www.theguardian.com/uk-news/2022/sep/09/queen-elizabeth-constitutional-role.

[65] Bogdanor (2022) How the Queen's constitutional role shifted over her reign'. The Guardian, 9 September 2022. Available at: https://www.theguardian.com/uk-news/2022/sep/09/queen-elizabeth-constitutional-role.

[66] The king had proposed a radio address in which he would speak to the people and state that he wished to marry. This was opposed by the Prime Minister as it would have pitted the king against his ministers and "It would have been unconstitutional for the king to ask his subjects to make a decision over the heads of his ministers" (Bogdanor 1995, p. 136). As Bogdanor noted, "the abdication crisis showed that the king's choice of a wife is limited not by statute but by convention. It firmly established the principle that the king cannot marry against the wishes of his ministers" (Bogdanor 1995, p. 136). Bogdanor is clear that Stanley Baldwin wanted to keep Edward VIII as king, rather than compel him to abdicate, p. 138. Nonetheless, Edward VIII's unwillingness to accept the advice of his ministers reflected a "non-legal principle" of the constitution, and thus he needed to abdicate (Blackburn 2013, p. 177). See also Blackburn 2016.

[67] Bogdanor 1995, p. 138. As Robert Blackburn has observed, "Political and religious objections drove Edward VIII from the throne and into exile in 1936." This was something which was eventually repeated in the case of Princess Margaret in the 1950s. (See Blackburn 2013, p. 177).

[68] Bogdanor 1995, p. 141.

Thus, in order for the constitution to muddle-through both the monarch and the Prime Minister must work together, respect the other's role, whilst accepting the limitations imposed on their own office. The key point is that the UK has a constitutional monarch who is expected to preside over the unwritten norms of our constitution and work above the political machination of the day, to offer continuity, support, and frank feedback to the Prime Minister. In return the Prime Minister and their government must not drag the monarch into political crisis and an inherent aspect of this is to respect the unwritten constitutional norms. Circumstances during the reign of Elizabeth II conspired to bring the monarch into political situations, namely the leadership Conservative Party and the role of the then monarch in choosing a successor to her outgoing Prime Minister.[69] But in the case of Elizabeth II and her Prime Minister no one acted improperly, even if it was, from a public relations viewpoint, uncomfortable to see the monarch have to exercise such an important choice.

However, the major failing of the Johnson administration was to present a dilemma to the monarch as how to respond to a maverick Prime Minister who either did not understand, or perhaps was willing to readily ignore, the constitution. There are allegations that Johnson's approach as Prime Minister concerned Buckingham Palace. According to Laura Kuenssberg, the former BBC Political Editor, "Senior government officials spoke to Buckingham Palace at the height of the pandemic to express their concern about Boris Johnson's conduct in office, the BBC has been told. Officials even discussed suggesting to the Queen she raise the concerns with Mr Johnson during private audiences".[70] Kuenssberg reported that "It's understood there were a number of phone calls and communications over and above routine communication between Number 10 and the Palace. One source said the then-prime minister 'had to be reminded of the constitution'... There had already been worries at Buckingham Palace about Mr Johnson's government's behaviour [relating to the prorogation of Parliament]".[71]

However, despite speculation in the press, what did Johnson actually do wrong from a constitutional perspective? It is alleged by his critics that Johnson's conduct was problematic. The *Independent* reported that Johnson "twice broke with convention and talked about their private audiences, and publicly apologised to the Queen and the country over events in Downing Street on the eve of the Duke of Edinburgh's funeral".[72] Revealing private correspondence between the Prime Minister and monarch was not new, as David Cameron had revealed Elizabeth II's reaction to him following the outcome of the referendum on Scottish Independence. Cameron had informed Michael Bloomberg that, "The definition of relief is being the prime

[69] See Steve Richards' account of how this played out for Rab Butler who narrowly lost out on becoming Prime Minister on two occasions (Richards 2021).

[70] Kuenssberg (2023) Boris Johnson: Officials discussed raising concerns about former PM to Queen. BBC News, 18 September 2023. Available at: https://www.bbc.co.uk/news/uk-politics-66839314.

[71] Ibid.

[72] Elston (2022) The Queen and Boris Johnson: Constitutional problems, parties and apologies. Independent, 31 August 2022. Available at: https://www.independent.co.uk/news/uk/boris-johnson-buckingham-palace-elizabeth-ii-prime-minister-dominic-cummings-b2156651.html.

minister of the United Kingdom and ringing the Queen and saying: 'It's alright, it's OK'. That was something. She purred down the line."[73] This revelation, albeit intended for a private conversation and unintentionally recorded by Sky News, was reportedly criticised by Buckingham Palace. It was not just Cameron's willingness to break convention, but that many believed the monarch had been asked to intervene in the days before the referendum by asking the people of Scotland to think very carefully about the future', i.e. about how they voted.[74] Subsequently Cameron revealed that he requested such an intervention from the monarch, as "[b]ut just a raising of the eyebrow, even you know a quarter of an inch, we thought would make a difference".[75] This in turn led to unofficial criticism from Buckingham Palace that by Cameron revealing private conversation, "it makes it very hard for the relationship to thrive".[76]

If revealing private discussions between monarch and Prime Minister was not new, the charge sheet for the Johnson administration is significant. A few examples will be considered below and ultimately these examples could lead to a breakdown of the relationship between a monarch and the Prime Minister—as circumstances may potentially necessitate the monarch's dismissal of the Prime Minister.

Firstly, Johnson's approach demonstrated a willingness to disregard the rule of law. An example of this was his suggestion that he would refuse to follow the requirement contained in s.1(4) of European Union (Withdrawal) (No.2) Act 2019 for the Prime Minister to "obtain from the European Council an extension of the period under Article 50(3) of the Treaty on European Union ending at 11.00pm on 31 October 2019" in the event that an agreement had not been reached with the European Union. The European Union (Withdrawal) (No.2) Act 2019 (otherwise known as the Benn Act, after Hillary Benn, the opposition politician) had been enacted without the consent of the government. This is a rare example of Parliament creating legislation in the face of government opposition, as usually the Westminster model necessitates the government having the confidence of the House of Commons and thus has a majority of MPs. The fact that the European Union (Withdrawal) (No.2) Act 2019 was enacted was due to the government not having a majority in the House of Commons and the impact of Brexit on party loyalty (i.e. MPs were willing to

---

[73] Mason (2014) David Cameron says Queen "purred down line: after Scotland no vote". The Guardian, 23 September 2014. Available at: https://www.theguardian.com/politics/2014/sep/23/david-cameron-queen-purred-down-line-scotland-no-vote.

[74] Watt (2014) David Cameron "embarrassed and sorry" for saying Queen purred. The Guardian, 28 September 2014. Available at: https://www.theguardian.com/politics/2014/sep/28/david-cameron-sorry-queen-purred. McKenzie and Said (2019) David Cameron reveals he asked the Queen to "raise an eyebrow" over Scottish referendum. CNN, 19 September 2019. Available at: https://edition.cnn.com/2019/09/19/uk/david-cameron-queen-scottish-referendum-gbr-intl/index.html.

[75] McKenzie and Said (2019) David Cameron reveals he asked the Queen to "raise an eyebrow" over Scottish referendum. CNN, 19 September 2019. Available at: https://edition.cnn.com/2019/09/19/uk/david-cameron-queen-scottish-referendum-gbr-intl/index.html.

[76] Chiara Giordano (2019) Buckingham Palace "displeased" by David Cameron's comments about seeking Queen's help during Scottish referendum. Independent, 20 September 2019. Available at: https://www.independent.co.uk/news/uk/politics/david-cameron-queen-comments-buckingham-palace-scottish independence-referendum-a9112796.html.

vote against their own government). Johnson's response was problematic. During a visit to see police recruits, Johnson (whilst standing in front of a cohort of new police officers) announced that "I'd rather be dead in a ditch" than seek the extension.[77] This was a clear statement of the Prime Minister's disregard for the rule of law, even if he would never intend to do this in reality, he gave the impression that he was. In response the then Speaker of the House of Commons, John Bercow, criticised Johnson, arguing that "Not obeying the law must surely be a non-starter. Period', and Johnson's statement was a 'terrible example to set to the rest of society".[78] Tellingly, Johnson's Lord Chancellor, Robert Buckland, felt compelled to say "[Johnson and I] have spoken over the past 24 hours regarding the importance of the Rule of Law, which I as Lord Chancellor have taken an oath to uphold".[79] Buckland's comments suggest implicit criticism of the Prime Minister from the minister tasked by Parliament with defending the rule of law.

Secondly, Johnson was willing to advise the monarch to prorogue Parliament in order to avoid parliamentary scrutiny and accountability during the final months of the Brexit negotiations with the European Union. The five-week prorogation of Parliament meant that parliamentarians could no longer scrutinise the government's Brexit policy. Yvette Cooper MP, a senior opposition politician, viewed the prorogation as showing "such disregard for the rule of law or tried to concentrate power in [his] own hands by cancelling Parliament…".[80] The decision to prorogue Parliament was challenged in the courts in both England and Wales, and Scotland. In *Cherry and others v Advocate General for Scotland*[81] the Inner House of the Court of Session held that it was unlawful. Lord Carloway was critical of the Prime Minister's advice to the monarch, as "Since scrutiny is a central pillar of the good governance principle, which is enshrined in the constitution, the decision cannot be seen as a matter of high policy or politics. It is one which attempts to undermine that pillar".[82] Therefore, "the true reason for the prorogation is to reduce the time available for parliamentary scrutiny of Brexit".[83] Ultimately, the UK Supreme Court in *R (on the application of Miller) v The Prime Minster (No. 2)*[84] held that the Prime Minister's advice to

[77] Proctor and Walker (2019) Boris Johnson: I'd rather be dead in ditch than agree Brexit extension. The Guardian, 5 September 2019. Available at: https://www.theguardian.com/politics/2019/sep/05/boris-johnson-rather-be-dead-in-ditch-than-agree-brexit-extension#:~:text=4%20years%20old.

[78] BBC (2019) Bercow warns Johns against disobeying Brexit law. BBC News, 13 September 2019. Available at: https://www.bbc.co.uk/news/uk-politics-49683797.

[79] Mairs (2019) Justice Secretary Robert Buckland warns Boris Johnson about following "rule of law" over no-deal bill. Politics Home, 8 September 2019. Available at: https://www.politicshome.com/news/article/justice-secretary-robert-buckland-warns-boris-johnson-about-following-rule-of-law-over-nodeal-bill.

[80] HC Deb 25 September 2019, Vol. 664, Col. 785.

[81] The Supreme Court of the United Kingdom, *Cherry and others (Respondents) v. Advocate General for Scotland (Appellant) (Scotland)*, judgement of 24 September 2019, 49.

[82] Ibid., 51.

[83] Ibid., 53.

[84] The Supreme Court of the United Kingdom, *R (on the application of Miller) v. The Prime Minster (No. 2)*, UKSC judgment of 2019, 41.

the monarch was unlawful. This was because whilst limiting Parliament's ability to be sovereign, it "frustrat[ed] or prevent[ed] the constitutional role of Parliament in holding the Government to account".[85]

Thirdly, Johnson as Prime Minister was expected to enforce Ministerial standards. Johnson arguably failed to enforce the standards set out in the Ministerial Code when Priti Patel, the Home Secretary, was accused of bullying civil servants. Crucially, as Prime Minister, it was Johnson who had the sole responsibility for enforcing the Code. His failure to enforce the Ministerial Code revealed an unwillingness to uphold the requisite standards expected by the constitution.[86]

Fourthly, Johnson misled the House of Commons over whether he knew about social gatherings in Downing Street during the time when Covid-19 restrictions made it unlawful to socialise. This was coined as Partygate, as pictures were to emerge of the Prime Minister holding alcoholic drinks at a small party to celebrate his birthday. Johnson denied that this had been the case. It is of paramount importance that the Prime Minister is truthful to the House of Commons and where he has made a mistake, that he immediately corrects the record and informs Parliament. This is an obligation underpinned by constitutional norms and its inclusion in the Ministerial Code. In her investigation on behalf of the Cabinet Office, Sue Gray stated that, "Many will be dismayed that behaviour of this kind took place on this scale at the heart of Government. The public have a right to expect the very highest standards of behaviour in such places and clearly what happened fell well short of this".[87]

Johnson was investigated by the Committee of Privileges which published its report in June 2023. Johnson had already resigned as Prime Minister (see below) and shortly before the report was published, he then resigned as a Member of Parliament. The Committee of Privileges was highly critical of Johnson:

> It is of paramount importance that Ministers give accurate and truthful information to Parliament, correcting any inadvertent error at the earliest opportunity. Ministers who knowingly mislead Parliament will be expected to offer their resignation to the Prime Minister... We conclude that when he told the House and this Committee that the Rules and Guidance were being complied with, his own knowledge was such that he deliberately misled the House and this Committee... He misled the House on an issue of the greatest importance to the House and to the public, and did so repeatedly.[88]

Johnson's departure from Downing Street risked causing a constitutional crisis, as faced with a deluge of senior ministerial resignations, Johnson might have been

---

[85] Ibid., 55–56.

[86] Haddon (2020) The handling of the Priti Patel bullying inquiry has fatally undermined the Ministerial Code. Institute For Government, 20 November 2020. Available at: https://www.instituteforgovernment.org.uk/article/comment/handling-priti-patel-bullying-inquiry-has-fatally-undermined-ministerial-code.

[87] UK Parliament (2022) Findings of Second Permanent Secretary's Investigation into Alleged Gatherings on Government Premises During Covid Restrictions. Cabinet Office, 25 May 2022. Available at: https://hansard.parliament.uk/commons/2019-09-25/debates/AD2A07E5-9741-4EBA-997A-97776F80AA38/PrimeMinisterSUpdate#contribution-EA9CC9DF-6E5D-4D84-A0C2-00E110D58BE3.

[88] Committee of Privileges 2023.

expected to offer his resignation to the monarch. However, Johnson's party enjoyed a majority in the House of Commons, thus Johnson could technically say that as party leader he enjoyed the confidence of the House of Commons. There was speculation that Johnson might request that the monarch use her personal prerogative powers to dissolve Parliament and trigger a general election, thus offering Johnson the prospect of going to the country and seeing if the electorate would support him. Whilst such a dissolution would be possible under the Dissolution and Calling of Parliament Act 2022, it would not be constitutional, given Johnson's tangible lack of support from within his party. This presented the monarch with a dilemma. As Sebastian Payne observed, "For the Queen to reject an election request outright would have prompted a full-blown constitutional crisis and put the monarch in the most perilous position of her reign." Therefore, if directly asked then the monarch would be bound to agree. The solution was controversial: "Another senior official confirmed it would be politely communicated to Downing Street that Her Majesty 'couldn't come to the phone' had Johnson requested a call with the intention of dissolving parliament."[89] Thus, the constitution would have muddled-through, with the monarch too busy to take the Prime Minister's calls. Nonetheless there was some speculation that the monarch might have declined Johnson's request (here a prorogation of Parliament), as apparently, "the Queen was ready to decline Mr Johnson's request due to the fact he did not have the support of his MPs".[90] A royal refusal would have been significant, regardless of the rationale for doing so and one royal insider is reported as saying "For Mr Johnson to have even attempted to put Her Majesty in such a position could have caused a very difficult constitutional situation."[91]

So, did Johnson reveal the inadequacy of the constitution? One view was that "Yes, the self-correction powers of the British political system have done their job, but barely". However, "For all his failings, his greatest favour to the public in the United Kingdom may have been to demonstrate the fragility of that nation's constitutional arrangement."[92] This is hardly a robust endorsement of the constitution. This fragility and long-term consequences are a theme addressed by Lisa James, who observed that "Perhaps the most significant legacy of Johnson's time in the office is the relative normalisation of such [unconstitutional] behaviour".[93]

In Hannah White's view "The most important lesson that Johnson's three years as prime minister have taught us is how uniquely vulnerable this type of constitution may be to concerted manipulation by a determined populist leader with a

---

[89] See Payne (2022) In the Bunker: Boris Johnson's last stand. Financial Times, 18 November 2022. Available at: https://www.ft.com/content/e6d6c253-45a1-4c53-9621-405e2e1507e6_.

[90] Parsley (2022) Queen would have refused Boris Johnson a general election for two key constitutional reasons, insiders say. I, 7 July 2022, available at: https://inews.co.uk/news/politics/queen-refused-boris-johnson-general-election-constitutional-reasons-royal-insider-1730372.

[91] Ibid.

[92] Maastricht University (2022) The fragility of the familiar: how Boris Johnson exposed the tenuous nature of the UK Constitution. 4 August 2022. Available at: https://www.maastrichtuniversity.nl/blog/2022/08/fragility-familiar-how-boris-johnson-exposed-tenuous-nature-uk-constitution.

[93] James (2022) Boris Johnson's constitutional legacy. The Constitution Unit, 4 September 2022. Available at: https://constitution-unit.com/2022/09/04/boris-johnsons-constitutional-legacy/.

large Commons majority and a calculated agenda."[94] However, White was keen to distinguish Johnson from an aspiring authoritarian ruler: "Johnson was not that. His testing of the limits of the constitution was mostly opportunistic, driven by a passion for self-preservation and bolstered by an instinctive self-regard rather than by any concerted political project save that of 'getting Brexit done'".[95] This is a fair assessment. White regards Johnson as being opportunistic and supporting his allies "as a means to the end of sustaining his premiership rather than himself being the driving force behind them".[96] The evolutionary nature of the uncodified constitution was highly problematic, as White warned, "[n]ot only is an evolving constitution easy to contest, but the fact that its rules, norms and conventions are located in a multiplicity of different places makes it vulnerable to subtle erosion without this necessarily generating widespread alarm".[97] There is no canary in the cage—an assault on the constitution can be gradual and hidden behind differing interpretations and flexibility. White's major criticism of Johnson's government was that "Even worse than simply setting norms aside, at times Johnson's ministers demonstrated a form of constitutional vindictiveness, using their majority to attempt to neuter any institution or individual who mounted a challenge to their plans". White draws upon example including the government's reaction to the Supreme Court's decision in *Miller No.2*.[98] Indeed, Johnson's last speech in the House of Commons as Prime Minister, contained this arguably vindictive and personal attack on the former President of the Supreme Court: "[w]ith iron determination we saw off Brenda Hale and we got Brexit done".[99]

Commenting on Johnson's fall from power, Mark Elliot remarked, "So has the constitution 'worked'? That depends on what we expected of it. However, based on the established understanding of how Government works and is sustained in the UK, it is difficult to see in what sense the constitution has failed to work". To Elliot the constitution and political mechanisms worked, and Johnson could be, and was, removed. However, Elliot rejected the view that a written constitution would have made things better: "in my view it is inaccurate to suggest that a written constitution would necessarily have dealt with this week's extraordinary political events differently, better or more efficiently than the existing constitution, at least if the goal is to ensure fidelity to the cardinal principle that the Prime Minister can govern only when he or she enjoys the confidence of the House of Commons".[100] The

[94] White (2022) What Boris Johnson taught us about the UK constitution. Prospect, 17 August 2022. Available at: https://www.prospectmagazine.co.uk/politics/38876/what-boris-johnson-taught-us-about-the-uk-constitution.

[95] Ibid.

[96] Ibid.

[97] Ibid.

[98] Ibid.

[99] HC Deb 18 July 2022, vol 718, col 726.

[100] Elliot 2022. A similar view was taken by Sir Stephen Laws, who argued that "The prediction that our constitutional arrangements could not deal with what was seen to be the developing crisis have proved to be wrong". Laws (2022) Forty-eight hours that proved the UK's unwritten constitution is fit for purpose. Policy Exchange, 8 July 2022. Accessed at: https://policyexchange.org.uk/blogs/forty-eight-hours-that-proved-the-uks-unwritten-constitution-is-fit-for-purpose/.

threat of Johnson was foiled by the public, as David Sanders argues that "Johnson has already inflicted considerable damage on Britain's constitutional practices. The crumb of comfort for supporters of democracy is that British voters in general appear to have understood how Johnson has violated Britain's inherently flexible unwritten constitution."[101] Johnson's conduct was scathingly attacked by Lord Hennessy, who condemned Johnson and his allies as "In pursuit of partisan advantage or personal gratification, they were often willing to bypass non-binding constraints to which those in their position should willingly subject themselves".[102]

4.3.2 Muddling-Through: Lessons from History

Constitutional crisis is not a new phenomenon. The 1780s must rank as one of the most turbulent periods in British constitutional history. This decade saw Britain make peace with its former American colonies and recognise American independence, an outcome which had caused the collapse of Lord North's long-serving ministry in 1782,[103] the rapid collapse of Lord Shelburne's ministry in 1783,[104] and the creation of the most controversial coalition government in British political history. The Fox-North coalition that emerged in 1783, brought together two unlikely allies, Charles James Fox and Lord North, who served under the premiership of the Duke of Portland. The ministry was regarded as reformist and a threat to the traditional constitution. The planned reforms of the East India Company, whereby Fox's India Bill would have increased government control of the Company, was regarded as an attempt to gain access to an importance source of patronage.[105] The crisis of 1783 illustrated the dramatic consequences of when the relationship between the monarch and their Prime Minister (here this breakdown related to key ministers in the government) broke down. The king's dislike of the coalition and his believe that this "unprincipled coalition" has been forced upon him precipitated a crisis that led to a showdown between the king and his ministers.[106]

George III accepted that he could not refuse royal assent to the India Bill and had he done so the coalition would still form the government.[107] Instead, the king acted extra-constitutionally and signalled through his ally Earl Temple that "whoever voted for the India Bill were not only not his friends, but he should consider them as his

---

[101] Sanders (2023) The Consequences of Boris Johnson's Assault on the British Political System. Political Quarterly, 26 June 2023. Accessed at: https://politicalquarterly.org.uk/blog/the-consequences-of-boris-johnsons-assault-on-the-british-political-system/.

[102] Hennessy (2022) Post-Johnson, constitutional combustion continues. But the fire can be extinguished. The Constitution Society, 10 November 22. Available at: https://consoc.org.uk/constitutional-combustion-continues/.

[103] Cannon 1970, pp. 1–2

[104] Ibid., pp. 36–37.

[105] Ibid., p. 139.

[106] Ibid., p. 80.

[107] Ibid., p. 124.

enemies".[108] The king was clear that his own government did not have his support. As John Cannon argued, "No constitutional defence of the king's action is possible, nor was any attempted at the time by his supporters". The problem was "Secret lobbying against his ministers was bound, as the coalition pointed out, to destroy the basis of responsible government: ministers could only be answerable for policy if it were their own."[109] If there was to be a defence to justify the king's unconstitutional conduct, then "The only possible defence of the intervention was the one… which assumed the constitution had virtually broken down, and that the king was entitled to use any means to defend his position".[110] Unsurprisingly the House of Lords rejected the Bill, which gave the king grounds to dismiss the coalition government and request that William Pitt form a government in late 1783.[111] This was despite the former government still enjoying a majority in the House of Commons.[112]

The subsequent general election was hard fought and the former coalition, who lost, regarded the outcome as tainted by corruption and the undue influence of the East India Company.[113] The fallout from the election was immense, in opposition the former coalition found that:

> Its heterogeneity made unity upon shared principles impossible, and its unpopularity made most of its members unwilling after the general election even to challenge their exclusion from office by what they considered to be the unconstitutional behaviour of George III and of the ministry of William Pitt. Burke was later to adduce this unwillingness as a major cause of difference between Fox and himself from 1784.[114]

As the decade dragged on the opposition led by Edmund Burke spearheaded the impeachment of Warren Hastings,[115] the former governor-general of Bengal, and constitutional crisis erupted over the madness of the king and his incapacity to rule. The Prince of Wales and the opposition favoured a Regency, and unsurprisingly this was opposed by the government. George III's recovery deferred the eventual establishment of a Regency until 1810. The constitution muddled-through this decade of crisis and even George III's intervention faded into the background.

The idea that there a *real* constitution though was contested. In *The Rights of Man* Thomas Paine responded to Edmund Burke's criticism of him by stating, "Can then Mr. Burke produce the English Constitution? If he cannot, we may fairly conclude, that though it has been so much talked about, no such thing as a constitution exists, or ever did exist, and consequently that the people have yet a constitution to form."[116]

---

[108] Ibid., p. 133.

[109] Ibid., p. 142.

[110] Ibid.

[111] Ibid., p. 144.

[112] Ibid., p. 149.

[113] Ibid., pp. 219–221.

[114] Hill 1974, p. 2.

[115] Ibid., pp. 10–11. For Charles James Fox the campaign against Warren Hastings was primarily aimed at embarrassing the government and Burke suspected "that political expediency rather than abstract principle was to be the first consideration" (Hill 1974, p. 12).

[116] Paine 1791.

Paine continued, "no such thing as a constitution exists in England. But it may be put as a question, not improper to be investigated, that if a constitution does not exist, how came the idea of its existence so generally established?". The reason given by Paine was the self-interest of those in power and the country believed it had a constitution because of the government to justify the status quo, "if the cry of constitution had not been set up by the government. It has got into circulation like the words bore and quoz [quiz], by being chalked up in the speeches of parliament, as those words were on window shutters and doorposts; but whatever the constitution may be in other respects, it has undoubtedly been the most productive machine of taxation that was ever invented".[117]

However, was the British constitution merely illusionary and borne out by expediency and self-interest of those in power? Arguably the American revolutionaries offer an important lesson in the fact that the revolution and drive for independence was motivated by them being denied their constitutional rights. Thus, they accepted there was a constitution from which they derived rights. Examples of this approach included the Stamp Act Congress when it petitioned George III to help them secure "the inherent Rights and Liberties of your Subjects here, upon the Principles of the English constitution".[118] As Reid observed, "Although one might object that there was, in 1765, no such thing as an English constitution, the claim could not be misunderstood. What was being sought was both English and British—English rights under the British constitution."[119] Consequentially, "Colonial Whigs might speak of American rights but they were thinking of English rights guaranteed to Americans by the British constitution".[120] The problem with English constitution rights were that these were 'vague', and this vagueness "was due in large part to the nature of British constitutional doctrine, arising from an unwritten constitution", however this vagueness did not prevent colonists from asserting these rights "as if they were clearly defined".[121]

As Gordon Wood observed, "Up to 1775 the colonists had carried on their debate with Great Britain within the confines of the English constitution. The rights that the colonists claimed were the rights of Englishmen, the rights embodied in Magna Carta and other English documents. But to members of the Continental Congress contemplating the possibility of independence… it became awkward to talk continually of English rights."[122] However, the revolution forced the colonists to rethink the idea of a constitution and how rights were protected. This resulted in a shift towards conceptualising rights as natural rights and not dependent on documents and case reports.[123] Wood is clear that the revolution saw a convergence in the meaning of a constitution, as "The American revolutionaries virtually established the modern idea

---

[117] Ibid. See also Whatmore 2014.

[118] Reid 1986, p. 9.

[119] Ibid.

[120] Ibid.

[121] Ibid., pp. 10–11.

[122] Wood 2021, p. 29.

[123] Ibid.

of a written constitution… they made written constitutions a practical and everyday part of governmental life", whereas "before the era of the American revolution a constitution was rarely distinguished from the government and its operation".[124] Wood cites Supreme Court Justice William Paterson who in the 1790s argued that "in England… there is no written constitution, no fundamental law, nothing visible, nothing real, nothing certain" and the constitution was "entirely at the mercy of the parliament".[125]

The constitution and how many of the colonists regarded their rights within it and their expectations of good government and representation, played a pivotal role in the revolution. The constitution laid out principles that the metropole was expected to extend to its colonists in the periphery, and a failure to acknowledge this by the government and monarch, proved decisive. In terms of the wider context Jack P Greene argues that the dispute needs to be considered within the broader debate about the constitutional relationship between the metropole and its empire.[126] This was problematic as the constitutional arrangements were uncertain and thus "The balance of authority between metropolis and colonies remained undefined".[127] Consequentially, Parliament's attempts to tax the colonies in the 1760s were met with resistance in America, but were viewed as constitutionally legitimate by Britain.[128] The solution proposed that of virtual representation, whereby Parliament would represent the interests of the colonists (who were not actually represented by their own MPs), was rejected in America as "the very concept was incompatible with that ancient and basic constitutional principle that no tax could be 'justly laid on any People… when the People taxed have not contributed to the Law, and agreed by their Representatives to receive it'".[129]

Arguably the muddling-through constitution was foiled by those within the metropole not being receptive to the significance relationship between the colonies and the British state. The flexible constitution could have evolved to meet this new challenge and a solution found to enable new constitutional arrangements to emerge and thus to permit the constitution to muddle-through. However, the constitution muddled on, and the lessons of America were to influence British attitudes to other colonies that were established by settlers.

---

[124] Ibid., p. 42.

[125] Ibid., p. 3.

[126] Greene 2011.

[127] Ibid., p. 67

[128] Ibid., pp. 67–70.

[129] Ibid., pp. 70–72.

4.4 Conclusion

This chapter has demonstrated the importance of the relationship between the monarch and the Prime Minister in the UK's constitution. The ability of these two key actors to effectively work together is the key ingredient for ensuring that the constitution can muddle through periods of political, societal, and constitutional change. It has been argued that the premiership of Johnson has shown the dangers posed by a willingness to disregard the accepted constitutional norms. Johnson's tenure as Prime Minister was short and he was removed by his own party, yet it raises a pertinent question: is the UK constitution robust enough to survive going forward? The answer is that the strength of the constitution is a willingness to muddle through, both by the institutions, and the actors within the constitution. The relationship between the monarch and the Prime Minister demonstrates this willingness, even if it can be tested in extraordinary times. Notwithstanding the Johnson premiership, the relationship between Prime Minister and monarch did not fracture. Indeed, it has been reported that some of those close to Johnson wished to draw upon this relationship between Johnson and the monarch, by proposing that the monarch should offer advice to her Prime Minister so as to advise Johnson to moderate his approach to the constitution.

In terms of the broader suitability of the constitution in its present form this chapter has argued that the muddling-through approach works. In the coming decade there will be no shortage of challenges that will test the UK's constitution. The question of whether future constitutional reform includes the introduction of a written constitution, or is confined to targeted reforms of specific areas, remains to be seen. The purpose of this chapter is not to refute the case for a written constitution, but rather to argue that the constitution has proved capable of muddling through and surviving challenges, such as the turbulent events of the 1780s. In recent years the constitution has survived the turmoil of the Brexit years, the Scottish independence referendum, coalition government, and increased polarisation in politics. The constitution has muddled through, and the evidence suggests that no matter the alarm bells being run by commentators, it will continue to muddle through. This chapter has sought to demonstrate this. The health of the constitution post-Johnson is sound, the Johnson administration may have raised the temperature of the constitution, but the remedy was ultimately provided by political events, much as has always been the case. If there is to be a fix, then this fix is not to introduce a written constitution, but to look at changing political culture and calming the hostile and divisive public debate that has worsened in the wake of the decision to hold a referendum on the UK's membership of the European Union. Arguably the more polarization in public debate, the more aggression in politics and public discourse, then the more likely it is that warnings of unconstitutional conduct by those in power will be drowned out by all the noise.

References

Allan TRS (2011) Questions of legality and legitimacy: Form and substance in British constitutionalism. International Journal of Constitutional Law 9(1):155–162.

Arvind TT, Kirkham R, Mac Síthigh D, Stirton L (eds) (2021) Executive Decision-Making and the Courts: Revisiting the Origins of Modern Judicial Review. Hart Publishing, Oxford.

Bagehot W (1963) The English Constitution. Fontana, London.

Barber NW (2008) Against a written constitution. Public Law 1:11–18.

Blackburn R (2013) Queen Elizabeth II and the Evolution of Monarchy. In: Qvortrup M (ed) The British Constitution: Continuity and Change. Hart Publishing, Oxford, pp. 165–177.

Blackburn R (2016) The Abdication of Edward VIII: Legal and Constitutional Perspectives. In: Glencross M, Rowbotham J, Kandiah M (eds) The Windsor Dynasty 1910 to the Present: 'Long to Reign Over Us?'. Palgrave Macmillan, London, pp. 159–194.

Blick A (2019) Stretching the Constitution: The Brexit Shock in Historic Perspective. Hart Publishing, Oxford.

Bogdanor V (1995) The Monarchy and the Constitution. Oxford University Press, Oxford.

Breay C, Harrison R (eds) (2015) Magna Carta: Law, Liberty and Legacy. British Library, London.

Cannon J (1970) The Fox-North Coalition: Crisis of the Constitution, 1782–1784. Cambridge University Press, Cambridge.

Committee of Privileges (2023) Fifth Report—Matter referred on 21 April 2022 (conduct of Rt Hon Boris Johnson): Final Report', HC 940 https://committees.parliament.uk/committee/289/committee-of-privileges/publications/.

Dickinson HT (1986) Caricatures and the Constitution, 1760–1832. Chadwyck-Healey, Cambridge.

Elliot M (2020) Constitutional Adjudication and Constitutional Politics in the United Kingdom: The *Miller II* Case in Legal and Political Context. European Constitutional Law Review 16(4):625–646.

Elliot M (2022) Boris Johnson's resignation: Did the constitution work? Public Law for Everyone.

Gaunt P (1989) Drafting the Instrument of Government, 1653–54: A Reappraisal. Parliamentary History 8(1):28–42.

Gordon R (2010) Repairing British Politics: A Blueprint for Constitutional Change. Hart Publishing, Oxford.

Greene JP (2011) The Constitutional Origins of the American Revolution. Cambridge University Press, Cambridge.

Griffith JAG (1979) The Political Constitution. Modern Law Review 42:1–21.

Grzybowski K (1959) The New French Constitution. The American Journal of Comparative Law 8(2):214–217.

Hailsham Q (1976) Elective Dictatorship. The Listener 496–500.

Hale B (2016) The Supreme Court: Guardian of the Constitution? Sultan Azlan Shah Lecture 2016, Kuala Lumpur.

Heffer S (1998) Power and Place: The Political Consequences of King Edward VII. Weidenfeld & Nicolson, London.

Hill BW (1974) Fox and Burke: The Whig Party and the Question of Principles, 1784–1789. The English Historical Review 89:1–24.

Jones BC (2020) Constitutional Idolatry and Democracy: Challenging the Infatuation with Writtenness. Edward Elgar, Cheltenham.

Jones BC (2023) In defence of the UK's unwritten constitution. Institute for Government, Bennett Institute for Public Policy, Cambridge.

Macinnes AI (2007) Union and Empire: The Making of the United Kingdom in 1707. Cambridge University Press, Cambridge.

Marshall G, Moodie GC (1967) Some Problems of the Constitution. Hutchinson University Library, London.

McLean I (2009) What's Wrong with the British Constitution? Oxford University Press, Oxford.

Monaghan C, Welsh J (2023) Questions of Control: Accountability in the Shadow of Prorogation. In: Flinders M, Monaghan C (eds) Questions of Accountability: Prerogatives, Power and Politics. Hart Publishing, Oxford 115–128.
Murkens JEK (2021) A Written Constitution: A Case Not Made. Oxford Journal of Legal Studies 41(4):965–986.
Neuberger D (2015a) Magna Carta: The Bible of the English Constitution or a Disgrace to the English Nation. Guildford Cathedral.
Neuberger D (2015b) UK Supreme Court decisions on private and commercial law: The role of public policy and public interest. Centre for Commercial Law Studies Conference 2015.
Norton P (2020) Governing Britain: Parliament, Ministers and our Ambiguous Constitution. Manchester University Press, Manchester.
Oliver D (2010) Repairing British Politics: A Blueprint for Constitutional Change—By Richard Gordon. Hart Publishing, Oxford. International Journal of Law in Context 6(4):399–403.
Paine T (1791) The Rights of Man. JS Jordan, London.
Popp KA (2000) The Impeachment of President Clinton: An Ugly Mix of Three Powerful Forces. Law and Contemporary Problems 63:223–243.
Rakove J (2024) Impeachment, Responsibility and Constitutional Failure. In: Monaghan C, Flinders M (eds) British Origins and American Practice of Impeachment. Routledge, Abingdon.
Reid JP (1986) Constitutional History of the American Revolution: The Authority of Rights. The University of Wisconsin Press, Madison.
Richards S (2021) The Prime Ministers We Never Had: Success and Failure from Butler to Corbyn. Atlantic Books, London.
Ridley FF (1988) There is No British Constitution: A Dangerous Case of the Emperor's Clothes. Parliamentary Affairs 41(3):340–361.
Ridley FF (1991) Defining Constitutional Law in Britain. Anglo-American Law Review 20:101–115
Scarman L (1974) English Law a New Dimension, Hamlyn Lectures. Stevens & Sons, London.
Sumption J (2015) Magna Carta then and now. Address to the Friends of the British Library.
Tarkow IN (1943) The Significance of the Act of Settlement in the Evolution of English Democracy. Political Science Quarterly 58(4):537–561.
Whatmore R (2014) Thomas Paine. In: Galligan D (ed) Constitutions and the Classics: Patterns of Constitutional Thought from Fortescue to Bentham. Oxford University Press, Oxford 414–438.
Wood GS (2021) Power and Liberty: Constitutionalism in the American Revolution. Oxford University Press, Oxford.
Woolf H (1995) Droit public—English style. Public Law 57–71.

Chapter 5
Militant Constitutionalism: Formal Institutions and Constitutional Practices

Ronald Tinnevelt

Contents

Abstract Constitutional democracy—representative democracy founded in a constitution and recognition of fundamental rights—is a fragile form of governance that can slowly disappear without protection, support and maintenance. What can make constitutional democracy more resilient and prevent it from turning into a form of illiberal democracy or authoritarian rule? Within legal and political theory, this question has received considerable attention from the 1930s onwards, leading to numerous studies on militant democracy. These studies, however, mainly focus on one of the two pillars of constitutional democracy, *democracy*, while the other pillar, *constitutionalism* and *rule of law,* has received far less attention. With some minor exceptions hardly any articles or books are dedicated to the question what the concept of militant constitutionalism entails (i) or what a legal theory of militant constitutionalism should look like (ii). Those publications that do address the concept of militant constitutionalism, moreover, primarily focus on *formal instruments* of constitutional defense (rule of law institutions) and not on *informal instruments* (norms, ethos, practices and culture). Yet, what kind of informal instruments or legal culture are needed to maintain and defend constitutional democracy (iii)? This chapter has two main goals. The *first* is to answer question (i) by mapping different understandings of the concept of militant constitutionalism. The *second* goal is to give a general

R. Tinnevelt (✉)
Department of the Philosophy of Law, Radboud University, Nijmegen, The Netherlands
e-mail: ronald.tinnevelt@ru.nl

M. De Visser et al. (eds.), *European Yearbook of Constitutional Law 2024*, European Yearbook of Constitutional Law 6, https://doi.org/10.1007/978-94-6265-699-4_5

response to question (iii) by distinguishing four possible elements of such a legal culture.

Keywords Rule of law backsliding · Militant constitutionalism · Militant democracy · Binding power · Constitutional practices · Legal trust · Rule of law · Unwritten legal rules and norms

> Constitutions are only sets of vague words proposing solutions that defy the natural tendencies of power aggrandizement.[1]

5.1 Introduction

In *Freedom in the World 2022*—the main annual report of Freedom House—two serious threats to liberal democracy and global freedom are mentioned. On the one hand, "authoritarian regimes have become increasingly effective at co-opting or circumventing the norms and institutions meant to support basic liberties (...)". On the other hand, democracies are increasingly threatened by internal "illiberal forces", politicians and parties seeking to undermine the democratic system from within.[2] This is not a temporary setback in a long process of democratization. The global increase in autocratic governance is the result of sixteen consecutive years of decline. A decline that not only effects democracy. The "enemies of liberal democracy", as the Freedom House report firmly puts it, focus their arrows not just on democratic governance but also on the rule of law; both can be attacked and consequently fall into disrepair.[3]

Freedom House is not the only organization to issue such a warning. Similar worries are widely shared, reflected in multiple statistics and reports, and clearly show that constitutional democracy—a representative democracy founded in a constitution and recognition of fundamental rights—is a fragile form of governance that can disappear without protection, support and maintenance. But what can make constitutional democracy resilient and prevent it from turning into a form of illiberal democracy or authoritarian rule?

Within legal and political theory, this question has received considerable attention from the 1930s onwards, especially during the last decade, leading to numerous studies on militant democracy. Strikingly, though, these studies mainly focus on one of the two pillars of constitutional democracy, *democracy*, while the other pillar, *constitutionalism* and *rule of law* (both principles for limiting and binding governmental power), is largely neglected. While it is true that within legal and political

[1] Sajó 2021, p. 17.

[2] Repucci and Slipowitz 2022.

[3] Repucci and Slipowitz 2022, p. 1.

science much is written about the problem of rule of law backsliding and constitutional decay in countries like Poland, Hungary, and the United States, the concept of militant constitutionalism is rarely being discussed. Hardly any publication is dedicated to the question what the concept of militant constitutionalism entails (i) or what a theory of militant constitutionalism should look like (ii). Those publications that do address the concept of "militant constitutionalism" (or "militant rule of law"[4]), moreover, primarily focus on *formal instruments* of constitutional defense (rule of law institutions) and not on *informal instruments* (norms, ethos, practices and culture). Following Loewenstein's famous quote—"The most perfectly drafted and devised statutes are not worth the paper on which they are written unless supported by [the] indomitable will to survive" (1937c: 657)—one can argue, however, that the informal instruments are just as important as the formal ones. Yet, what kind of "political and legal culture within (…) society"—as the Venice Commission describes this—is needed to maintain and defend constitutional democracy (iii)?[5]

This chapter has two main goals. The *first* is to answer question (i) by mapping different understandings of the concept of militant constitutionalism. The *second* goal is to give a general response to question (iii) by distinguishing four possible elements of such a legal culture. The aim of this chapter, however, is not to develop a normative argument for militant constitutionalism nor to present a theory of militant constitutionalism (question ii). A second disclaimer: although this chapter will analyze militant constitutionalism by comparing it with and distinguishing it from militant democracy, both are needed to make constitutional democracies resilient and stable. Section 5.2 provides a general analysis of militant constitutionalism on the basis of a comparison with the notion of militant democracy. Section 5.3 addresses the question what conception of rule of law is presupposed by militant constitutionalism. Section 5.4 argues that stable constitutional practices are crucial for the resilience of constitutional democracies and distinguishes four possible elements of these practices: acceptance of and dialogue on unwritten legal rules and norms; public and professional mentality; legal trust; and civic and professional education. Section 5.5, finally, briefly summarizes the main finding of this chapter.

5.2 Militant Democracy and Militant Constitutionalism

The concept of militant constitutionalism is rarely used or analyzed in the current literature on "illiberal democracy" and "rule of law backsliding". What is the best way to get to the heart of this concept? An obvious route is by first studying how the concept of militant *democracy* is defined in the literature (Sect. 5.2.1), in order to draw lessons for the delineation of the concept of militant *constitutionalism* (Sect. 5.2.2).

---

[4] Sajó 2019; Sajó and Tuovinen 2018; Sajó 2023a and 2023b.

[5] European Commission for Democracy Through Law (Venice Commission) *The Netherlands, Opinion on the Legal Protection of Citizens*, opinion no 1031/2021, 18 October 2021, p. 8.

After all, militant democracy bears clear similarities to militant constitutionalism and can be seen as it counterpart.

5.2.1 *Militant Democracy*

The concept "militant democracy" was first used in the mid-1930s by German jurist and political scientist Karl Loewenstein in two articles: "Militant Democracy and Fundamental Rights I and II".[6] Loewenstein—who fled Nazi Germany in late 1933 and who lived and worked in the United States consequently—described the rise of international fascism, showed how European democracies threatened to turn into autocracies and why the Weimar Republic could not defend itself against the National Socialist dictatorship. "Democracy and democratic tolerance", Loewenstein claimed with regard to the Weimar republic, "have been used for their own destruction".[7] The cause, he believed, was a strong form of relativism and formalism: "It is the exaggerated formalism of the rule of law which under the enchantment of formal equality does not see fit to exclude from the game parties that deny the very existence of its rules".[8]

What is his answer to this problem? The enemies of democratic institutions must be suppressed: at the national level by the state, at the global level by a coalition of democratic states.[9] Representative democracies must be militant and the concept of democracy redefined as "the application of disciplined authority, by liberal-minded men, for the ultimate ends of liberal government: human dignity and freedom".[10] After the war, the importance of Loewenstein's analysis of militant democracy was recognized and incorporated into the draft constitution of the Federal Republic of Germany (see, for example, Articles 20(4) and 79(3)).[11]

A general definition of militant democracy is given by Jan-Werner Müller. Militant democracy, he writes, "refers to the idea of a democratic regime which is willing to adopt pre-emptive, prima facie illiberal measures to prevent those aiming at subverting democracy with democratic means from destroying the democratic regime".[12] A less battle-worn definition is given by Samuel Isscharoff. It refers to "the ability of democratic regimes to restrict forms of debate, political organization, or political participation that pose an existential threat to democracy itself".[13]

This difference between both definitions immediately shows a problem of terminology. The unambiguity regarding the origins of the concept "militant democracy",

[6] Loewenstein 1937a, 1937c, p. 656; see also Loewenstein 1937a, 1936.

[7] Loewenstein 1937a, p. 423.

[8] Ibid., p. 424.

[9] Greenberg 2015, p. 179.

[10] Loewenstein 1937b, p. 658.

[11] Müller 2012b, p. 1258; Papier and Durner 2003.

[12] Müller 2012b, p. 1253.

[13] Issacharoff 2015, p. 18.

does not translate directly into a similar unambiguity regarding its name and content. Different interpretations and translations have been used. If we look at the scientific research on militant democracy, Bastiaan Rijpkema claims that it is striking that the term has a different meaning in English and German.[14] According to Rijpkema, the English term "militant democracy" expresses a strong "militant or aggressive attitude": the active combating of undemocratic elements and forces ("Fire is fought with fire," as Loewenstein puts it).[15] By contrast, the concepts of "Streitbare Demokratie" and "Wehrhafte Demokratie" that are being used in German primarily imply a defensive attitude in which strong consideration is given to the legitimacy and rule of law character of the means of protection deployed. Put differently, "militant" leaves open the possibility that illegitimate means (such as a strong curtailment of rights) may be deployed to fight undemocratic forces, whereas "defensive" takes the normal constitutional order as its limit.

It is important to keep the difference between "defensive" and "militant" in mind. A difference which, according to Rijpkema, disappears in the English-language literature because people cling to the concept of "militant democracy" as it was originally introduced by Loewenstein. "Defensive democracy", Rijpkema claims, is a more appropriate term to refer to the general notion of resilient democracy. Although a valuable suggestion, the problem is that in the English literature "militant democracy" and "defensive democracy" are sometimes used interchangeably. It might be better, as Müller suggests, to express the difference by speaking of two paradigms: "militant democracy" and "defending democracy" (or "democratic self-defense"). The latter paradigm has received increasing attention in recent years as it explores a broader pallet of democratic defense tools. The emphasis shifts from party bans and restrictions on freedom of speech to the importance of public deliberation and civic education.[16] This shift is important because we will see below that resilience—whether regarding democracy or rule of law—can never rely solely on the establishment of formal institutions (think of the constitution) or the deployment of rule of law instruments (such as constitutional review). An important interaction exists between formal structures, informal instruments and personal attitudes.

5.2.2 *Militant Constitutionalism*

Determining what concept to use for the general idea of the resilience of the rule of law poses an interesting puzzle. This is partly because it is not immediately clear which of the existing (or perhaps possible) notions from the current scientific literature best catches this general idea. In the German literature, both "Streitbare" and "Wehrhafte Rechtsstaat" can be found,[17] while in the English-language literature

---

[14] Here I follow Rijpkema 2018, p. 10.

[15] Loewenstein 1937c, p. 656.

[16] Müller 2012b, p. 1262; see also: Müller 2019, p. 13.

[17] See for instance: Rill 2003.

"militant constitutionalism" and "militant rule of law" are used interchangeably.[18] Although both constitutionalism and rule of law can be seen as principles for limiting and binding governmental power, they are certainly not identical. Given, though, that militant constitutionalism and militant rule of law are used interchangeably I will—for reasons of elegance—opt for the shortest one in terms of words: militant constitutionalism.

But what about the content of the concept of militant constitutionalism? In "Is the Rule of Law an Essentially Contested Concept" Jeremy Waldron argues that the Rule of Law is an "solution-concept" instead of an "achievement-concept". As he writes: "it is the concept of a solution to a problem we're not sure how to solve; and rival conceptions are rival proposals for solving it or rival proposals for doing the best we can in this regard given that the problem is insoluble".[19] Martin Krygier argues something similar. Jurists and legal scholars have been too occupied with giving lists of the elements that constitute the rule of law as a virtue of the law and tend to neglect the fact that the rule of law is the response to a specific problem: the arbitrary use of power. Arguing against giving recipes with different ingredients Krygier claims that we should first of all focus on the telos of the rule of law by posing the question "What is the rule of law problem?".[20] Like "rule of law", one can argue, militant constitutionalism is also primarily a solution-concept and not an achievement-concept. What is the problem, though, that militant constitutionalism is trying to solve?

Three different answers and consequently three different conceptions of militant constitutionalism can be distinguished. The *first conception* can be found, for example, in the response of the US government in the years following the September 11, 2001 attacks. Rule of law resilience in that context implied being able to protect constitutional democracies against domestic and foreign terrorist without sacrificing the fundamental importance of civil liberties. Such an understanding of militant constitutionalism can be found in books like *Before the Next Attack* by Bruce Ackerman or Richard Posner's *Not a Suicide Pact*.[21] A more classic reference regarding the issue of (constitutional) emergency powers is of course Carl Schmitt's work. Already in the twenties of last century Schmitt forcefully discussed the issue of the "state of exception" in, among else, *Die Diktatur* (1921) and *Politische Theologie* (1922).[22] Interestingly, certain parallels exist between Schmitt's and Loewenstein's

---

[18] Gutmann and Voigt 2023. Sajó uses both concepts. Compare Sajó 2019 and 2023a.

[19] Waldron 2002, p. 158.

[20] Krygier 2019, p. 759.

[21] Compare: "Der streitbare Rechtsstaat sollte dabei allerdings vermeiden, im Namen der Rechtssicherheit durch die Verkleinerung von Freiheitssphären seine eigene rechtsstaatliche und demokratische Substanz zu zerstören" [However, the militant constitutional state should avoid destroying its own constitutional and democratic substance by reducing spheres of freedom in the name of legal certainty], Cavallar 2017.

[22] Schmitt 2006; Schmitt 2009. For an interesting comparison between both books, see McCormick 1998. For an analysis of the conceptual affinities between the work of Schmitt and Loewenstein, see: Górnisiewic 2023.

writings. Górnisiewic, for example, claims that "the conceptual world of Loewenstein's militant democracy agrees with surprisingly many of Schmitt's constitutional insights into the nature of the Weimar crisis".[23] Schmitt's "theory of the constitution", according to Górnisiewic, "may serve the aim of a 'militant constitutionalism,' not necessarily a liberal democratic one".

To prevent another 9/11 terrorist attack Ackerman proposes an "emergency constitution". Such a constitution "allows for effective short-term measures that will do everything plausible to stop a second strike—but which firmly draws the line against permanent restrictions". It "makes sense", Ackerman claims, "to tie ourselves to the mast as a precaution against deadly enticements". Even in a race against time it is important to design "a limited state of emergency".[24] So although the focus is on preventing "politicians from exploiting momentary panic to impose long-lasting limitations on liberty"[25] the aim of these politicians was not to establish an electoral autocracy. Posner also focuses on the "constitutional rights that impinge on the measures for the protection of national security".[26] "The more numerous or dangerous the nation's enemies are believed to be", he argues, "the greater the pressure to curtail civil liberties in favor of executive discretion and unity of command, in order to enable the government to wield its great power more effectively, if less responsibly".[27] Whereas Ackerman, however, discusses a variety of controls Posner emphasizes that "law must adjust to necessity born of emergency".[28] The problem that Ackerman and Posner address closely resembles the democratic paradox (or democratic dilemma) that is entailed in Loewenstein's concept of militant democracy: "the possibility of a democracy destroying itself in the process of defending itself".[29] Militant constitutionalism is confronted with a similar paradox—a constitutional paradox or constitutional dilemma: "the possibility of a constitution destroying itself in the process of defending itself".

The *second conception* of militant constitutionalism starts from a different problem. To understand this specific problem it is helpful to take a short look at two different threats to constitutional democracy that Aziz Z. Huq and Tom Ginsburg distinguish: "authoritarian reversion" and "constitutional retrogression".[30] The former involves a process of rapid and complete transition from constitutional democracy toward authoritarian rule. Think of a coup d'état or the sudden declaration of a state of emergency.[31] The relapse toward authoritarian rule, however, need not happen suddenly but can also occur through a long process of small and gradual

[23] Górnisiewicz 2023, p. 2.
[24] Ackerman 2006, p. 3.
[25] Ibid., p. 3.
[26] Posner 2006, p. 1.
[27] Ibid., p. 5.
[28] Cited in Posner 2006, p. 158.
[29] Müller 2012a, pp. 536–537.
[30] Huq and Ginsburg 2018.
[31] Ibid., p. 83.

changes.[32] The object of the second model of militant is precisely this *incremental erosion* of constitutional democracy. The current call for rule of law resilience with regard to countries like Hungary and Poland should be understood in light of this notion of constitutional retrogression. Laurent Pech and Kim Lane Scheppele, two well-known authors in the debate on authoritarianism in Europe, give the following definition of constitutional retrogression with regard to constitutional democracies: "the process through which elected public authorities deliberately implement governmental blueprints which aim to systematically weaken, annihilate or capture internal checks on power with the view of dismantling the liberal democratic state and entrenching the long-term rule of the dominant party".[33]

The gradual dismantling of constitutional democracies, however, does not necessarily need to be the result of the deliberate attempt of populists or authoritarian leaders to create a one-party state. Not all forms of constitutional retrogression are intentionally and systematically pursued, they can also occur as a consequence of the inadequate protection of citizens in the face of the negative effects of government measures. This *third and last conception* of militant constitutionalism emerges if we, for example, take a look at the effects of the childcare benefit scandal in the Netherlands. This scandal entailed institutional racism and racial profiling by the Dutch Tax and Customs Administration and other legal and political institutions. The content of this scandal is concisely described in one of the parliamentary questions posed by the European parliament: "In order to create risk profiles of individuals applying for childcare benefits, the Dutch Tax and Customs Administration used algorithms in which 'foreign sounding names' and 'dual nationality' were used as indicators of potential fraud".[34] Thousands of low- and middle-income families were consequently falsely accused of fraud and had to pay back their benefits. The main task of the current State Commission on the Rule of Law—"Staatscommissie Rechtsstaat"—directly follows from this. It needs to "analyze the functioning of the rule of law and make proposals for strengthening the rule of law" with particular attention to the "protection of citizens against unforeseen and undesirable consequences of government measures".[35] The focus, therefore, is not on the threats posed by populists posed on entrenching their power or a president or Congress suspending habeas corpus but on the consequences of governments not taking seriously their protective duties.

---

[32] Ibid., p. 94.

[33] Pech and Scheppele 2017, p. 10. The ruling party, according to them, deliberately tries to establish an electoral autocracy. See Scheppele K L and Pech L (2018) What is Rule of Law Backsliding? Verfassungsblog, 2 March 2018. Available at: https://verfassungsblog.de/what-is-rule-of-law-backsliding/.

[34] Parliamentary question, The Dutch childcare benefit scandal, institutional racism and algorithms, 28 June 2022. Available at:https://www.europarl.europa.eu/doceo/document/O-9-2022-000028_EN.html.

[35] Rijksoverheid (2022) Kabinet stelt Staatscommissie Rechtsstaat in [Cabinet establishes State Commission on the Rule of Law]. Rijksoverheid, 25 November 2022. Available at: https://www.rijksoverheid.nl/actueel/nieuws/2022/11/25/kabinet-stelt-staatscommissie-rechtsstaat-in.

Constitutional retrogression, in that sense, not only concerns the horizontal relationship between state powers but also the vertical relationship between government and citizen.

Given these three conceptions, is there a common denominator? Is there a core problem to which the theory of militant constitutionalism seeks to provide an answer? I think there is. Going back to Pech and Scheppele's definition, I would argue that militant constitutionalism's main focus is on finding defense mechanisms to guard against "the process through which public authorities implement governmental policies and laws that systematically weaken, annihilate or capture the rule of law with the effect of seriously endangering or dismantling constitutional democracy". Important to emphasize is that this definition is not only focused on the *abuse* of governmental power. It also entails the possibility that the rule of law can be threatened by governments systematically neglecting their positive duties.

The second of these three conceptions is used by authors like Sajó, Gutmann and Voigt—authors that actually use the phrase "militant constitutionalism"—and can be seen as the dominant conception of militant constitutionalism with regard to discussions on rule of law backsliding. The second conception of militant constitutionalism differs in three important regards from the notion of militant democracy that was discussed in the previous section; differences dealing with timing (a), choice of means (b) and actors involved (c). Regarding "timing", militant democracy seeks to identify the enemies of democracy *ex ante* and prevent them from coming to power, whereas militant constitutionalism seeks to encapsulate these enemies *ex post* by curtailing their ability to abuse government power to undermine the achievements of the rule of law. Militant constitutionalism, in that sense, only becomes relevant after populist politicians come to power.[36] The goal is to curb their power and prevent damage to legal institutions.[37]

Among the "means" offered to make democracy resilient militant democracy discusses party bans, the restriction of political freedoms and democratic debate. Examples of "means" in the domain of militant constitutionalism are: separation of powers, limitation of terms of office, curtailment of government power to make executive orders, the constitutional protection of judicial independence, a strong form of constitutional review, the constitutional enshrinement of fundamental rights and liberties, and perhaps "eternity clauses and doctrines of unconstitutional constitutional amendments".[38]

With regard to the "actors" charged with implementation militant constitutionalism is not only aimed at actors within the government but also "actors well beyond the government",[39] like NGOs or the media. These actors need to be "protected by the

[36] Gutmann and Voigt 2023.

[37] Sajó 2019, p. 187 makes a similar claim: "Once populists grab power, the issue is how much resistance can be provided by mechanisms of constitutional self-defense institutions. This question rarely informs constitutional design".

[38] Suteu 2021, p. 264. Suteu, however, is critical of these clauses and amendments. She points to the deep tension that exists between unamendability and democratic constitutionalism.

[39] Gutmann and Voigt 2023, p. 379.

constitution against would-be autocrats"[40] but they also share in the responsibility of containing the power of would-be autocrats, for example by criticizing power abuse.

5.3 Rule of Law: Formal and Substantive

Defining the main problem of militant constitutionalism in this way is a step forward but immediately raises more questions: what conception of rule of law is presupposed in a coherent theory of militant constitutionalism (a) and how to distinguish "rule of law" from "militant constitutionalism" (b)? To address the first issue, it is helpful to take a short look at the literature on militant democracy. Whether democracies should defend themselves against antidemocratic enemies "subverting democracy with democratic means" is a question whose answer heavily depends on our understanding of democracy.[41] Or put another way: "A study of militant democracy touches on the concepts of democracy: what sort of democracy are we defending?"[42] In a general sense, a distinction is often made between formal and substantive notions of democracy. According to formal notions, democracy is a neutral procedure for arriving at political decisions. Democracy constitutes "a 'marketplace of ideas,' in which all ideas are equal".[43] According to substantive notions, democracy is more than just a procedure it also contains substantive moral values—like equality or mutual respect. Thus, not all ideas are equal.

A coherent theory of militant democracy presupposes a value laden or substantive notion of democracy. How substantive is content for debate. It makes little sense, after all, to call for militant measures if democracy is merely a decision-making procedure in which the majority principle determines which decisions are legitimate and which are not. Starting with a purely procedural concept of democracy the democratic dilemma will not even arise. A democratic system that dissolves itself by democratic means will simply not be viewed as a problem in itself. What about a theory of militant constitutionalism? Should a coherent theory of militant constitutionalism also presuppose a substantive concept of rule of law? To answer this question, we need to take a brief look at the difference between formal and substantive notions.

Research on the rule of law and its values has a long tradition and contains a rich variety of different understandings. In his survey work *On the Rule of Law* (2004) Brian Tamanaha describes the difference between formal and substantive notions as follows: "formal theories focus on the proper sources and form of legality, while substantive theories also include requirements about the content of the law (usually that it must comport with justice or moral principle)".[44] Tamanaha distinguishes six notions of the rule of law; three formal and three substantive. With respect to the

---

[40] Ibid., p. 381.

[41] Müller 2016, p. 251.

[42] Rijpkema 2018, p. 8.

[43] Rijpkema 2018, p. 8.

[44] Tamanaha 2004, p. 92.

formal notions of the rule of law, these are (from thin to thick): "rule-by-law", "formal legality" and "democracy+legality". With respect to the substantive notions, these are (again from thin to thick): "individual rights", "right of dignity and/or justice" and "social welfare".

Let us briefly review these six notions and begin with the formal ones. *Rule-by-law* (1) asserts the requirement that government should act on the basis of law. *Formal legality* (2) adds the idea that the form of the law must meet certain conditions and that government is bound to rules and limits, such as that laws must be general and comprehensible, may not have retroactive effect and must guarantee legal certainty.[45] Finally, *Democracy + legality* (3) adds democracy to the importance of formal legality. Democracy not in a material sense, but as a decision-making procedure to arrive at laws on the basis of consent—even if it is given indirectly. All three substantive notions of the rule of law incorporate all the elements of the formal conceptions and add certain requirements regarding the content of laws. Laws should safeguard individual liberty rights (such as the right to property, contract, privacy or autonomy) (4), respect human dignity and political equality (5), or guarantee socio-security rights (6). The latter view imposes a positive duty, a duty of care on governments.

Returning to the question whether a coherent theory of militant constitutionalism—like a coherent theory of militant democracy—should also minimally presuppose a substantive notion of rule of law, the answer is "no" because even a formal notion of rule of law contains moral value and consequently contains reasons for a form of constitutional self-defense. A theory of militant constitutionalism, however, should entail more than just "rule-by-law". If we start from a political understanding of law and put the will of the sovereign at the center, such a formal notion of "rule of law" seems quite meaningless, as in Neumann's formulation: "all utterances of the sovereign, because they are utterances of the sovereign, are law".[46] Law in this sense "is *voluntas* and nothing else".[47] Rule-by-law has little to do with rule of law as implying that government not only has to act on the basis of law, but is also be bound by law. A theory of militant constitutionalism consequently should minimally presuppose a form of "formal legality" (notion 2).[48] Whether such a theory should entail more than just "formal legality" is topic for discussion. Looking at the three conceptions of militant constitutionalism discussed in Sect. 5.2.2, however, it is easy to see that all three presuppose that laws should safeguard individual liberty rights (notion 4). The third conception of militant constitutionalism, in fact, entails notion 6, guaranteeing socio-security rights.

---

[45] Ibid.

[46] Neumann 1957, p. 26. Also cited in Tamanaha 2004, p. 92.

[47] Neumann 1957, p. 26.

[48] What 'formal legality' requires, however, depends on whether it is merely a morally neutral instrument that can be used for both good and bad (i), or an instrument with moral value that can contribute to a more just society (ii). Whether (i) or (ii) is the desired interpretation of legality, however, is not a question I want to address here. Compare Raz 1979, p. 226.

Although I agree that there are good reasons to claim that militant constitutionalism only makes sense if we at least presuppose a substantive conception of the rule of law (concept 4), this is not a claim that needs to be addressed here. It suffices to argue that depending on one's notion of the rule of law and on the specific problem militant constitutionalism needs to address, different instruments and mechanisms will be proposed to protect constitutional democracy. I will return to this issue in Sect. 5.4.1.

How to distinguish between "rule of law" and "militant constitutionalism" (question b above)? This question becomes especially relevant if we take Krygier's analysis of the rule of law problem as our starting point. The rule of law problem for Krygier is the arbitrary exercise of power, its main aim "reducing the possibility of arbitrary exercise of power".[49] Rule of law and militant constitutionalism, in that sense, seem to formulate the same goal: tempering power. So how to separate both concepts? Gutmann and Voigt's definition of militant constitutionalism, unfortunately, is not helpful in this regard. They "propose to refer to any constitutional design feature that aims at safeguarding constitutionalism as 'militant constitutionalism' to document its close relationship with the idea of "militant democracy".[50] This definition seems overly inclusive. Sajó—who uses militant constitutionalism and militant rule of law interchangeably—gives a more useful description of militant rule of law: "The term refers to the aggressive use of tried-and-tested rule of law standards and rules tailored to specific circumstances. Militant rule of law allows for exceptions to the rule of law which are already recognized in rule of law standards and a principled reinterpretation of rule of law precepts". These exceptions, Sajó adds, need to be "temporary, subject to proportionality and independent control".[51] So militant constitutionalism tries to protect the rule of law by either creating new "guardrails and norms"[52] or further strengthening and stretching existing ones in order to prevent public authorities from implementing laws that systematically weaken, annihilate or capture the rule of law.

This way of distinguishing "rule of law" from "militant constitutionalism" can be directly applied to the first and second conception of militant constitutionalism that were discussed in Sect. 5.2.2. The third conception—governments neglecting their protective duties towards their citizens–, however, can only be partially connected to the theme of the abuse or arbitrary use of power because its main aim is much broader than this. The third conception of militant constitutionalism more closely resembles the idea of "defensive democracy" than that of "militant democracy" (see Sect. 5.2.1 above). This conception will not refer to the "aggressive use of tried-and-tested rule of law standards" needed to bind power but to the institutions, constitutional practices

[49] Krygier 2019, p. 789. See pp. 762–763 for three different ways in which the exercise of power can be arbitrary.

[50] Gutmann and Voigt 2023, p. 378.

[51] Sajó 2023b. See also Sajó 2023a, p. 65: "The rule of law does not contain a mechanism of self-defense, a kind of militant rule of law, apt to prevent and combat systemic abuse, and it does not provide a system for its self-restoration that would not endanger, perhaps severely, its own normal functioning".

[52] Smibert 2024, p. 1112.

and perhaps virtues that are needed to protect the rule of law as an instrument of socio-economic rights protection. I will return to this issue in Sect. 5.4.1.

5.4 Constitutional Practices

What mechanisms and instruments are available to make the rule of law more resilient? In Sect. 5.3 I mentioned a few: separation of powers, limitation of terms of office, curtailment of government power to make executive orders, or the constitutional protection of judicial independence. In terms of a toolkit such formal mechanisms seem to be the first to turn to. Do constitutional rules or formal rule of law mechanisms, however, actually constitute effective instruments to prevent forms of constitutional retrogression? According to Gutmann and Voigt, there is little empirical evidence for this. This is not to say that the form and structure of constitutional institutions are not important, but rather that their effect on resilience is limited. According to Gutmann and Voigt, the best antidote is still what Loewenstein pointed out: a strong democratic and—this I add to their claim—rule-of-law tradition.[53] With regard to militant democracy Loewenstein gives the example of the UK: "In no country do better prerequisites for a successful stand against fascist doctrine and practice exist than in Great Britain. Two factors contribute to the expectation that England will be immune from fascism. One is the time-honored acceptance of democratic ideals and institutions in the country in which free government originated".[54] The other, Loewenstein, claims is "that England, having apparently reached the deepest point of the depression, seems on the way to recovery".[55] I will come back to this last point in Sect. 5.5.

Rules are only respected when a large part of the population—both citizens and officials—accepts their value and rational. In the absence of such support, it becomes all the easier for politicians and legislative jurists to disregard constitutional constraints. More research is therefore needed on what kind of constitutional or rule-of-law practices can help protect the rule of law. Unfortunately, current research and reports are sometimes vague about the content of these practices or use different conceptions to present very general guidelines. In addition, depending on the problem that militant constitutionalism tries to address a different interpretation of these necessary practices will emerge. To indicate how this works I will distinguish two possible frameworks for interpreting the content of these practices in Sect. 5.4.1 and in Sect. 5.4.2 I will describe four different elements of these practices.

---

[53] Gutmann and Voigt 2023, p. 379.

[54] Loewenstein 1935, p. 776. Also quoted in Gutmann and Voigt 2023, p. 380.

[55] Loewenstein 1935, p. 776.

5.4.1 Binding Power and Protecting Socio-Economic Rights

In Sect. 5.2.2 I distinguished three problems that militant constitutionalism might try to answer: a president or Congress suspending habeas corpus to deal with national emergencies (1), threats posed by democratically elected populists posed on entrenching their power (2), and the consequences of governments neglecting their protective duties towards their citizens (3). Taking these different problems seriously partially explains why some authors primarily argue for the strengthening of formal defense mechanisms as a way to deal with rule of law backsliding, whereas others also emphasize a specific set of virtues or a specific ethos as necessary defense mechanisms. To make this claim I will briefly construct two perspectives to look at the constitutional practices that are needed to protect constitutional democracies: "rule of law as an instrument of binding power" (I) and "rule of law as an instrument of socio-economic rights protection" (II).

To introduce the *first perspective* I want to return to the quote by Ackerman I cited above: "Given the clear and present danger, it makes sense to tie ourselves to the mast as a precaution against deadly enticements".[56] The idea of tying oneself to the mast goes back to the encounter of Odysseus with the Sirens in Homer's *Odyssey*. Leaving the island of *Aeaea* Kirke gives Odysseus the following advice to avoid being killed by the Sirens: "You must sail past, having stopped the ears of your companions with sweet wax kneaded and pressed into them, so that none of the others should hear. But if you yourself want to hear, then have your men tie you hand and foot in the fast ship, upright against the mast holder with the ropes attached to the mast itself—thus you can take your pleasure in hearing the voice of the Sirens. And if you beg your companions and order them to release you, then they must put yet further ropes on you".[57]

What does this encounter between Odysseus and the Sirens have to do with the rule of law and militant constitutionalism? Many legal scholars and philosophers have used this encounter to answer the question of constitutional legitimacy: why does a political society need a constitution? The rope with which Odysseus is tied to the mast to resist the seductive song of the Sirens is a metaphor for the constitution. Stephen Holmes expresses this as follows: "Citizens need a constitution, just as Ulysses needed to be bound to his mast. If voters were allowed to get what they wanted, they would inevitably shipwreck themselves. By binding themselves to rigid rules, they can better achieve their solid and long-term collective aims".[58] Thus, the primary purpose of the constitution—as a function of protecting the rights and autonomy of the citizen—is to constrain the capricious will of the majority by imposing rule of law limitations. Of course, there is a clear difference between individual and collective self-binding, as authors such as Holmes, Jeremy Waldron and also Jon Elster show.[59] But this does not alter the fact that the idea of self-binding is a core idea for many of

[56] Ackerman 2006, p. 3.

[57] Homer 2000, p. 128.

[58] Holmes 1997, p. 135.

[59] Elster 1985; Waldron 1999, pp. 261–266.

us when we talk about constitution and rule of law. The exercise of power is bound by the rules and principles of law through a constitution. Krygier, as we saw above, argues something similar. "Tempering power" is the point of the rule of law, "the arbitrary exercise of power" its specific antipathy.[60]

If tempering power is the umbrella term—as Krygier claims—to refer to the telos of the rule of law this will have implications for the specific form and content of the constitutional practices that are needed to protect the rule of law. "Many aspects of the rule of law", Krygier writes, "are intended to generate virtues of moderation and thoughtful self-knowledge, that are encouraged by constitutional and rule of law practices and institutions, not contained or constrained by them".[61] Such a form of tempering consists on the one hand of an *institutional* form of moderation—balancing or blending of power—and on the other on certain *personal virtues*.[62] Krygier specifically focuses on "Temperantia" as one of the four cardinal virtues that can be applied in this case. Militant constitutionalism along this line of thinking will stress mechanisms of defense whose main aim is to bind and guide power.

Shifting the focus from "rule of law as an instrument of binding power" to "rule of law as an instrument of socio-economic rights protection", however, can lead to a different perspective on the institutions, constitutional practices and perhaps virtues that are needed to protect constitutional democracies and make them more resilient. In *Political Emotions* (2013) Martha Nussbaum discusses the value and danger of public emotions—like anger, fear, love or sympathy—for liberal democracies, specifically for the political goals they want to reach. "They can give the pursuit of those goals new vigor and depth", according to Nussbaum, "but they can also derail that pursuit, introducing or reinforcing divisions, hierarchies, and forms of neglect or obtuseness".[63] Focusing on the first she argues that the "political cultivation of emotion" can fulfil several important tasks for liberal democracies that spire "justice and equal opportunity for all".[64] The one I want to address here is that the political cultivation of emotions can "engender and sustain strong commitment to worthy projects that require effort and sacrifice—such as social redistribution, the full inclusion of previously excluded or marginalized groups, the protection of the environment, foreign aid, and the national defense".[65] Liberal democracies, in that sense, should not only protect rights but also cultivate good attitudes. Attitudes that are not only relevant for citizens but also for public officials themselves.

If we return to the third conception discussed in Sect. 5.2.2—rule of law decline as a consequence of governments neglecting their protective duties towards their citizens—the cultivation of certain emotions and their accompanying attitudes seems to be an important element of militant constitutionalism. Take the capacity for empathy. Cultivating empathy—"the ability to imagine the situation of the other, taking the

60 Krygier 2019, p. 760.

61 Ibid., p. 782.

62 Krygier's interpretation of balancing as a chemical process will not be discussed.

63 Nussbaum 2013, p. 2.

64 Ibid., p. 3.

65 Ibid., p. 3.

other's perspective" or to see "the world through the eyes of others and to recognize their individuality"[66]—as a capacity for judges, legislative jurists and politicians would have had a tempering effect regarding the Childcare Allowance Case in The Netherlands. Militant constitutionalism along this line of thinking will stress mechanisms of defense whose aim is not merely to bind and guide power but also to make sure that the government takes its positive duties and responsibilities seriously, accepting its role in the ensuring of effective human rights protection. The ethos that belongs to such a responsibility is more than one of moderation and critical vigilance against the possibility of the abuse of power. It implies a willingness to actively protect the inherent moral worth of each individual.[67]

5.4.2 Four Possible Elements

Given the focus of both perspectives on stable constitutional and political practices, one can argue—like Sadurski and Gutmann and Voigt do—that the importance of a well-designed constitution should not be overestimated. Of course, legal rules and institutions erect a dam against the danger of constitutional retrogression, and well-designed and well-functioning institutions contribute to the creation and maintenance of a well-functioning democratic and rule-of-law practices. However, this does not alter the fact that these institutions can only fulfill their protective role insofar as they are sustained and supported by officials and citizens alike; insofar as the constitution also has a cultural and societal anchorage. Sadurski quotes Huq and Ginsburg to drive this point home: "Constitutions are, after all, only pieces of paper that derive their power from the intersubjective views of elites and citizens".[68] Loewenstein already argued the same in 1936—as also quoted above: "The most perfectly drafted and devised statutes are not worth the paper on which they are written unless supported by [the] indomitable will to survive".[69] So what are the structuring elements of this "indomitable will to survive" when applied to militant constitutionalism? Unfortunately, and as far as I am able to determine, there are no publication in legal and political theory extensively discussing this question. Given limited space I will not present a thorough analysis of this issue but merely mention four likely candidates for these "structuring elements": the acceptance of and dialogue on unwritten legal rules and norms (1), a public and professional mentality (2), legal trust (3) and civic and professional education (4). These elements will not be discussed in detail. On some there already exists a large body of literature, on others not. The main aim of this section is to tie these elements to the idea militant constitutionalism and not to

[66] Ibid., pp. 145, 198.

[67] Whether 'empathy' is a virtue or an ability or a skill is a question I will not address here, compare: Battaly 2011. For a discussion of the issue of political and legal ethos in connection to the notion of militant constitutionalism, see: Tinnevelt 2025.

[68] Huq and Ginsburg 2018, p. 68, cited in Sadurski 2019, p. 17.

[69] Loewenstein 1937c, p. 657.

fully elaborate their meaning and potential. In that sense this section is somewhat speculative.

According to Sadurski it is important to point out the importance of the acceptance of and dialogue on the *unwritten legal rules and norms* (1) that underpin the rule of law, giving it meaning and providing it with a solid foundation. These are the rules and norms that indicate why certain laws and structures are important.[70] Failure to comply with these rules and norms has a destabilizing effect on the edifice of the democratic rule of law. Sadurski provides a long list of examples, some from Polish politics, others from American politics. To name two: When Poland's current president, Andrzej Duda, pardoned ex-minister Mariusz Kamiński in 2015, he was formally entitled to do so, but still violated an unwritten rule: "a pardon is a means of last resort, which can be applied only to those sentenced in *final* judgments".[71] If a pardon could be granted at any time during legal proceedings, it would jeopardize the separation of executive and legislative powers. Or take the norm that electoral commissions must be able to operate independently of politics: "When PiS adopted the law on electoral commission, which replaced the key figures in the electoral machine from judges to administrators subordinate to the minister for interior, it acted within a lacuna left by the Constitution but against a norm that the apparatus of electoral commissions should be independent of politicians".[72] These examples illustrate not only that the unwritten rules and norms underlying the democratic legal system need to be made explicit over and over again, but also that politicians, judges and officials need to internalize and abide by them.[73]

The next element is *public and professional mentality* or ethos (2). The "principal problem of [rule of law] restoration"—Sajó claims—"is not just insufficient self-correction. It is also a problem of public and professional mentality. The rule of law is not just a principle, or a set of principles, generating standards and ultimately rules. It is also about the spirit, the morality that motivated and generated the principle, anchored in shared social experience".[74] Such a morality covers more than just written and unwritten constitutional rules and norms, it implies a certain "consciousness, culture, habitus, etc…".[75] In "The Netherlands Opinion on the Legal Protection of Citizens"—adopted by the Venice Commission in October 2021 and written to address the Childcare Allowance Case in The Netherlands—a similar claim can be found: "maintaining the rule of law is not only about institutions and formal legal safeguards, but also about maintaining an enabling environment for the rule of law through the political and legal culture within the society". What is required? The Commission argues for "a political culture with a high degree of awareness of the rule of law consequences of political decisions and exercise of self-restraint when

[70] Sadurski 2019, p. 253.

[71] Ibid., p. 253. Needless to say, the existence of unwritten rules is not self-evident.

[72] Ibid., p. 254.

[73] Ibid., p. 256.

[74] Sajó 2023a, p. 65.

[75] Ibid.

politically desired measures are contrary to the rule of law".[76] Something similar also applies to legislative jurists, judges, public servants etc. Awareness and self-restraint are also important for them—including the willingness to act as a countervailing power and the ability to look beyond immediate political self-interest and focus on something like the common good or the community.[77] In the previous section (Sect. 5.4.1) I presented two perspectives to look at some of the virtues or abilities needed by government officials. For a convincing analysis different roles and responsibilities need to be distinguished and explained what can be expected from each of these.

The importance of *legal trust* (3) can be explained by returning to Sadurski's claim about unwritten norms. According to Sadurski: "Unwritten norms prevent interpreting legal rules in ways which would be contrary to their original and/or best rationales".[78] Although some of these norms will be controversial and their proposed meanings contested, in a healthy constitutional democracy a certain degree of consensus is essential. But there is also a second element Sadurski addresses: "What is required is not just knowledge of the norms, but also knowing that others know them, and that they will abide by them, and, if they do not, they will know that they have violated them".[79] The Venice Commission makes a similar point by claiming that a resilient constitutional democracy needs to have "a legal culture in which the rule of law is accepted as a framework for and limit to democratic decisions and policies".[80] Such a form of legal trust not only applies to political and legal officials, but also to the wider public. In an interesting analysis of the different dimensions of trust Kevin Vallier emphasized this point and connects it also to the second structuring element I have distinguished ("a public and professional mentality"). Vallier writes: "a public exhibits legal trust to the extent that its participant members generally believe that (i) legal officials are necessary or helpful for achieving public goals, (ii) legal officials are generally willing and able to do their part to achieve those goals, knowingly or unknowingly, by playing their prescribed legal role, and (iii) moral reasons normally motivate the legal officials to play that role".[81] Such a form of legal trust creates constitutional stability.

About the last structuring element—*civic and professional education* (4)—I want to be brief. In Sect. 5.2.1 I discussed the difference between two paradigms: "militant democracy" and "defending democracy" (or "democratic self-defense"). The latter paradigm includes a broader pallet of democratic defense tools, ranging from party bans and restrictions on freedom of speech to the importance of public deliberation

---

[76] European Commission for Democracy Through Law (Venice Commission) *The Netherlands, Opinion on the Legal Protection of Citizens,* opinion no 1031/2021, 18 October 2021, p. 8.

[77] Given the limited space available, I am unable to pay fair attention to the huge literature that exists on the ethics rules for civil servants and the codes of conduct for judges and legislative jurists.

[78] Sadurski 2019, p. 256.

[79] Ibid.

[80] European Commission for Democracy Through Law (Venice Commission) *The Netherlands, Opinion on the Legal Protection of Citizens,* opinion no 1031/2021, 18 October 2021, p. 8.

[81] Vallier 2021, p. 37.

and civic education. Civic education or democratic education with regard to militant democracy would minimally imply that citizens have knowledge about and certain competencies regarding the democratic system in which they live and regarding the status of being a citizen in a democracy. Civic education regarding militant constitutionalism would extend this knowledge and these competencies to also include the rule of law (a) and include not only primary and secondary education but also the way education is being organized at our law faculties (b). A strong link, in that sense, exists between the first, second and last structuring elements of a stable constitutional tradition.

5.5 Concluding Remarks

A stable constitutional tradition is thus an important pillar for the resilience of the legal institutions of constitutional democracies. Just as, conversely, well-designed legal institutions are essential to the creation and maintenance of such a tradition. An important interaction, in other words, exists between formal institutions and (in)formal practices and attitudes. How the aforementioned four structuring elements are given shape and form will partially depend on the problem that "militant constitutionalism" tries to address and the concept of rule of law from which one starts.

The conceptions of militant constitutionalism that I discussed in Sect. 5.2.2, however, are not unrelated. This specifically applies to the second and third conception. Governments structurally neglecting their responsibility to uphold and effectively implement a system of basic rights and liberties can create a fragile and unstable political context in which populists and autocrats can successfully gain political power and subsequently try to dismantle constitutional democracies. Heraclitus, not a democrat himself, once claimed: "the townspeople must fight for the law just as they do for their city-wall".[82] Having a duty to fight for the law and actually being willing to do so, however, can sometimes be two separate things. Certain prerequisites, therefore, need to be met in order for citizens being willing to fight for the law and for constitutional democracies to be resilient and stable. According to Loewenstein the "time-honored acceptance of democratic ideals and institutions" is related to socio-economic circumstances and the way governments deal with these ("England, having apparently reached the deepest point of the depression, seems on the way to recovery"[83]). Under all economic circumstances "practice[s] of rights protection"[84] are needed in which basic rights and freedoms are not merely enshrined in the constitution but where it is clear to all citizens that these are also successfully protected in everyday life. This requires effective public policies aimed at ensuring real equality of opportunity and a dignified and decent life for all citizens: "observable acts of

[82] White 2021, Book 9.2, p. 363.

[83] Loewenstein 1935, p. 776.

[84] Vallier 2021, p. 103.

publicly protecting and exercising basic rights".[85] Consequently, income, wealth and power inequality need to be critically examined again and again. At all times a situation must be avoided in which citizens have the same rights on paper but in practice do not possess the same opportunities, influence and dignity.[86] "[T]rust-increasing liberal rights practices", in other words, are needed in which "basic liberal rights, recognized in constitutional law, exercised regularly by the people, and embodied in public policy, are the principal drivers of trust".[87]

This argument regarding the link between two of the conceptions discussed in Sect. 5.2.2, however, needs further substantiation and is not an argument I need to make here given the two main goals of this chapter: clarifying the concept of militant constitutionalism (i) and giving a general description of the political and legal culture that is needed to maintain and defend constitutional democracy (ii). I have argued that militant constitutionalism's main focus is on finding defense mechanisms to guard against "the process through which public authorities implement governmental policies and laws that systematically weaken, annihilate or capture the rule of law with the effect of seriously endangering or dismantling constitutional democracy". Section 5.2.2 discussed three conceptions of militant constitutionalism. Section 5.4, subsequently, showed that stable constitutional practices—in addition to formal institutional safeguards, are required to make constitutional democracies more resilient (a) and presented a sketch of four structuring elements of these constitutional practices (b).

Important to emphasize, finally, are two concluding remarks. The first is that "militant constitutionalism" does not replace "militant democracy". To make constitutional democracies resilient both "militant constitutionalism" and "militant democracy" are needed. Secondly, it is equally important to emphasize that the aim of both militant democracy and militant constitutionalism is not to sketch the groundwork for a just constitutional democracy. Militant democracy and militant constitutionalism are normatively dependent concepts that build on wider theories of democracy and rule of law "to gain substantive normative content".[88] Their focus is on the barriers that need to be erected and the practices and ethos that need to be sustained to defend constitutional democracies.

References

Ackerman B (2006) Before the Next Attack. Preserving Civil Liberties in an Age of Terrorism. Yale University Press, New Haven/London.

Battaly HD (2011) Is Empathy a Virtue? In: Coplan A, Goldie P (eds) Empathy. Philosophical and Psychological Perspectives. Oxford University Press, Oxford, pp. 277–301.

[85] Ibid., p. 22.

[86] Compare the distinction that Michael Sandel makes between "equality of opportunity" and "equality of condition": Sandel 2020.

[87] Vallier 2021, p. 9.

[88] Müller 2007, p. 11 makes this claim with regard to the concept of constitutional patriotism.

Cavallar G (2017) Islam, Aufklärung und Moderne. Ein Plädoyer [Islam, Enlightenment and Modernity. A Plea]. W. Kohlhammer, Stuttgart.
Elster J (1985) Ulysses and the Sirens Studies in Rationality and Irrationality. Cambridge University Press, Cambridge.
Górnisiewic A (2023) Personal enemies, conceptual friends. Karl Loewenstein and Carl Schmitt on self-destructive legalism. Journal of Political Ideologies 1–20.
Greenberg U (2015) Militant Democracy and Human Rights. New German Critique 3:169–195.
Gutmann J, Voigt S (2023) Militant constitutionalism: a promising concept to make constitutional backsliding less likely? Public Choice 195(3–4):377–404.
Holmes S (1997) Passions and Constraint: On the Theory of Liberal Democracy. University of Chicago Press, Chicago.
Homer (2000) The Odyssey (Hammond M (transl.)). Bloomsbury Academic, London.
Huq AZ, Ginsburg T (2018) How to Lose a Constitutional Democracy. UCLA Law Review 1:79–169.
Issacharoff S (2015) Fragile Democracies. Contested Power in the Era of Constitutional Courts. Cambridge University Press, New York.
Krygier M (2019) What's the Point of the Rule of Law? Buffalo Law Review 67(3):7843–791.
Loewenstein K (1935) Autocracy versus democracy in contemporary Europe II. The American Political Science Review 29(5): 755–784.
Loewenstein K (1936) Law in the Third Reich. The Yale Law Journal 1936 5:779–815.
Loewenstein K (1937a) Dictatorship and the German Constitution: 1933–1937. University of Chicago Law Review 4:537–574.
Loewenstein K (1937b) Militant Democracy and Fundamental Rights, I. American Political Science Review 3:417–432.
Loewenstein K (1937c) Militant Democracy and Fundamental Rights, II. American Political Science Review 4:638–659.
McCormick JP (1998) The Dilemmas of Dictatorship Carl Schmitt and Constitutional Emergency Powers. In: Dyzenhaus D (ed) Law as Politics. Carl Schmitt's Critique of Liberalism. Duke University Press, Durham/London, pp. 217–251.
Müller JW (2007) Constitutional Patriotism. Princeton University Press, Princeton
Müller JW (2012a) A "Practical Dilemma Which Philosophy Alone Cannot Resolve"? Rethinking Militant Democracy: An Introduction. Constellations 19(4):536–539.
Müller JW (2012b) Militant Democracy. In: Rosenfeld M, Sajó A (eds) The Oxford Handbook of Comparative Constitutional Law. Oxford University Press, Oxford.
Müller JW (2016) Protecting Popular Self-Government from the People? New Normative Perspectives on Militant Democracy. Annual Review of Political Science 1:249–265.
Müller JW (2019) Individual Militant Democracy. In: Malkopoulou A, Kirshner AS (eds) Militant Democracy and Its Critics. Populism, Parties, Extremism. Edinburgh University Press, Edinburgh.
Neumann F (1957) The Democratic and The Authoritarian State. Essays in Political and Legal Theory. Free Press of Glencoe, London.
Nussbaum M (2013) Political Emotions. Why Love Matters for Justice. The Belknap Press of Harvard University Press, Cambridge.
Papier H, Durner W (2003) Streitbare Demokratie. Archiv des öffentlichen Rechts 3:340–371.
Pech L, Scheppele KL (2017) Illiberalism Within: Rule of Law Backsliding in the EU. Cambridge Yearbook of European Legal Studies 19:3–47.
Posner R (2006) Not a Suicide Pact: The Constitution in a Time of National Emergency. Oxford University Press, New York.
Raz J (1979) The Authority of Law: Essays on Law and Morality. Clarendon Press, Oxford.
Repucci S, Slipowitz A (2022) Freedom in the World 2022. The Global Expansion of Authoritarian Rule. Freedom House. Available at: https://freedomhouse.org/report/freedom-world/2022/global-expansion-authoritarian-rule.
Rijpkema B (2018) Militant Democracy. The Limits of Democratic Tolerance. London/New York.

Rill B (ed) (2003) Terrorismus und Recht—Der wehrhafte Rechtsstaat. Hans Seidel Stiftung, Munich.
Sadurski W (2019) Poland's Constitutional Breakdown. Oxford University Press, Oxford.
Sajó A (2019) Militant Constitutionalism. In: Malkopoulou A, Kirshner AS (eds) Militant Democracy and Its Critics. Populism, Parties, Extremism. Edinburgh University Press, Edinburgh, pp. 187–206.
Sajó A (2021) Ruling by Cheating. Governance in Illiberal Democracy. Cambridge University Press, Cambridge.
Sajó A (2023a) On the Difficulties of Rule of Law Restoration. In: Södersten A, Hercock E (eds) The Rule of Law in the EU: Crisis and Solutions. Swedish Institute for European Policy Studies, Stockholm, pp. 60–65.
Sajó (2023b) Militant Rule of Law. VerfBlog, 20 December 2023. Available at: https://verfassungsblog.de/militant-rule-of-law/.
Sajó A, Tuovinen J (2018) The Rule of Law and Legitimacy in Emerging Illiberal Democracies. Osteuropa Recht 64(4):506-529.
Sandel M (2020) The Tyranny of Merit. What's Become of the Common Good? Penguin, London.
Schmitt C (2006) Die Diktatur. Von den Anfängen des modernen Souveränitätsgedankens bis zum proletarischen Klassenkampf [The Dictatorship: From the Beginnings of the Modern Idea of Sovereignty to the Proletarian Class Struggle], 7th edn. Duncker & Humblot, Berlin.
Schmitt C (2009) Politische Theologie. Vier Kapitel zur Lehre von der Souveränität [Political Theology: Four Chapters on the Doctrine of Sovereignty], 9th edn. Duncker & Humblot, Berlin.
Smibert J (2024) Defensive Rule of Law. Emory Law Journal 73(5):1111–1172.
Suteu S (2021) Eternity Clauses in Democratic Constitutionalism. Oxford University Press, Oxford.
Tamanaha B (2004) On the Rule of law. History, Politics, Theory. Cambridge University Press, New York.
Tinnevelt R (2025) Militant constitutionalism and the paradoxes of liberalism. Kantian Review (forthcoming).
Vallier K (2021) Trust in a Polarized Age. Oxford University Press, New York.
Waldron J (1999) Law and Disagreement. Oxford University Press, Oxford.
Waldron J (2002) Is the Rule of Law an Essentially Contested Concept (In Florida)? Law and Philosophy 21(2):137–164.
White SK (ed) (2021) Diogenes Laertius, Lives of Eminent Philosophers. Cambridge University Press, Cambridge.

Chapter 6
Rights, Remedies and Paradigms of Constitutionalism—Same-Sex Marriage Before the Courts

Kushagr Bakshi

Contents

Abstract Courts in various jurisdictions have relied on either the right to privacy or the right to equality to offer protections to the LGBTQ+ community. While the use of different rights to achieve similar ends may seem like a distinction without a difference, the difference in the nature of each right along with the accompanying remedies, points to the difference in the nature of constitutionalism practiced across various jurisdictions. Courts operating in the traditional liberal democratic constitutional paradigm tend to construct privacy as a negative right, restricting the state from interfering in the intimate relationships between individuals. However, courts operating within a transformative constitutional framework rely on the right to equality to impose duties upon the state to guarantee equal moral membership to all members of society. This is not a mere theoretical distinction, as the remedies granted by these courts vary based on the paradigm they operate under. This chapter examines the reliance on these rights in the context of legalizing same-sex marriages. It shows that courts in the transformative constitutional paradigm have interpreted equality to abandon default verticality, that is the legal tradition of situating private relationships and community conventions outside of the constitutional mould, instead subjecting societal mores to constitutional morality.

K. Bakshi (✉)
Law School, University of Michigan, Ann Arbor, MI, USA
e-mail: kushagrb@umich.edu

M. De Visser et al. (eds.), *European Yearbook of Constitutional Law 2024*, European Yearbook of Constitutional Law 6, https://doi.org/10.1007/978-94-6265-699-4_6

Keywords Equality · India · LGBTQ+ Rights · Marriage · Positive and Negative Rights · Privacy · Transformative Constitutionalism

6.1 Setting the Scene: Same-Sex Marriage Before Courts

In April 2023, the Supreme Court of India heard petitions in *Supriyo v. Union of India*, which sought legal recognition for same-sex marriages.[1] These hearings marked the latest episode in the decades old struggle for LGBTQ+ rights in India.[2] Where efforts at legislative and social reform had proven to be laborious and unsuccessful, the courts had emerged as a venue for the LGBTQ+ community[3] to defend their rights.[4] Decades of protracted litigation had resulted in previous vindicative decisions, such as *NALSA v. Union of India*[5] where the Court found a constitutional right to a third gender identity, and *Navtej Johar v. Union of India*[6] where the Court decriminalized homosexuality. Relying on these judgements, the petitioners in *Supriyo* demanded legal recognition for same-sex marriages and all the concomitant benefits under Indian law.

The Indian Supreme Court is not alone in adjudicating such cases. Many courts, including those in the United States, Europe,[7] Brazil and South Africa have previously had to adjudicate rights based challenges to restrictive marriage and civil union

---

[1] Supreme Court of India, *Supriyo a.k.a Supriya Chakraborty & Abhay Dang v. Union of India*, judgement of 17 October 2023, W.P.(C) No.1011/2022.

[2] Aids Bhedbhav Virodhi Andolan 1991.

[3] I am using the term "LGBTQ+" as an umbrella term to refer to the diversity of identities and the broader rights claims made by gender and sexual minorities. However, for the purposes of this chapter, I acknowledge that I have limited myself by only dealing with cases about sexual orientation, specifically same-sex couples. For a brief overview of transgender rights in India, see, generally, Suresh 2011.

[4] Rai 2021.

[5] Supreme Court of India, *NALSA v. Union of India*, judgement of 15 April 2014, AIR 2014 SC 1863.

[6] Supreme Court of India, *Navtej Johar v. Union of India*, judgement of 6 September 2018, AIR 2018 SC 4321.

[7] Throughout this chapter, I use the term "Europe" to refer to the Council of Europe and its member states. My analysis is focused on the jurisprudence of the principal supranational judicial authority charged with human rights protection by the Council—that is, the European Court of Human Rights (ECtHR). Of course, one can disaggregate the constitutional regimes and courts within the member states of Council, given the vast differences in their national jurisprudence, but I do not do so here. I also put aside the debates regarding the human rights regime instituted by the European Convention on Human Rights and defended by the ECtHR, specifically whether this regime can be considered "constitutionalism proper". For my purposes, it is sufficient to note that the ECtHR engages in human rights interpretation within a constitutional paradigm, in a similar fashion to other supreme or constitutional courts. Therefore, focusing on the ECtHR's judgments provides valuable insights into judicial rights interpretation in constitutional paradigms, which is this chapter's primary concern. For detailed arguments on the constitutional nature of the ECtHR, see Ulfstein 2021; Harmsen 2007.

laws and broader LGBTQ+ rights claims. Yet, the rights in question in each of these cases have differed. Mirroring the distinction in these courts, the petitioners in the Indian case too, sought legal recognition for same-sex marriage by grounding such demands in two different constitutional rights, i.e. the right to privacy and the right to equality.

The Indian Supreme Court had previously ruled that the right to privacy includes within it sexual decisional autonomy.[8] Drawing on this conception of privacy, the petitioners argued that decisional autonomy must include within it the freedom to choose a partner and have the state offer legal recognition for such a choice. Similar arguments grounded in the right to privacy have found favour with other courts seeking to protect LGBTQ+ rights. In the U.S. for instance, the Supreme Court relied on the right to privacy under the due process and equal protection clause to strike down Texas's sodomy laws.[9] The European Court of Human Rights (ECtHR) also held that states must provide legal recognition to civil unions of same-sex couples, as part of their right of privacy guaranteed under Article 8 of the European Convention on Human Rights.[10]

The use of privacy by the European and U.S. courts to protect LGBTQ+ rights is predicated on default verticality, that is the legal tradition of situating private relationships and community conventions outside of the constitutional mould. Relying on default verticality, these courts have interpreted the right to privacy as creating a shield against undue state intrusion. On this basis, these courts have made findings such as the illegality of the restriction on same-sex intimacy or the illegality of the Defense of Marriage Act which restricted the definition of marriage to one man and one woman, holding that such laws violate the liberty interests inherent in the privacy rights of individuals.[11]

Yet this conceptualization of privacy also creates a situation where the state is not required to provide a positive content to the right, even in private settings. For instance, in the context of abortion funding, the U.S. Supreme Court held that while the government may not place obstacles in the path of a woman's exercise of her freedom of choice, it need not remove those not of its own creation.[12] It is a very short step from that which the government has a duty *not* to intervene in to that which it has *no* duty to intervene in.[13] By situating institutions like the family in the private domain and therefore outside the domain of the state, courts do not provide any positive protections to individuals seeking them. For instance, European courts have found that while privacy protects a couple's choice to cohabitate, it does not grant

---

[8] Supreme Court of India, *Justice K.S. Puttuswamy and Another v. Union of India & Others*, judgement of 24 August 2017, AIR 2017 SC 4161.

[9] United States Supreme Court, *Lawrence v. Texas*, judgment of 26 June 2003, 539 U.S. 558.

[10] European Court of Human Rights, *Oliari and Others v. Italy*, judgement of 21 July 2016, App No. 18766/11 and 36030/11.

[11] European Court of Human Rights, *Dudgeon v. U.K.*, judgement of 22 October 1981, App No. 7525/76. United States Supreme Court, *United States v. Windsor*, judgement of 26 June 2013, 570 U.S. 744.

[12] United States Supreme Court, *Harris v. McRae*, judgement of 30 June 1980, 448 U.S. 297.

[13] MacKinnon 1987.

them access to the rights and benefits that flow from marriage or family.[14] Therefore, even in the landmark case legalizing same-sex marriage—*Obergefell*—, the U.S. Supreme Court had to step outside of privacy and rely on the dignity of marriage to find a positive obligation upon the state to legalize same-sex marriages.[15] Privacy then, has been conceptualized as a negative right which imposes no obligation upon the state to act.

On the other hand, courts in Brazil, South Africa and India have relied on the right to equality when defending LGBTQ+ rights. When decriminalizing homosexuality, the Indian Supreme Court articulated a vision of substantive equality by holding that the impugned section of the penal code institutionalised decades of discrimination against the LGBTQ+ community.[16] Similarly, the South African Constitutional Court and the Brazilian Federal Supreme Court formulated a substantive right to equality when constitutionally guaranteeing the right to a same-sex marriage and civil unions.[17] Drawing on this conception of equality, the petitioners in the same-sex marriage case before the Indian Supreme Court argued that the gendered provisions of marriage laws in India discriminated amongst people based on their sexual orientation and gender identity.

By articulating a substantive vision of equality, courts in Brazil, India and South Africa amongst others have rejected the notion of principled distance from the private domain. Rejecting default verticality, these court pay attention to societal mores and subject those to constitutional tests of equality.[18] Hence, when ruling that the common law criminalization of sodomy was unconstitutional, the Constitutional Court of South Africa considered the position of the applicants in society to evaluate the effects of the discriminatory law.[19] It held that gay men had been discriminated against in society and the sodomy provisions institutionalised this discrimination by penalizing those who failed to conform to the moral and religious views of a section of society. By articulating a substantive vision of equality which accounts for social realities, these courts have pierced domains traditionally considered private, to ensure a greater degree of constitutional protection for LGBTQ+ individuals. Hence the Constitutional Court of South Africa, departing from the ECtHR, held that persons in permanent same-sex relationships ought to receive equal treatment as that given to married heterosexual persons under immigration law, thereby allowing

---

[14] European Commission of Human Rights, *X and Y v. U.K.*, decision of the commission (admissibility) of 3 May 1983, App No. 9369/81, para 221.

[15] Ewing 2023; Rao 2013.

[16] See n. 6 above.

[17] Constitutional Court of South Africa, *Minister of Home Affairs v. Fourie*, judgement of 1 December 2005, ZACC 19; Federal Supreme Court of Brazil, *Action for Failure to Comply with Fundamental Principle (Governor of the State of Rio de Janeiro v. Court of Justice)*, judgement of 5 May 2011, ADPF No. 132.

[18] See Bhatia 2019, Chap. 1 and 2.

[19] Constitutional Court of South Africa, *National Coalition for Gay and Lesbian Equality v. Minister of Justice*, judgement of 9 October 1998, ZACC 15.

them to access the benefits and privileges of the institution of marriage and family.[20] Courts in Brazil,[21] Namibia[22] and India have also relied on a substantive vision of equality, recognizing indirect discrimination and social realities when adjudicating cases involving protections for LGBTQ+ people. By using equality, these courts have been able to craft remedies which impose positive obligations upon the state.

Despite some facial similarities, there is fundamental difference in the nature of the right to privacy and the right to equality as used by these courts, expressly visible through the difference in the obligations imposed upon the state. Flowing from differing interpretations of the right of privacy and the right of equality, courts have crafted different remedies for each right. Courts which interpret privacy as a negative right to prohibit the state from interfering in society do not enjoin the state to remedy the systemic discrimination faced by LGTBQ+ people which prohibits them from exercising their rights and freedoms in any substantial sense. On the other hand, courts using substantive equality, craft remedies which impose positive obligations upon the state to rectify hierarchical social inequities thereby ensuring that LGBTQ+ people can enjoy the substantive content of their freedoms. Functionally then, the content of the rights and the protections offered by courts to LGBTQ+ people, varies in these different jurisdictions, based on the choice between privacy and equality.

This chapter contends that the conceptual difference in the choice between privacy and equality points to the different types of constitutionalism practiced across these jurisdictions. While constitutionalism in the U.S., Europe, South Africa and India can broadly be understood as belonging to the liberal tradition, there are critical differences in the structural interpretations of rights and remedies. Constitutionalism in the U.S. and Europe exemplifies the *traditional liberal democratic* paradigm which is grounded in the notion of negative rights, prohibiting the state from actively discriminating between individuals. However, South Africa, Brazil and India amongst others practice a vision of *transformative constitutionalism* which requires the state to not only protect the fundamental rights of individuals but also advance and promote constitutional values, often referred to as constitutional morality.[23] Crucially, transformative constitutionalism seeks to order relations not just between the state and the individual, but also between individuals. The comparative examples herein show that the interpretive schema courts follow to enforce rights guarantees in transformative constitutional projects leads them to eschew legal formalism in favour of interpretations that acknowledge and respond to the reality of hierarchical structures and power relationships within society.

The rest of the chapter proceeds in three sections. First, it considers the development of the right to privacy as a tool to protect the rights of LGBTQ+ people

---

[20] Constitutional Court of South Africa, *National Coalition for Gay and Lesbian Equality v. Minister of Home Affairs*, judgement of 2 December 1999, ZACC 17.

[21] Federal Supreme Court of Brazil, *The Direct Action of Unconstitutionality by Omission*, judgement of 13 June 2019, (ADO) No. 26.

[22] Supreme Court of Namibia, *Digashu and Another v. GRN and Others; Seiler-Lilles and Another v. GRN and Others*, judgement of 16 May 2023, SA 6/2022; SA 7/2022, NASC 14.

[23] Nayak 2023.

(Sect. 6.2). This section explains how the usage of the right to privacy exemplifies the traditional liberal democratic paradigm of constitutionalism and analyses its shortcomings. Second, the chapter considers the development of equality jurisprudence by various courts in the context of LGBTQ+ rights (Sect. 6.3). By recognizing indirect discrimination and adopting a measure of substantive equality, these courts have exemplified the practice of transformative constitutionalism and crafted remedies to offer more effective protection to LBGTQ+ people. Finally, this chapter argues that these paradigms, while sometimes entrenched in constitutional texts, are a product of legal cultures and interpretive choices and thus leave open the space for transplants and transformations (Sect. 6.4). In *Supriyo* for instance, despite the transformative inheritance of the Indian Constitution, the Indian Supreme Court relied on a negative rights conception of privacy and replicated the shortcomings of the traditional liberal democratic paradigm in denying relief to the petitioners. Surely then, the converse is also possible. Analysing select decision of the U.S. Supreme Court and the ECtHR shows us that courts in a liberal democratic constitutional paradigm are not bound to negative rights interpretation of privacy and can evaluate LGBTQ+ rights through the lens of substantive equality, thereby practicing a version of transformative constitutionalism.

6.2 The Inadequacy of Privacy in the Traditional Liberal Democratic Paradigm

6.2.1 Privacy as a Negative Right

Courts across various jurisdictions have regularly relied on the liberty interests inherent in the right of privacy to protect the rights of LGBTQ+ people.[24] Most of these decisions have pivoted on ensuring that the right to privacy acts as a restraint on the state, preventing it from interfering in the private sphere, most notably the bedroom. For instance, privacy doctrine in the United States which stems from cases concerning the use of contraceptives[25] and abortion rights,[26] embodies judicial limitations on state power by demarcating the threshold of state intrusion into domains traditionally considered free, namely the private sphere. This conception of privacy as a limitation was explicitly articulated in *Lawrence v. Texas*,[27] where the U.S Supreme Court struck down Texas' sodomy law. In the majority opinion, Justice Kennedy held that the petitioners were entitled to respect from the state in their private lives. Arguing that the liberty interest in the right to privacy gave the petitioners the full right to engage in private conduct without the interference of the state, Justice Kennedy ruled

[24] Eskridge 1993; Hohengarten 1994; D'Aloia 2014.

[25] United States Supreme Court, *Griswold v. Connecticut*, judgement of 7 June 1965, 381 U.S. 479.

[26] United States Supreme Court, *Roe v. Wade*, judgement of 22 January 1973, 410 U.S. 113.

[27] United States Supreme Court, *Lawrence v. Texas*, judgement of 26 June 2003, 539 U.S. 558.

that the state could not advance any legitimate interest which justified its intrusion. Emphatically using privacy to demarcate the limits of state authority, the Court held that "It is a promise of the Constitution that there is a realm of personal liberty which the government may not enter."[28]

Courts in the U.S. are not alone in relying on this liberty protecting conception of the right to privacy as a shield against the state. The ECtHR has also relied on this conception of privacy to defend LGBTQ+ rights. In *Dudgeon v. United Kingdom*,[29] the ECtHR adjudicated the validity of indecency laws in Northern Ireland which criminalized male intimacy. It held that private sexual acts could not be regulated by the state and therefore the impugned law violated the liberty interests guaranteed by right to privacy in the European Convention for the Protection of Human Rights and Fundamental Freedoms.[30]

This construction of the right to privacy aims to protect an individual's liberty interests. The judicial remedies meant to allow an individual to exercise their liberty, often extend to protecting *personhood*, or the individual's freedom of self-definition. In addition to protecting the ability of an individual to define their own identity, privacy has been interpreted to include the right to not have an identity imposed upon them by the state.[31] This interpretation of privacy is exemplified by the U.S. Supreme Court in *United States v. Windsor*.[32] In *Windsor*, the Court considered the constitutionality of the Defense of Marriage Act,[33] specifically section 3 which defined marriage as the legal union between one man and one woman. According to the Court, the Act and by extension the state demeaned the moral and sexual choices of individuals, which were protected by the Constitution. The Court went on to hold that the liberty interest in the Fifth Amendment, withdrew from the government, the power to degrade or demean individuals in the way that it had through the Act, thereby finding it unconstitutional. This articulation of the liberty interest of the individual drew from the right to privacy upheld in *Lawrence*, in so far as it prevented the state from interfering or imposing itself in the private domain.[34]

[28] Ibid, para 578.

[29] European Court of Human Rights, *Dudgeon v. United Kingdom,* judgement of 22 October 1981, App No. 7525/76, para 60.

[30] The Convention for the Protection of Human Rights and Fundamental Freedoms 1950, art 8, 213 U.N.T.S 221.

[31] Tribe 2004, pp. 1918–1932; Rubenfeld 1989, pp. 782–805.

[32] United States Supreme Court, *United States v. Windsor*, judgement of 26 June 2013, 570 U.S. 744.

[33] Defense of Marriage Act 1996, 1 U.S.C, section 7.

[34] To be fair, when considering whether the state had a legitimate interest to interfere, the court held that the principle purpose and effect of DOMA was to identify a subset of state sanctioned marriages and make them unequal. This imposition of inequality deprived couples of their rights and dignity. In a sense, this goes so far as recognizing indirect discrimination, which is otherwise taboo in U.S. constitutional doctrine. Yet the judgement only recognised limits upon state power and imposed no positive obligation upon the state. The judgement also touches upon many other aspects of constitutional doctrine. See United States Supreme Court, *United States v. Windsor*, judgement of 26 June 2013, 570 U.S. 744, paras 22–26; Siegel 2014.

Similarly, in India too, the right to privacy has been used as a shield to protect LGBTQ+ people. While the Indian Constitution does not contain a textual provision guaranteeing the right to privacy, the Indian Supreme Court has read the right to personal liberty and privacy into the right to life and due process guarantees of the Indian Constitution.[35] The most emphatic assertion of this came in 2017 when the Supreme Court unanimously held that the right to privacy was a standalone fundamental right guaranteed by Article 21.[36] In a plurality opinion, Justice Chandrachud observed that sexual orientation, as a function of decisional autonomy, was a core aspect of the right to privacy. Relying on this conception of decisional autonomy as the core of the right to privacy, the Court separately declared Section 377 of the Indian Penal Code, which criminalized consensual "unnatural" sex, unconstitutional.[37] The Court reasoned that such a restriction on expressing an individual's sexuality was an infringement of their liberty interest. The Court's reasoning can be distilled down to Justice Chandrachud holding that "the right to privacy, founded on the right to autonomy of a free individual, must capture the right of persons of the homosexual community to navigate spaces on their own terms, *free from state interference*".[38]

In addition to liberty, the Indian Supreme Court interpreted privacy to protect autonomy. Much like in the U.S. and Europe, the Indian court's conception of privacy restricts the state from unjustly intervening in private lives and personal decisions. The Court has relied on this conception of privacy in cases concerning marriage as an exercise of the individual's decisional autonomy. In *Shafin Jahan v. Asokan*,[39] the Supreme Court heard an appeal arising from the decision of the Kerala High Court, which had granted custody of an adult, competent Hindu woman to her father. The High Court had annulled her marriage to a Muslim man holding that she had been brainwashed into the marriage, despite her explicit statements to the contrary. Finding that the woman did not suffer from mental incapacity or coercion, the Supreme Court reversed the decision of the High Court, holding that her decisional autonomy, an essential component of her privacy right, had been restricted by the High Court.[40] As articulated by the Supreme Court, this individual autonomy centric view of privacy, which protects the individual's liberty interests, functions to the exclusion of a collective. By exclusion, it prevents third parties, notably the state, from interfering with marriage or sexual acts without a legitimate aim.

---

[35] Constitution of India 1950, art 21.

[36] See United States Supreme Court, *Lawrence v. Texas*, judgment of 26 June 2003, 539 U.S. 558.

[37] See note 7, pp. 96–111.

[38] Ibid, para 471.

[39] Supreme Court of India, *Shafin Jahan v. Asokan*, judgement of 8 March 2018, 16 SCC 368.

[40] Justice Chandrachud held that "The right to marry a person of one's choice is integral to Article 21 of the Constitution... Intrinsic to the liberty which the Constitution guarantees as a fundamental right is the ability of each individual to take decisions on matters central to the pursuit of happiness". Ibid, p. 21. *Cf.* United States Supreme Court, *Loving v. Virginia*, judgement of 12 June 1967, 388 U.S. 1 (where the U.S. Supreme Court relied on the right to equality and freedom from discrimination to find anti-miscegenation statutes unconstitutional).

This conception of privacy, as a restriction upon the state functionally creates a *liberty interest*.[41] Simply put, a liberty interest does not obligate a third party (in this case, the state) to intervene. Rather it imposes a duty upon the third party to not intervene, thereby ensuring the liberty and autonomy of the right holder.[42] Because the protection of a liberty interest requires nothing of the state except inaction, rights which guarantee such interests are often called negative rights.[43] Fundamentally then, these courts have constructed privacy as a negative right, that is, as a shield against the state.[44] Negatively constructed privacy rights play a significant role in cases which involve decriminalization of homosexual acts, primarily because they enable courts to limit the state from interfering in private acts.

6.2.2 Negative Rights and the Impoverishment of Traditional Liberal Democratic Constitutionalism

The construction of privacy as a negative right, points to an underlying conception of constitutionalism and the nature and function of rights. By constructing privacy, amongst other rights, as a negative right, courts interpret their constitutional structure as one where rights act as exclusions.[45] Inspired by a Lockean fear of an overawing state, constitutional rights guarantees are interpreted as demarcating the boundary between state and society. This approach to rights interpretation, predicated on ensuring the protection of the private sphere (where the liberty interest of the individual is at its strongest) by deeming that public interest (operationalized through the state) does not pierce this domain, exemplifies the paradigm of traditional liberal democratic constitutionalism. Within this paradigm, upholding default verticality, court interpret rights as protections from or against the state to protect the liberty interests of an individual. While this approach originated in the United States,[46] negative rights as protections from the state have now come to define the practice of traditional liberal democratic constitutionalism in many jurisdictions.[47]

While some initial elements of this paradigm of constitutionalism can be found in the structure of the bill of rights of a particular jurisdiction, they are also products of a legal culture. Moving beyond the structural construction in a bill of rights, Ran Hirschl

---

[41] Hohfeld 1919.

[42] See Hurd and Moore 2018; Singer 1982; Schlag 2015.

[43] Fried 1978, pp. 110–114; the classic discussion of the distinction between positive and negative liberties is Berlin 1969, pp. 118–172. See also Fabre 2000, pp. 40–66.

[44] Schmitt 2009, pp. 163–170 (calling such rights defensive rights).

[45] Grimm 2016, p. 57.

[46] United States Supreme Court, *Barsky v. Board of Regents of University of State of New York*, judgement of 26 April 1954, 347 U.S. 442, para 473 (Douglas J noting that the US Bill of Rights is about what Government "may not take away").

[47] Dowdle and Wilkinson label it the "structural-liberal" approach to constitutionalism, and trace its roots to the founding of the US Constitution. Dowdle and Wilkinson 2017. On supranational European institutions as typical liberal constitutional democracies, see Schütze 2020, pp. 90–98.

demonstrates that courts operating under the traditional liberal democratic constitutional paradigm systematically uphold a negative or non-interventionist conception of rights in favour of more expansive positive interpretations.[48] In its most powerful form, the justification for such a non-interventionist conception of rights emphasises an individualistic conception of a just society, postulating that liberal democracies, by limiting the scope of government action to the public sphere, encourage the preservation of a heterogenous private sphere which enhances the autonomy of citizens.[49] The interpretation of privacy as a negative right, that is a limitation on state action,[50] embodies this justification.

Courts in this constitutional paradigm value some version of *stasis*. While they react to infringements of liberty interests by the state, they are usually loath to impose obligations upon the state to interfere in society.[51] And while I have used privacy to demonstrate a negative rights interpretation, it is certainly not the only right to be interpreted as such. Hirschl demonstrates how similar constitutional provisions, given generous interpretations in context of negative rights, are routinely constructed narrowly in the context of positive claim rights which would impose obligations upon the state.[52] Premised on Lockean individualism and a dyadic, anti-statist conception of rights, these courts have regularly conceptualised the objective of rights and by extension constitutionalism as the protection of an individual's liberty and autonomy from the interference of the collective.

But what should also be apparent, is that this conception of autonomy and liberty which a negative rights interpretation seeks to protect, is an abstracted a priori conception which does not account for the lived reality of the individual. By limiting the understanding of autonomy and liberty to the absence of coercive state power,[53] courts do not interrogate whether these individuals enjoy autonomy in any meaningful way. Instead, this conception leads courts to privilege a formalist interpretation of rights which takes the existing conditions of liberty as natural, thereby reproducing the existing conditions of social inequity.[54] This interpretation gives rise to a tension between the restriction on governmental intrusion on one hand and the substantive content of the right on the other. Restricted from interfering in the private sphere, the state is rendered incapable of securing the autonomy sought to be guaranteed, especially for groups facing social inequities in hierarchically organised societies. This dichotomy does not represent two facets of the same right, rather a tension in the construction of the right itself.

In the context of the right to privacy, this tension presents itself when the state uses the right to secure for individuals *an inviolable personality* by ensuring that they have

[48] Hirschl 2000.

[49] Gardbaum 2003, pp. 394–395.

[50] Krotoszynski 2016.

[51] Damaska 1991, p. 73. See also Somek 2014, pp. 36–78.

[52] See, e.g., Minow 2022; MacNaughton 2001.

[53] This understanding of autonomy goes back to at least Hobbes and still holds sway today. See Hobbes 1968, part II, chapter 21. See also Atiyah 1985, p. 43.

[54] Grimm 2016, p. 86. See generally Sunstein 1998.

autonomy over their intimacy.[55] To do so, courts regularly instruct the state to centre its self-restraint on the body and the home, most notably the bedroom. By staying out of the private, including marriage and the family, this construction of privacy seeks to guarantee an individual's bodily integrity, personal exercise of moral intelligence, and freedom of intimacy. But if one asks whether a marginalized group's access to these values in material terms has been guaranteed, it is evident that the law of privacy translates traditional social values, in this case heteronormative standards and expectations, into the rhetoric of individual rights as a means of subordinating a group's access to those rights, to specific social imperatives. In doing so, privacy reproduces patterns of heterosexual dominance over LGBTQ+ people.[56]

There are two interrelated critiques I'm advancing here. First, a negative privacy right, by only acting as a restraint against the state, fails to guarantee liberty or autonomy, even within the private space it claims to protect.[57] For instance, in an early case, the former European Commission of Human Rights (a precursor to the ECtHR) held that the relationship between a gay couple did not fall within the scope of "family" under Article 8 of the convention and was instead a matter of their private life. As such, while a state was obligated to not interfere with their private life, it was not obligated to provide any material support to the couple, so that they may effectively exercise their right to a private life. In this case, the Commission upheld the United Kingdom's refusal to permit a Malaysian national man to remain in the UK with his UK-national male partner.[58] The reliance on a negative rights interpretation of privacy failed to allow the couple in question to exercise their autonomy in any substantive sense.

Second, in addition to not guaranteeing autonomy, the focus on privacy as a negative right also relegates queer identities to the mere acts of sexual intimacy and thereby the private space. Since the state is not expected to intervene to correct social inequities, queer individuals are subjected to the majoritarian heterosexual standard in their attempts to access public spaces or institutions. Their rights are subjugated to social imperatives.[59] Take the institutions of marriage and family.

---

[55] MacKinnon 1987, pp. 96–97.

[56] On the "heteronormative standard", see Berlant and Warner 1998, pp. 547–566; Mandal 2009.

[57] Schauer 2018, p. 35.

[58] European Commission of Human Rights, *X and Y v. United Kingdom,* decision of the commission (admissibility) of 3 May 1983, App No. 9369/81. The couple eventually left for Sweden. According to the Commission, because they were both "professionally mobile", and had not shown that there was no country in the world apart from the UK in which they could live together, the deportation order did not even constitute an "interference" with their Article 8 right to respect for their private lives, and therefore required no justification. See also European Court of Human Rights, *Karner v. Austria,* judgement of 24 October 2003, App No. 40016/98. See generally Crisafulli 2014, pp. 417–419.

[59] A perfect example of this is: Singapore High Court, *Ong Ming Johnson v. Attorney General,* judgement of 30 March 2020, SGHC 63, para 175–195. Considering a colonial era legislation which criminalized acts of gross indecency by two male persons, the Singapore High Court upheld the validity of the legislation. It observed that there had been no significant change in "societal disapproval towards male homosexual conduct". Clearly, it subjected LGBTQ+ people's free exercise of rights to public morality. However, I do not wish to rely excessively on this example since Singapore's liberal democratic bona fides are questionable. See Thio 2019; Huat 2022.

The ECtHR has regularly privileged heteronormative interpretations of family when considering the claims brought by same-sex couples demanding legal recognition of their relationship as marriage.[60] Initially the court restricted the definition of family using gender essentialism, that is marriage between a man and woman, [61] although it has recently changed that view to account for changes to the social character of the institution of family and marriage.[62] But even this "evolved" interpretation subjects the attempts of LGBTQ+ individuals to access public institutions to heteronormative social standards.

The ECtHR does this by relying on a doctrine called the "margin of appreciation". According to the Court, marriage has deep rooted social and cultural connotations which differ from one state to another. Hence, the Court defers to national assessments of whether such a right can extend to same-sex couples. By relying on this heteronormative interpretation of marriage, the ECtHR does not scrutinize the legitimacy of government aims in restricting access to marriage and by extension the proportionality requirements, instead presuming them to be valid as expressions of local social and cultural norms, and therefore within the state's margin of appreciation.[63] For instance, in *Schalk*,[64] the ECtHR found that there was no overwhelming European consensus favouring same-sex marriage. As such, the ECtHR held that Austria was justified, within its margin of appreciation, in offering same-sex couples access to a registered partnership instead of marriage. Alternatively, in *Oliari*,[65] the Court compelled Italy to offer some form of recognition to same-sex couples. Here too, it relied on public sentiment and morality, albeit differently. Where in *Schalk*, the Court had zoomed out to examine the existence of a consensus (or lack thereof) amongst all member states, in *Oliari* the Court zoomed in to examine the social consensus in Italy. Observing that a majority of the Italian population expressed popular acceptance of homosexual couples, the Court found that there were no valid community interest which restricted Italy from offering such protections.[66] Even if

---

[60] It has routinely upheld decisions by various states to not extend the institution of marriage to same-sex couples. It seems to rely on social consensus by evaluating whether a majority of the states in the European Union extend marriage to same-sex couples. See Soucek 2017.

[61] European Commission of Human Rights, *S v. United Kingdom*, decision of the commission (admissibility) of 14 May 1986, App No. 11716/85; European Court of Human Rights, *Rees v. The United Kingdom*, judgement of 17 October 1986, App No. 9532/81; European Commission of Human Rights, *C & L.M. v. The United Kingdom*, decision of the commission (admissibility) of 9 October 1989, No. 14753/89.

[62] European Court of Human Rights, *Christine Goodwin v. The United Kingdom*, judgement of 11 July 2002, App No. 29857/95, paras 62–70. See Pustorino 2014, pp. 400–405.

[63] Shahid 2017.

[64] European Court of Human Rights, *Schalk and Kopf v. Austria*, judgement of 24 June 2010, App No. 20131/04.

[65] See note 1011, paras 144–185.

[66] *Oliari* also goes further than the ECtHR's previous finding in *Vallianatos* because the Court does impose a positive obligation upon Italy to provide some form of recognition to same-sex relationships. But the Court instantly qualifies this by highlighting the failure of Italian legislators to heed the conclusions of the domestic courts, as well as the changing social attitudes about homosexuality. Hence, the Court makes it clear that the "positive obligation" established by the

you find the outcome laudable, it is evident that LGBTQ+ people's access to the values sought to be guaranteed by the privacy doctrine are subordinated to social imperatives, in this case the heterosexual standard.[67]

This twofold criticism also explains why courts in the liberal democratic constitutional paradigm have had to augment the right to privacy to compel the state to offer legal recognition to same-sex marriages. In its landmark judgement affirming the right of same-sex couples to get married, the U.S. Supreme Court stepped outside the traditional privacy doctrine to rely on a claim of dignity.[68] Like the ECtHR, the Court held that marriage was intimately tied to social and cultural norms and was the bedrock of American society. That is where the similarities end. Diverging from the ECtHR, the U.S. Supreme Court held that the value of forming an intimate, two-person union lay in the dignity that came from the public recognition of the union, that is a dignity inherent to the institution of marriage.[69] The Court held that exclusion from the institution of marriage had the effect of teaching same-sex couples and their children that they were unequal in important respects. Hence the Court ruled that all couples otherwise eligible were entitled to the dignity of marriage, regardless of gender.[70] It was this reliance on dignity that allowed the Court to move beyond

---

judgment cannot simply be applied to other States, such as the Russian Federation. Ibid, para 186. It is, therefore, the "changing conditions in Italy" which are decisive to the Court's judgment. In fact, in their concurring opinion, Judges Mahoney, Tsotsoria and Vehabović are careful to point out that this *new* positive obligation exists "on the basis of a combination of reasons not necessarily found in all the Contracting States" (§ 10). Mahoney, Tsotsoria and Vehabović would have preferred to have found a *negative* violation of Article 8 based on a classic analysis of whether the Italian state, in interfering with Article 8(1), had any justification under Article 8(2). See also European Court of Human Rights, *Vallianatos & Others v. Greece*, judgement of 7 November 2013, App No. 29381/09 and 32684/09.

67 I understand that some scholars point to the recent decisions by the ECtHR in *Fedotova* and *Buhuceanu* to show that by guaranteeing the right to civil unions in countries where there was staunch social opposition to the same, the ECtHR is moving beyond social morality. But that strikes me as an incorrect reading of the judgements. In *Fedotova* for instance, the ECtHR relied on a clear ongoing trend within contracting states to supersede the margin of appreciation (zooming out instead of zooming in like in *Oliari*). It seems to me that the Court is refusing to move beyond privileging social morality. In this case, rather dishonestly in my view, it zoomed out to find a social morality which it was keen to uphold. While I am thrilled with the outcome, the reasoning seems suspect to me. European Court of Human Rights, *Fedotova and Others v. Russia*, judgement of 17 January 2023, App No. 40792/10, 30538/14 and 43439/14. European Court of Human Rights, *Buhuceanu and Others v. Romania*, judgement of 23 May 2023, App No. 20081/19. See also Vikarska Z (2023) The Many Troubles of the Fedotova Judgement. VerfBlog. Available at: <https://verfassungsblog.de/the-many-troubles-of-the-fedotova-judgment/>. Accessed on 21 November 2023.

68 See United States Supreme Court, *Lawrence v. Texas*, judgment of 26 June 2003, 539 U.S. 558, para 2594. United States Supreme Court, *Obergefell v. Hodges*, judgement of 26 June 2015, 576 U.S. 644.

69 Bhagwat 2016, pp. 390–398. For a general overview of dignity in LGBTQ+ cases, see Fink 2016.

70 As Justice Kennedy held, "They ask for equal dignity in the eyes of the law. The Constitution grants them that right". See United States Supreme Court, *Lawrence v. Texas*, judgment of 26 June 2003, 539 U.S. 558, para 2608.

the negative rights conception of privacy, to impose a positive obligation upon the state to guarantee same-sex couples access to marriage.[71]

The use of a negative rights conception of privacy in the traditional liberal democratic constitutional paradigm to defend the rights of LGBTQ+ people suffers from conceptual flaws. Due to the structural constraints imposed by negative-rights conceptions of privacy, these courts fail to provide any substantial guarantee of liberty or autonomy to the LGBTQ+ community to enjoy their rights. These courts end up subjecting the exercise of freedoms by LGBTQ+ people to public morality. Guided by the incorrect assumption that the life of law is abstracted logic and not experience, courts' subsequent restrictions on states actually reproduce social hierarchies and leave LGBTQ+ people without their full bouquet of freedoms. This leaves but one question: if not privacy, then what?

6.3 The Reach of Equality in a Transformative Paradigm

6.3.1 A Substantive Vision of Equality

Equality! Many courts in the Global South, which practice post liberal[72] forms of constitutionalism have instead looked to equality provisions in their constitutions when seeking to protect LGBTQ+ rights. In doing so, these courts have moved beyond the negative rights interpretation of privacy. Importantly, they have crafted a substantive conception of equality—instead of a merely formal one—that acknowledges the lived reality of LGBTQ+ individuals and, as a result, imposed positive obligations upon the state to intervene.[73]

Courts in the traditional liberal democratic constitutional paradigm often use a formal conception equality to defend LBGTQ+ rights.[74] Formal equality functions on the simply formulated abstract precept of "treating likes alike and unalikes unalike", more helpfully "sameness". Based on this precept, courts rely on identity characteristics to differentiate between people and justify findings which in fact lead to

---

[71] Justice Kennedy's reliance on dignity has been critiqued extensively, particularly his focus on the institution of marriage. Critics argue that by deifying the institution of marriage, such a decision encourages assimilation into existing patriarchal social institutions. Such assimilation prioritizes existing family institutions such as marriage and the nuclear, biological family, that have had a long history of being oppressive to women and LGBTQ+ individuals, over alternative family arrangements such as non-marital relationships thereby disregarding the radical transformational possibilities such alternative arrangements offer. See Murray 2016; Strauss 2018.

[72] Klare 1998, pp. 151–156.

[73] MacKinnon 2019, p. 306; MacKinnon 2020. On how Europe still relies on a version of formal equality, see Tobler 2014, p. 529.

[74] Supreme Court of Israel, *El Al Airlines Ltd. v. Danilowitch,* judgement of 30 November 1994, 48(5) P.D. 749, H.C. 721/95 (Where the Court held discrimination based on sexual orientation to be unconstitutional. While terming Israel a liberal constitutional democracy, is a stretch at the best of times, its Supreme Court sometimes engages in liberal rights interpretation).

discrimination.[75] To explain the inadequacy of "sameness" in the context of sex, MacKinnon demonstrates how courts perceive sex as a differentiating characteristic and therefore reject calls for equal treatment of men and women under law. Reliance on this abstracted conception has allowed courts to hold that criminal sodomy laws do not violate equality as they equally restrict homosexual and heterosexual conduct. Formal equality has led courts to conclude "both that a gay marriage prohibition law does not discriminate against gay men and lesbian women based on sex because both men and women equally cannot marry persons of their own sex, and that it does discriminate against them based on sex because each person who wishes to marry a person of their own sex could do so but for their sex".[76]

However, some courts have repudiated this vision of formal equality to articulate a vision of substantial equality. The Constitutional Court of South Africa laid down the first brick in the vision of substantive equality in the queer rights space when determining the statutory and common law criminalization of sodomy to be unconstitutional.[77] Moving beyond the traditional doctrine of "suspect classification", the Court paid particular attention to the position of LGBTQ+ people in society. Finding that gay men were a permanent minority in society and had suffered repeated patterns of discrimination, the Court held that the sodomy laws only served to subjugate the identity and acts of gay men to the moral and religious views of a section of society. By shifting the focus from the sameness or difference of an individual to the lived reality of the individual due to their group identity, the South African Constitutional Court moved beyond formal equality to articulate an anti-stereotyping principle. The Court recognized that the discrimination in question was not a mere prohibition of a private sexual act, rather, such criminalization, based on sex stereotypes, affected the lives of a group of people by permanently relegating them to an inferior status in society. As Justice Sachs stated, "*Only in the most technical sense was this a case about who may penetrate whom where. At a practical and symbolic level it was about*

[75] The right to equality is not encompassed in formal equality where all persons are treated alike irrespective of the unequal socioeconomic status but in substantive equality. See Aids Bhedbhav Virodhi Andolan 1991, p. 122. See also Supreme Court of India, *State of Kerala v. N.M. Thomas*, judgement of 19 September 1975, 1976 SCR (1) 906.

[76] MacKinnon 2019, p. 93. ("The legal doctrine that corresponds to this [formal equality] says that what equality is about is treating likes alike and unalikes unalike. The main rule is, if you are "alike" you get equality, and if you are "unalike" you don't. At the same time, the social definition of disadvantaged groups is based on their unlikeness to advantaged groups. In other words, we are told that to the extent you are disadvantaged you are different, and to the extent you are different you are not entitled to equality, because you are only entitled to equality if you are the same. The way one is socially defined and shaped is in direct conflict with what one needs to show legally to succeed in an equality claim.")

[77] Constitutional Court of South Africa, *National Coalition for Gay and Lesbian Equality & Another v. Minister of Justice & Others*, judgement of 9 October 1998, CCT 11/98. To be fair, the Canadian Supreme Court is widely credited with the first judicial articulation of rejection of the sameness criteria and articulating substantive equality. However, this is the first case I can find which articulates a substantive equality vision in the context of LGBTQ+ rights. See, Supreme Court of Canada, *Andrews v. Law Society of British Columbia*, judgement of 2 February 1989, 1 SCR 143.

the status, moral citizenship, and sense of self-worth of a significant section of the community".[78]

The Indian Supreme Court built on a similar vision of substantive equality in *Navtej Johar*.[79] In addition to upholding the group based vision of discrimination,[80] one of the plurality opinions moved beyond the *discriminatory intent*[81] test for legislation by rejecting the reasonable classification doctrine. Examining the classification doctrine, Justice Chandrachud held that equating the content of equality with the reasonableness of a classification enabled legal formalism by elevating form over substance. Instead, he searched for the substantive content of equality by examining the effects of a provision upon the lives of people, in their proper socio-economic context. Just like the South African Constitutional Court, he found that the effect of the impugned provision was to criminalize behaviour that did not conform to the heterosexual expectations of society. In doing so, it perpetuated a cycle of homophobic legislation that was predicated upon traditional gender stereotypes, in this case, the societal conviction that certain behaviour is appropriate for members of one sex but not the other.[82] The effect of this stereotyping, enforced by legislation, was decades of discrimination, prejudice and harassment which obliterated queer identities by outlawing any form of their expression.[83] Therefore, for Justice Chandrachud, the impugned provision was emblematic of an indirectly discriminatory law, neutral in form but discriminatory in effect. By holding it unconstitutional because of its effects on a group of people, the Indian Supreme Court expanded the vision of substantive equality to include the indirect effects test.

This vision of substantive equality holds that the substance of equality rests in recognizing the discriminatory effects of laws that reinforce social stereotypes. Relying on this, courts around the world have arrived at vastly different conclusions from the American and European courts discussed above, when considering the same questions. For instance, in the context of immigration law, the Namibian Supreme Court was asked to consider whether the term "spouse" encompassed same-sex partners lawfully married in foreign jurisdictions.[84] The Court held that denying the recognition of same-sex spouses under immigration law was unfair discrimination and therefore fell afoul of the constitutional guarantee of equality. In the context of family law, specifically adoption, the South African Constitutional Court read the right to equality as protecting LGBTQ+ rights. It held that the denial of second parent adoption rights was a violation of the equality provisions of the constitution.

---

[78] Ibid, para 107.

[79] See note 7. This decision of the court reads as a comparative exercise in dialogue with the reasoning of the South African Constitutional Court and many other courts. See Choudhry 2012.

[80] A similar anti-stereotyping principle has been previously upheld by the Indian Supreme Court. See Bhatia 2019, pp. 38–74.

[81] United States Supreme Court, *Washington v. Davis*, judgement of 7 June 1976, 426 U.S 229. See Huq 2018.

[82] See note 7, pp. 448–451.

[83] Devi and Bhat 2020; Atrey and Bhatia 2023.

[84] See Nayak 2023.

Its reasoning rested on the anti-stereotyping principle when it held that such a denial perpetuated the fiction or myth of family homogeneity based on the one father/one mother model.[85] It relied on the same principle when dealing with the situation of guardianship of children born via artificial insemination. It ruled that partners who were not biological parents were to be regarded as natural parents and guardians and ordered the state to register both partners as parents.[86] Evidently then, courts relying on a substantive vision of equality have been able to offer better protections to LGBTQ+ people than courts relying on the right to privacy.

The key difference from the privacy based paradigm arises when we look at the nature of remedies these courts have crafted. Recognizing that the substantive equality guarantee requires state intervention to correct the discriminatory effects of social stereotypes, these courts have regularly imposed obligations upon the state to ensure that individuals are able to enjoy the substantive content of their rights. In a case concerning immigration law,[87] the Constitutional Court of South Africa held that those in same-sex relationships were capable of forming intimate relationships and sharing love much like heterosexual individuals and differentiating between the two amounted to unfair discrimination. Therefore, the Court held that partners of LGBTQ+ people in long term partnerships were entitled to the same immigration protections as those in heterosexual relationships. In their ruling, instead of reading down the impugned provisions to deny both types of couples immigration benefits, the Court cured the impugned law to impose a positive obligation upon the state to provide the same immigration benefits as those available to married heterosexual couples, to partners in same-sex relationships. Similarly, in the context of employment benefits, the Court imposed a positive obligation upon the state to provide same-sex partners of South African judges, the same employment benefits as those provided to opposite sex spouses.[88] Disappointed with state inaction, the Court stated that it was unsatisfactory for courts to grant piecemeal relief to members of the LGBTQ+ community as and when aspects of their relationships were found to be prejudiced by unconstitutional legislation, instead exhorting the legislature to give a positive content to the equality provisions of the Constitution through law reform.

This conception of substantive equality functionally creates a *claim right,* which entitles the right holder to impose a duty upon a third party. [89] In the case of claim rights against the state, the right holder is entitled to impose obligations upon the state, to provide mechanisms to ensure that the right holder is able to enjoy the substantive content of the right in question. Commonly used in the context of socio-economic rights, these rights are also called positive rights. Apart from imposing obligations

---

[85] Constitutional Court of South Africa, *Du Toit & Another v. Minister of Welfare and Population Development and Others*, judgement of 10 September 2002, (2) SA 198 (CC).

[86] Constitutional Court of South Africa, *J and B v Director-General, Department of Home Affairs and Others*, judgement of 28 March 2003, ZACC 3.

[87] Constitutional Court of South Africa, *National Coalition for Gay and Lesbian Equality & Another v. Minister of Home Affairs & Others*, judgement of 2 December 1999, (2) SA 1 (CC).

[88] Constitutional Court of South Africa, *Satchwell v. President of Republic of South Africa*, judgement of 25 July 2002, (6) SA 1 (CC).

[89] See note 42; Currie 1986; Wenar 2005.

upon the state to act, these may sometimes even impose duties upon other private individuals to act, thereby transcending the traditional barrier of verticality.[90] Such positive rights have played a significant role in cases concerning the social status and conditions of LGBTQ+ individuals as they have imposed obligations upon the state to recognize discrimination and take steps to alleviate its impact.

6.3.2 Equal Moral Membership and Transformative Constitutionalism

Clearly then, courts in constitutional democracies like India, South Africa, Brazil and Namibia by relying on equality instead of privacy, have guaranteed LGBTQ+ people access to the substantive content of the rights they are entitled to. The distinction between the usage of the right to privacy and the right to equality points to the underlying difference between the negative and positive construction of the right in question and subsequently the different reliefs each right entails. The question we are left to confront is, what, if anything, explains this difference?

An underlying difference in the nature of constitutionalism practiced in these different jurisdictions. Let me explain. In the case considering the constitutionality of the provisions criminalizing sodomy before the South African Constitutional Court, Justice Albie Sachs crystallised what was at stake, "*At a more general and conceptual level, it concerns the nature of the open, democratic, and pluralistic society contemplated by the Constitution.*"[91] Similar commitments to constitutionally mandated social engineering have been made by the Indian and Brazilian Supreme Court as well.[92] Instead of relying on the demarcated boundaries between state and society, these courts interpret their constitutions as envisioning and providing a roadmap to a particular vision of society. This roadmap, operationalised through fundamental rights jurisprudence, imposes positive obligations upon the state to take steps towards creating the society envisioned by these constitutions. This brand of constitutionalism, which marks a sharp break from the traditional liberal democratic constitutional paradigm, is commonly referred to as transformative constitutionalism.[93]

Transformative constitutionalism has so far escaped attempts to capture it in a single cohesive comparative theory. Yet, while the underlying political projects and paths to constitutionalism vary in each jurisdiction,[94] they all envision a transition

---

[90] Jackson 2016. See generally Bhatia 2023.

[91] See Constitutional Court of South Africa, *Satchwell v. President of Republic of South Africa*, judgement of 25 July 2002, (6) SA 1 (CC), para 107.

[92] See Krishna Iyer 1978, pp. 24–42.

[93] Baxi 2013, pp. 20–23.

[94] In South Africa and India, it was successful revolutionaries seeking to entrench their vision for change in a constitution to be enforced by courts whereas in Brazil, it was political elites attempting to change national fortunes for the better with less public attention and support. See Ackerman

to a democratic society,[95] or as Murienik posited, they are bridges from a culture of authority to a culture of justification, the latter being a normative commitment for a democratic society.[96] But that is not what sets this project apart from the traditional western liberal democratic constitutional project. After all, change is a commitment of any transitional project and most constitutions are interested in entrenching some version of democratic society as a building block for the project of state building.[97] The core of the claim to transformative constitutionalism then, lies in the nature of the change envisioned.

At its core, transformative constitutionalism entails a foundational constitutional commitment to social and political change at a fundamental level which is aimed at ensuring a more equal and just society. In other words, it entails a commitment to a radical reimagination of a society, which is freed from various forms of prescribed social hierarchy, by law. These hierarchies and consequently, the specific commitments vary based on the jurisdiction involved. For instance, in South Africa, it entails a commitment to a way of looking at the world which creates a space where contestation and dialogue are truly possible.[98] In India, it envisions a large-scale transformation of a society marred by divisions on the lines of class, caste, religion, gender and creed.[99] In Latin America it entails a commitment to socio-economic rights aimed at alleviating poverty through institutional measures.[100] But commonly, at a bare minimum, transformative constitutionalism consists of ideas of material redistribution and symbolic recognition. Importantly, it envisages a state that actively pursues this change.[101]

Within this broader emancipatory project, courts take on a role of heightened significance. While they remain arbiters of legal questions common to all constitutional projects, they also become the interpreters of this transformative project, imbued with the duty of pointing to the new society envisioned by the constitution. Their jurisprudence with regards to right adjudication, operationalized through new and old constitutional tests, offers the means to and justifications of this new society.[102] These courts have interpreted their constitutional projects, operationalised through fundamental rights jurisprudence, as imposing positive obligations upon the

---

2015. In contrast, Ackerman's third category of constitutional legitimacy, the insider model, makes a more unlikely context for transformative constitutionalism.

[95] From colonialism in India, autocracy in South Africa and authoritarianism in Brazil.

[96] Murienik 1994.

[97] The American Constitution is perhaps the first example of a genuinely revolutionary constitution aimed at a transition towards a democratic (no matter how flawed) society. See Tietel 2000.

[98] Langa 2006, p. 354.

[99] Mehta 2010, pp. 15–19.

[100] Arguelhes 2020, p. 165. See generally Fawkes 2017.

[101] Vilhena 2013, pp. 617–620. See also Klare 1998, pp. 153–156.

[102] Choudhry 2020, pp. 192–197. As the Constitutional Court of South Africa has held, the South African Constitution is not merely a formal document regulating public power. It also embodies an objective normative value system. It requires the Court to develop the law within the metric of this objective normative value system. Constitutional Court of South Africa, *K v. Minister of Safety and Security*, judgement of 13 June 2005, ZACC 8.

state to create a more equitable society. This interpretation of rights guarantees, offers us a paradigmatically different vision of constitutionalism in which the nature and function of rights differs from the traditional liberal democratic constitutional paradigm: *transformative constitutionalism.*

The difference in the nature and function of rights is best reflected in the proportionality analysis conducted by courts in the transformative constitutional paradigm. Proportionality analysis is a globally practiced constitutional framework used to assess the validity of the infringement of rights.[103] Broadly speaking, proportionality analysis generally consists of considering the following factors: the legitimacy of the purpose of the impugned law (or other rights restricting measure), whether the means (that is the law in question) bear a rational nexus to the purpose, whether these were the least restrictive means available and finally balancing the benefits of the impugned law with the infringements of the rights in question.[104] In the context of same-sex marriage cases, the first aspect of this test points to the critical difference between the traditional liberal democratic constitutional paradigm and the transformative constitutional paradigm. While courts in the former paradigm are content to accept the preservation of the existing social morality as a legitimate purpose, courts in the latter paradigm subject the stated purpose to a test of constitutional morality. Which is to say that instead of being guided by social morality, courts check whether the stated purpose, in this case the preservation of the social order, aligns with the transformative project the constitution mandates. In doing so, they refuse to subject the exercise of rights by LGBTQ+ people to existing social mores, instead subjecting these community conventions to judicial review based on constitutional principles.

The Indian Supreme Court, in *Navtej* exemplified such a use of proportionality analysis. When considering the purpose of the statute criminalizing same-sex sexual acts (Section 377 of the erstwhile Indian Penal Code), the Court held that the purpose of the Indian Constitution was to supplant a hierarchical society (undergirded by private social relations and norms, or social morality) by a new value system envisioned by the constitution. Therefore, the legitimacy of the government's aim in enacting this section could not be measured against precepts of social morality, rather had to be measured against the new value system envisioned by the constitution (constitutional morality). This constitutional morality, as articulated by the Court was a guarantee of equal concern and respect for all citizens to ensure the heterogenous fibre of society.[105] Measured against this guarantee, the Court found that the impugned section discriminated against individuals based on their "intrinsic and core" individual traits in furtherance of a majority perception. Laws which could only be justified by invoking reasons such as furthering the majority perception,

---

103 Stacey 2019. See generally Cohen-Eliya and Porat 2019.

104 In some jurisdictions, courts also add a final step after this: which is to check, after all of the above questions are answered in favour of the rights restricting measure, whether the right still meaningfully available to individuals. Which is to say after the restriction, is the essential content of the right still preserved. In many cases, this final step is folded into the balancing exercise. See Grimm 2007; Moller 2012.

105 See note 7, pp. 116–124. Dworkin 1986, chapter 8.

which were at variance with constitutional morality could not stand the scrutiny of the Court, and therefore could not have a legitimate aim.[106]

Considered cumulatively then, substantive equality in a transformative constitutional paradigm entails four aspects, namely, an affirmation of anti-stereotyping, a recognition of indirect discrimination, a rejection of social morality in favour of constitutional morality and the imposition of a positive obligation upon the state. All of these principles are best operationalized by the Constitutional Court of South Africa in *Fourie*, a landmark judgement legalizing same-sex marriage.[107]

Hearing challenges to the common law and statutory restriction of marriage to heterosexual couples, the Court first considered the symbolic impact of this restriction. According to the Court, such restrictive legislation had the effect of telling same-sex couples that they were outsiders, and that their need for affirmation and protection of their intimate relations as human beings was somehow less than that of heterosexual couples, by law. Additionally, such legislation reinforced the wounding notion that same-sex couples ought to be treated as biological oddities, as failed or lapsed human beings who do not fit into normal society, and, as such, do not qualify for the full moral concern and respect that the Constitution seeks to secure for everyone. Finally, such legislation also signified that the capacity of same-sex couples to love, commit and accept responsibility was by legal definition less worthy of regard than that of heterosexual couples. The Court held that this exclusion of same-sex couples, ultimately served to reinforce harmful and hurtful stereotypes of gays and lesbians by classifying them as exclusively sexual beings reduced to one dimensional creatures defined by their sexuality.[108]

The Court also recognised the material damage to the LGBTQ+ community which this "facially neutral" law caused. By excluding same-sex couples from the institution of marriage, in material terms, it deprived the couples of the full benefits of marriage including state protection, adoption benefits, inheritance and tax benefits. For the Court, it was self-evident that the denial of the status, entitlements and responsibilities of marriage to same-sex couples constituted a denial of their right to equality under the law. It went on to hold that their right to equality could not be so thinly construed as only mandating the preservation of their private space. Instead, the Court emphasized the right of same-sex couples to be acknowledged and embraced as equals within the law. This right obliged the state to take all necessary steps to ensure that the substantive content of their right was provided to them.[109] Finally,

---

[106] See note 7, pp. 247 and 673.

[107] Constitutional Court of South Africa, *Minister of Home Affairs v. Fourie,* judgement of 1 December 2005, ZACC 19.

[108] Ibid, paras 63–74.

[109] Ibid, para 78. It is also important to point out that dignity played an important role in the Court's reasoning as well. However, where they differ distinctly from the US Supreme Court is in their choice of locating dignity. Unlike Justice Kennedy, who located dignity in the institution of marriage, Justice Sachs located dignity in the availability of choice to the individuals who would want to opt in to the institution of marriage. In doing so, Justice Sachs also responded to the feminist and queer critiques of the heteronormative nature of the institution of marriage. See Lau 2017, p. 2618.

when considering whether such limitation of the rights of same-sex couples was justified, [110] the Court stated that arguments drawing from social morality (that is the belief held by certain sections of society that marriage as defined between a man and a woman was a pillar of South African society) were in fact arguments of prejudice which did not reflect the constitutional values of the country. As such, they could not be accepted as a legitimate justification for such a restriction.[111] With all of this in mind, the Court concluded that common law and the statutory provisions, in so far as they failed to offer same-sex couples the option to enjoy the same status, entitlements and responsibilities accorded to heterosexual couples through marriage, were unconstitutional.

The most emphatic difference from the negative rights approach of courts in the traditional liberal democratic constitutional paradigm is in the nature of the remedies that courts in the transformative paradigm craft. In *Fourie*,[112] after finding the common law and statutory restriction of marriage to be unconstitutional, the Court issued a suspended declaration of invalidity.[113] Essentially, the Court's order of unconstitutionality was to be suspended for one year, within which time, parliament was directed to cure the deficiencies of the law. To ensure that substantive equality was achieved, the Court ordered a levelling up of marriage by issuing two mandatory principles to guide parliament in its task. The first principle prohibited parliament from ending the state's role in marriage and the second prohibited the state from producing a separate but equal formulation of marriage, like a civil union. The Court held that erasing the state's role in marriage or offering a lower status of recognition

---

[110] This form of proportionality analysis is built into the rights jurisprudence of the Constitutional Court through Article 36 of the Constitution of South Africa. The test for legitimate aim has been elaborated upon in various cases. See Constitutional Court of South Africa, *Prinsloo v. Van der Linde,* judgement of 18 April 1997, ZACC 5; Constitutional Court of South Africa, *Harksen v. Lane,* judgement of 7 October 1997, ZACC 12 (any legitimate government purpose must be a defensible vision of the public good).

[111] "Prejudice can never justify unfair discrimination. This country has recently emerged from institutionalised prejudice. Our law reports are replete with cases in which prejudice was taken into consideration in denying the rights that we now take for granted. Our constitutional democracy has ushered in a new era – it is an era characterised by respect for human dignity for all human beings. In this era, prejudice and stereotyping have no place. Indeed, if as a nation we are to achieve the goal of equality that we have fashioned in our Constitution we must never tolerate prejudice, either directly or indirectly. SAA, as a state organ that has a constitutional duty to uphold the Constitution, may not avoid its constitutional duty by bowing to prejudice and stereotyping." See note 108, para 113. See also Constitutional Court of South Africa, *Hoffman v. South African Railways*, judgement of 28 September 2000, ZACC 17.

[112] See Constitutional Court of South Africa, *Minister of Home Affairs v. Fourie,* judgement of 1 December 2005, ZACC 19, paras 147–161.

[113] Such remedies have previously been crafted by the Indian Supreme Court. The Court has held that it has the power to issue directions or guidelines when there is a vacuum in existing law. However, they have not been used to remedy discrimination or unconstitutionality in an existing law. *See*, Supreme Court of India, *Vishaka and Others v. State of Rajasthan*, judgement of 13 August 1997, AIR 1997 SC 311. Supreme Court of India, *Common Cause v. Union of India*, judgement of 9 March 2018, 5 SCC 1.

would reproduce the marginalisation of the private sphere which would deny same-sex couples the substance of equality. The focus on substantive equality required the South African Court to impose obligations upon the state that would ensure that LGBTQ+ people enjoyed the full content of their freedoms.

Courts in the transformative constitutional paradigm have sometimes gone further than imposing obligations only upon the state. Drawing on the same principles, these courts have sometimes recognised horizontally applicable positive rights. Such rights impose duties upon other private individuals and not only the state, in this case duties upon individuals to afford equal concern and respect to members of the LBGTQ+ community. In 2019, the Federal Supreme Court of Brazil was confronted with rising discrimination against LGBTQ+ people.[114] Declaring homophobia to be a crime akin to racism, the court relied on the concept of full citizenship or equal moral membership. Writing for the court, Justice De Mello argued that discrimination based on sexual orientation denied affected individuals the substantive content of their rights to equality and autonomy. By criminalizing homophobia, the Court imposed duties upon all Brazilians to act in such a manner than they created the social conditions enabling LGBTQ+ people to enjoy the substantive content of their rights. This criminalization functionally created a horizontal positive right as it imposed upon all members of society, a duty to treat individuals equally. Thus, in cases concerning the rights of LGBTQ+ people, courts in the transformative constitutional paradigm use substantive equality as a route to acknowledge and remedy the reality of hierarchical structures and power relationships within society and ensure that LGBTQ+ people are able to exercise their freedoms.

The differences in the nature and operationalisation of the right to privacy and right to equality are brought to the fore if one compares the decision in *Fourie* to *Oliari*. On a fundamental level, this comparison shows us the position occupied by an individual in their respective constitutional paradigm. In the traditional liberal democratic constitutional paradigm, negative rights interpretations of privacy only serve to allow an individual to maintain their position within the existing social hierarchy. However, the promise of the transformative constitutional paradigm lies in positive rights interpretations which guarantee and affirm the "equal moral membership" of each individual. The transformative interpretation of substantive equality requires courts to abandon default verticality and subject societal mores to constitutional morality. In doing so, courts can pierce domains traditionally considered private by interpreting the content of rights guarantees to issue remedies which impose positive obligations upon the state, and sometimes even impose horizontally applicable duties, thereby ensuring a greater degree of constitutional protection for LGBTQ+ individuals. Through material and symbolic transformations, courts and the state are entrusted with the project of erasing social hierarchy and affirming equal moral membership in a substantive sense.

---

[114] Supreme Court of Namibia, *Digashu and Another v. GRN and Others; Seiler-Lilles and Another v. GRN and Others*, judgement of 16 May 2023, SA 6/2022; SA 7/2022, NASC 14.

6.4 The Elasticity of Paradigms: A Discussion on Transplants

The transformative constitutional paradigm engenders the use of substantive equality to guarantee LGBTQ+ rights. Alternatively courts in the traditional liberal democratic paradigm use privacy and sometimes formal equality when confronted with similar cases thereby offering far more limited relief to LGBTQ+ people.[115] This has led some to contend that these formalist interpretations of privacy and equality arise due to structural limits imposed by the constitutional text.[116] Therefore, one would be justified in questioning whether courts in liberal democratic constitutional paradigms are capable of transcending the barrier of default verticality to impose positive obligations upon the state? Put differently, one could ask if these rights choices and paradigms of constitutionalism are firmly embedded in these different jurisdictions due to constitutional texts and history?

A closer analysis of the nature of bills of rights and interpretative methods suggests that this is not the case. Courts are not constrained to any one constitutional paradigm due to the form, structure or substance of their constitutional texts. Structurally, most bills of rights do not naturally obligate judges to arrive at any one particular conclusion. Instead, the content of these bills of rights are often open ended or indeterminate.[117] As Hirschl demonstrates, the open ended wording of the constitutional catalogues of rights allows courts to interpret the very same rights provisions in different manners.[118] Interpreting the content of a bill of rights often requires judges and courts to look beyond formalist interpretations of rules in search of the principled or moral content of the rights.[119] There is no textual imposition of particular interpretations of this moral content, rather contextual reasons which engender particular interpretations. These paradigms of constitutionalism are as much a product of the text and history of a constitution as they are a product of interpretive choices and constitutional cultures.[120] These cultures and interpretive choices are not ironclad and are open to change. Essentially, constitutional catalogues of rights are vaguely worded and there is value to this vagueness in as much as it leaves space for judges to make interpretive choices.[121]

---

[115] MacKinnon 2011. Supreme Court of Canada, *Vriend v. Alberta,* judgement of 2 April 1998, 1 S.C.R 493. Eyer 2010.

[116] See, e.g., Barnard and Hepple 2000 (Contending that the legislative frameworks of the UK and the European Community are not in themselves capable of leading to greater substantive equality and hence pointing out the need for a new framework).

[117] Kennedy 1987, pp. 1729–1732; Kennedy 1997, p. 19; Unger 1996, p. 65. See Tushnet 1983.

[118] Hirschl 2000, pp. 1095–1098.

[119] Waldron 2009; Dworkin 1978, p. 81; Green 2016, p. 323.

[120] Klare 1998, pp. 150–151; Bhatia 2019.

[121] Chadha-Sridhar 2021; Endicott 2005.

This rather fluid dichotomy between the paradigms of constitutionalism then arises from interpretive choices made by judges and courts.[122] The contextual factors leading to these choices vary from legal cultures to the influence of neoliberal economics, but they do not create a presumption of a static and unwieldy rights interpretation. Essentially, these are not fixed boundaries. Rights in what are otherwise considered traditional liberal democratic constitutional paradigms can be interpreted in a transformative manner and vice versa. The texts provide ample space for such changing interpretations by judges while maintaining interpretive fidelity to the constitutional project. For instance, German constitutional doctrine has embraced the values of transformative constitutionalism while making the necessary alterations to maintain fidelity to the legal culture in Germany.[123] Similarly, the judiciary in Australia has interpreted various rights regimes to give effect to large scale social transformation.[124] This is to say that courts in the liberal democratic constitutional paradigm are not bound to negative rights interpretation of privacy and can evaluate LGBTQ+ rights through the lens of substantive equality, as some have. Conversely, courts in a transformative constitutional paradigm can also interpret their constitutional catalogues of rights in a formal, traditional liberal manner. One need only return to the India Supreme Court's decision in *Supriyo* to see this fluidity in action.

In *Supriyo*, the Indian Supreme Court abandoned substantive equality and chose to rely on privacy, which is visible through its hesitance to enter into the domain of religious personal laws. In the oral hearings, the Court restricted the challenge to the recognition of same-sex marriages under the Special Marriage Act, 1954 (SMA). The SMA, explicitly framed as a secular law, sets up a separate marriage regime outside the aegis of religious personal laws. By restricting the constitutional challenge to the SMA, the Court essentially restricted the constitutional challenge to the state-created existing secular marriage regime. Through this restriction, the question before the Court shifted from whether the state had an affirmative duty to grant the petitioners access to marriage as a public institution to whether there was a fundamental right to marriage and consequently, whether the state had infringed upon the petitioners' liberty interests by denying them access to marriage. By changing the question before it, the Court instructed the petitioners to rely only on the sphere of privacy and the permissible scope of state intrusion into it.

Restricted to privacy, the petitioners drew upon the U.S Supreme Court's decision in *Windsor* to argue that the restrictive gendered definition of marriage in the SMA imposed a regime predicated upon heteronormative identity on LGBTQ+ people. According to the petitioners, it followed from the right to privacy that individuals must have the autonomy to enter into intimate relationships and the state ought to

[122] After all, what a constitution means, can never be completely separated from what the interpreter hopes and aspires it to mean. This is not to suggest that judges are not normatively and subjectively constrained, which is to say that a constitution cannot simply mean what a judge wants it to mean. Instead it is to suggest that the strategic pursuit of transformative projects through adjudication is not inconsistent with the principle of interpretive fidelity. In other words, indeterminacy does not lead to anarchy.

[123] Hailbronner 2017.

[124] De Villiers 2023. See generally Goldsworthy 2006.

maintain neutrality between various forms of intimate relationships and the diverse arrangement which they encompass. For them the gendered provisions of the SMA infringed upon this neutrality and they urged the Court to find it constitutionally invalid. In opposition, the Government of India argued that privacy jurisprudence only recognizes same-sex intimate relationships and does not include any claim to public recognition of marriage.[125] The majority opinion of the Supreme Court agreed with the government, refusing to find a positive obligation upon the state to grant to the petitioners, the right to marry.

The Court began by reiterating the findings of Indian and foreign courts regarding the fundamental privacy interest that guaranteed an individual the right to choose a partner. Denying the existence of a fundamental right to marry, however, the Court held that marriage as a social institution was based in personal and religious customs and preceded the state. Its status was not conferred by the state and hence, while the state had a legitimate interest in regulating it, the state could not move beyond the traditional purposes and perceptions sought to be protected by personal laws. According to the Court, while the right to privacy protected the choice of individuals, it did not impose a positive obligation on the state to open access to social institutions which were governed by custom and therefore beyond the state. Therefore, the Court refused to impose upon the state, any obligation to grant the petitioners a right to marriage or even civil unions.[126] For the Court, the right to be left alone could not entail the imposition of an obligation upon the state to "create" a social institution.

The Court also refused to read gender neutral language into the SMA by arguing that the object of the statute was to regulate heterosexual marriages and hence it could not accommodate a gender neutral provision. It went on to say that gender neutral provisions would deny women the protection afforded by the SMA, thereby reinforcing the heteronormative standard of marriage.[127] It ultimately concluded by asking Parliament to form a committee to re-evaluate the legal framework for marriage. By choosing the right to privacy, the Court subjected the rights of LGBTQ+ people to social standards and refused to find a positive obligation on the state. The Court's imposition of the heteronormative standard becomes expressly visible when you notice that the Court upheld the rights of transgender individuals to marry under the SMA as they conformed to the gender binary. In doing so, the Court expressly relegated queer identities to private spaces and refused to allow them a substantive content of autonomy, even in those private spaces.[128]

---

[125] Affidavit on file with Author.

[126] According to the Court, while the petitioners had a right to relationships, they did not have the right to compel the state to grant any recognition to these relationships. See Aids Bhedbhav Virodhi Andolan 1991, pp. 290–304.

[127] This is also evident from the Court, much like the ECtHR, stating that transgender people could get married under the SMA as they fit within the gendered provisions of the SMA. Ibid, p. 327.

[128] What is truly frustrating is that the majority opinion recognizes the material aspects of the indirect discrimination faced by queer couples who do not have access to the benefits and privileges flowing from the institution of marriage. Yet instead of finding a positive obligation upon the state to remedy this discrimination, they are content to note that the state shall, at some point of time, form a committee to explore these effects. Ibid, pp. 321–326.

The critical choice—error—of this Court arose from it its threshold determination that limited the challenge to the existence of a fundamental right to marriage and the SMA, thereby limiting itself to the privacy doctrine. This initial choice—and it was an interpretive choice—to stay out of the social domain of marriage laws limited the Courts ability to provide any substantive relief. This choice hamstrung the Court from the beginning as under the negative rights framework of privacy, the Court would have only been able to provide limited remedies even if it had legalised same-sex marriage.[129] Even if the Court had legalized same-sex marriage, it would have been confronted with the SMA's structural issues.[130] Additionally by restricting its marriage analysis to the purely secular law, the Court was precluded from ensuring access to the benefits and privileges of marriage that flow from personal religious laws.[131] The framing of the constitutional challenge as a negative privacy-rights case

[129] The Supreme Court has interpreted a limited number of socio-economic rights such as the right to food and the right to education which impose positive obligations on the State as flowing from Article 21's guarantee of life and personal liberty. While none of these have flown from the right to privacy, in India the right to privacy is housed under Article 21. Therefore, with some judicial creativity, one could make a plausible, albeit improbable argument to impose positive obligation upon the state to recognise samesex marriage. See Agarwal 2022.

[130] The SMA is notoriously riddled with procedural hurdles that regularly pose barriers for individuals trying to get married under its aegis. For instance, the SMA requires that a notice of an intended marriage be published publicly and displayed prominently. Thereafter, any person can object to the proposed marriage and subsequently the marriage officer can refuse to solemnize the union. This procedure often results in threats of violence, ostracism, and persecution of interfaith and inter-caste couples, which would also likely be perpetrated against LGBTQ+ couples. By denying anonymity to those who need it most, the SMA subjects couples to social pressure and stigma. Despite its aims, the SMA fails to afford such couples any substantial sense of autonomy, which it so desires to protect. So even if the Court had legalized same-sex marriage under the SMA, it would be faced with ensuring that LGBTQ+ couples enjoyed the full benefits and privileges of marriage. To guarantee this, it would have had to impose duties upon the state to both rectify the SMA to guarantee autonomy to LGBTQ+ couples as well as order the state to step in and amend personal religious law. A negative rights conception of privacy would prevent the Court from crossing this divide and ordering the state to interfere in the private domain. This is to say that the emphasis on the right to privacy to guarantee same-sex marriage in India not only failed in legalizing same-sex marriage but more importantly, even on its best interpretation, would result in limited remedies which impose heteronormative standards upon same-sex couples. Section 5, 6, 7, & 8, Special Marriage Act 1954. Bhandare and Karwa (2020) How The Special Marriage Act is Killing Love. Article 14. Available at: <https://www.article-14.com/post/how-the-special-marriage-act-is-killing-love>. Accessed on 21 November 2023; Canada: Immigration and Refugee Board of Canada (2012) India: Situation of Inter-Religious Couples from both Urban and Rural locations, including societal attitudes, treatment by government authorities and the treatment of their children (2005–April 2012). Available at: <https://www.refworld.org/docid/50b4a36c2.html>. Accessed on 10 October 2023.

[131] By limiting the constitutional challenge to a secular law, the Court disregarded the complex intersectional identities of LGBTQ+ people in India. Religion-based personal laws form an intrinsic part of the cultural identity of many Indians. In the context of marriage, a large number of same-sex couples use the rituals of their community to locate their relationships in their local, cultural and religious context. Additionally, this limited challenge also ignores the larger plural landscape of Indian family law. Given that marriage remains critical in determining the applicability of other laws related to inheritance, parenthood, etc., the limitation of marriage to the SMA created tangible roadblocks for LGBTQ+ people seeking the concomitant benefits that flow from marriage. For instance, Hindu couples married under the SMA are still subject to Hindu personal law, especially

ensured that the Court would not have been able to impose any positive duties upon the state (i.e. direct it to take action) to remedy these issues, even if it had legalized same-sex marriage. Therefore, the emphasis on negatively constructed privacy rights under the traditional liberal democratic constitutional paradigm not only failed in legalizing same-sex marriage but more importantly, even on its best interpretation, would result in limited remedies which impose heteronormative standards upon same-sex couples.

This decision of the Indian Supreme Court shows that transformative interpretations are not the only interpretations of the Indian constitutional text. Similarly, scholars argue that while the South African Constitution has the makings of a transformative document, it is up to the courts and other constitutional actors to give it meaning. Transformative constitutionalism does not reside in the text of the law, rather it must become a social practice for communities and cultures practising it.[132] This is all to say that while textual catalogues of rights are a starting point for such projects, the interpretive choices of courts which are undeniably influenced by social pressures and legal cultures are a constituting factor in paradigms of constitutionalism.

In the context of LGBTQ+ rights then, courts can, and must, evaluate their claims through the lens of transformative constitutionalism, positive rights and substantive equality. The use of substantive equality offers courts a route to acknowledge and respond to the reality of hierarchical structures and power relationships within society. Substantive equality enjoins the courts to abandon default verticality, and instead subject societal mores to constitutional morality. In doing so, courts can pierce domains traditionally considered private by interpreting the content of traditional rights guarantees to impose positive obligations upon the state and even horizontally applicable duties, thereby ensuring a greater degree of constitutional protection for LGBTQ+ individuals.

And some courts in otherwise traditional liberal democratic constitutional paradigms are beginning to recognize and implement substantive equality albeit tentatively. In *Lawrence*, Justice O'Connor's concurring opinion grounded the unconstitutionality of sodomy laws in the equality provisions of the U.S Constitution. In *Loving v. Virginia*, when evaluating whether the prohibition of interracial marriages, the U.S Supreme Court held that anti-miscegenation statutes employed a (quasi-) suspect classification, subjecting interracial couples to degradation, thereby violating the constitutional guarantee of equal protection.[133] As the Hawaii Supreme Court demonstrated in *Baehr v. Lewin*,[134] the question of same-sex marriages can be viewed as an equal protection question without any inquiry into the nature of marriage itself. The most emphatic declaration of substantive equality in the U.S. constitutional

---

with regard to succession and guardianship. Given that Hindu personal laws proceed on assumptions based in the gender binary, there remains considerable confusion regarding their application to same-sex couples. Section 6, Hindu Minority and Guardianship Act 1956. See also Agarwal 2022, pp. 176–180; Vanita 2005; Saxena 2021, chapter 10.

132 Spieker and Von Bogdandy 2023.

133 United States Supreme Court, *Loving v. Virginia*, judgement of 12 June 1967, 388 U.S. 1.

134 Supreme Court of Hawaii, *Baehr v. Miike* (originally *Lewin)* judgement of 9 December 1999, 852 P.2d 44.

context came in *Romer v. Evans*, in which the U.S. Supreme Court held that an amendment to the Colorado Constitution which blocked the state and its local governments from providing antidiscrimination protections based on sexual orientation was unconstitutional.[135] In a brief yet powerful judgement, the Court in *Romer* moved away from the traditional rational basis test to present a modified three stage review when judging whether the impugned law or action fell afoul of the equal protection clause of the U.S Constitution. It asked if (i) the impugned action implicated a classification based on a group's identity or conduct; (ii) the group was unpopular or lacked functional access to the political process; and (iii) if the impugned act was motivated by an animus. By setting forth this test, the U.S. Supreme Court recognises the anti-hierarchical principle which undergirds substantive equality. Finally, in *Bostock v. Clayton County*, the Court also pierced the public private divide when it held that acts of discrimination by private employers based on sexual orientation were prohibited under law.[136] To some extent then, courts in the United States have embraced anti-stereotyping, disparate impact and even broken through the tradition of default verticality.[137] To a degree, they have begun to recognize the disadvantaged position of LGBTQ+ people in society and are taking steps to ensure that the state steps in to offer the full protection of laws.

Even the ECtHR, has recently applied equality provisions of the convention in defence of LGBTQ+ rights. In the dissenting opinions in *Fedotova*, Judges Pavli and Modoc noted that law could serve to shape a society's moral views. According to them, national legal regimes that discriminated on impermissible grounds reinforced prejudice and social segregation. Providing equal recognition to same-sex couples signified acceptance of same-sex couples and validated them as equal members of society, irrespective of differences.[138] In *Maymulakhin and Markiv v. Ukraine*,[139] the ECtHR emphasized the "intrinsic value" of recognition as a symbol of inclusion and equality of same-sex couples. It held that allowing same-sex couples to be granted legal recognition and protection undeniably served the convention's ideals and values, as recognition and protection of this kind conferred legitimacy on same-sex couples and promoted their inclusion in society, regardless of sexual orientation. According to the Court, a democratic society within the meaning of the convention must reject any stigmatisation based on sexual orientation, and instead be built on the equal dignity of individuals, sustained by diversity. Furthermore, the Court noted that the core of the applicants' grievance was "to be treated with equal dignity" and that "the State would confer a sense of legitimacy on their relationship by legally recognising its existence and by ensuring its adequate protection". While the Court did not go so far

[135] United States Supreme Court, *Romer v. Evans*, judgement of 20 May 1996, 517 U.S. 620.

[136] United States Supreme Court, *Bostock v. Clayton County*, judgement of 15 June 2020, 590 U.S. 1618.

[137] Notes 2023.

[138] European Court of Human Rights, *Fedotova and Others v. Russia*, judgement of 17 January 2023, App No. 40792/10, 30538/14 and 43439/14, para 5 of dissenting opinion.

[139] European Court of Human Rights, *Maymulakhin and Markiv v. Ukraine*, judgement of 1 June 2023, App No. 75135/14, paras 64–77.

as to impose positive obligations upon the state, it advocated for social engineering through substantive equality, a core premise of transformative constitutionalism.

The strict dichotomy between these two paradigms is not so strict after all. As evidenced through the rulings of the ECtHR and the U.S Supreme Court, courts in what are traditionally considered liberal democratic constitutional paradigms, can use substantive equality provisions to voice transformative commitments and offer better protections to LGBTQ+ people. While the substantive equality paradigm has not yet been completely transplanted to these jurisdictions,[140] these early signs show promise. Transplanting substantive equality as a means of protecting LGBTQ+ rights offers a route to a constitutional revolution,[141] that is the establishment of a new legal paradigm which offers better protections for the LGBTQ+ community.

When confronted with questions regarding LGBTQ+ rights, specifically access to marriage, courts rely on either the right to privacy or the right to equality. By examining comparative jurisprudence, this chapter demonstrates that these judicial choices are a product of courts privileging differing interpretive paradigms. These jurisdictional differences between a negative rights conception of privacy and a positive rights conception of substantive equality have varied the content of the freedoms and remedies offered to LGBTQ+ people. This chapter unpacks the limits of privacy, as constructed in traditional liberal democratic constitutional paradigms and advances a transformative conception of substantive equality as a means to ensure material and symbolic remedies for LGBTQ+ people. Ultimately, it argues that transformative interpretations, operationalized through substantive equality, contain the promise of equal moral membership in society for LGBTQ+ people.

Acknowledgements My thanks to Rehan Abeyratne, Eric Christiansen and an anonymous reviewer for helpful comments on an earlier draft. This chapter draws on my previous work, Bakshi 2025. The views represented herein, and all errors, are my own.

References

Ackerman B (2015) Three Paths to Constitutionalism: And the Crisis of the European Union. British Journal of Political Science 45(4):705–714

Agarwal A (2022) Marriage Equality in India: Thinking Beyond Judicial Challenges to Secular Marriage Law. Indian Law Review 6(2):170–188

Aids Bhedbhav Virodhi Andolan [AIDS Anti-Discrimination Movement] (1991) Less than Gay. New Delhi

Arguelhes DW (2020) Transformative Constitutionalism: A View from Brazil. In: Dann P, Bonneman M, Reigner M (eds) The Global South and Comparative Constitutional Law. Oxford University Press, Oxford

Atiyah PS (1985) The Rise and Fall of the Freedom of Contract. Oxford University Press, Oxford

[140] Watson 1978.

[141] Lipkin 1989; Lipkin 2000, pp. 138–147.

Atrey S, Bhatia G (2023) In Search of Principle: 70 Years of Gender Jurisprudence in India. In: Chang WC, Loper K, Malagodi M, Rubio-Marin R (eds) Gender, Sexuality and Constitutionalism in Asia. Hart Publishing, Oxford, pp 259–280.
Bakshi K (2025) Marriage, Courts and Substantive Equality: A Transformative Interpretation. Michigan Law Review 123:519
Barnard C, Hepple B (2000) Substantive Equality. Cambridge Law Journal 59(3):562–585
Baxi U (2013) Preliminary Notes on Transformative Constitutionalism. In: Vilhena O, Baxi U, Viljoen F (eds) Transformative Constitutionalism: Comparing the Apex Courts of Brazil, India and South Africa. Pretoria University Law Press, Pretoria, pp 19–47
Berlant L, Warner M (1998) Sex in Public. Critical Inquiry 24(2):547–566
Berlin I (1969) Two Concepts of Liberty. In: Berlin I (ed) Four Essays on Liberty. Oxford University Press, Oxford, pp 118–172
Bhagwat A (2016) Liberty or Equality? Lewis & Clark Law Review 20:381–398
Bhatia G (2018) Case Comment: Navtej Singh Johar v. Union of India: The Indian Supreme Court's Decriminalization of Same-Sex Relations. Max Planck Yearbook of U.N. Law 22(1):218–233
Bhatia G (2019) The Transformative Constitution: A Radical Biography in Nine Acts. Harper Collins, India
Bhatia G (2023) Horizontal Rights: An Institutional Approach. Hart Publishing, Oxford
Chadha-Sridhar I (2021) The Value of Vagueness: A Feminist Analysis. Canadian Journal of Law & Jurisprudence 34(1):59–84
Choudhry S (2012) How to Do Comparative Constitutional Law in India? In: Khilnani S, Raghavan V, Thiruvengadam A (eds) Comparative Constitutionalism in South Asia. Oxford University Press, Oxford, pp 45–85
Choudhry S (2020) Postcolonial Proportionality. In: Dann P, Bonneman M, Reigner M (eds) The Global South and Comparative Constitutional Law. Oxford University Press, Oxford, pp 190–209
Cohen-Eliya M, Iddo Porat I (2019) Proportionality and Constitutional Culture. Cambridge University Press, Cambridge
Crisafulli F (2014) Same Sex Couples' Rights Before the ECtHR. In: Gallo D, Paladini L, Pustorino P (eds) Same Sex Couples before National, Supranational and International Jurisdictions. Springer, Berlin/Heidelberg
Currie D (1986) Positive and Negative Constitutional Rights. University of Chicago Law Review 53(3):864–890
Damaska M (1991) The Faces of Justice and State Authority: A Comparative Approach to Legal Process. Yale University Press, New Haven
D'Aloia A (2014) From Gay Rights to Same-Sex Marriage: A Brief History Through the Jurisprudence of US Federal Courts. In: Gallo D, Paladini L, Pustorino P (eds) Same Sex Couples before National, Supranational and International Jurisdictions. Springer, Berlin/Heidelberg, pp 33–71
de Villiers B (2023) Breathing Life into the Constitution: The Role of Courts to Give a Unique Identity to a Constitution. Constitutional Review 9(1):109–141
Devi KTG, Bhat SR (2020) Navtej: A Queer Rights Jurisprudential Revolution? NUJS Law Review 13(3):490–515
Dowdle MW, Wilkinson MA (2017) Introduction. In: Dowdle M W, Wilkinson M A (eds) Constitutionalism beyond Liberalism. Cambridge University Press, Cambridge, pp 1–14
Dworkin R (1978) Taking Rights Seriously. Harvard University Press, Massachusetts
Dworkin R (1986) A Matter of Principle. Harvard University Press, Massachusetts
Endicott T (2005) The Value of Vagueness. In: Bhatia V, Engberg J, Gotti M, Heller D (eds) Vagueness in Normative Texts. Peter Lang, Bern, pp 27–48
Eskridge Jr. W (1993) A History of Same Sex Marriage. Virginia Law Review 79:1419–1513
Ewing C (2023) Dignity Disputed. Journal of Law and Courts 11:370–388
Eyer K (2010) Have We Arrived Yet? LGBT Rights and the Limits of Formal Equality. Law and Sexuality 19:160–166

Fabre C (2000) Social Rights Under the Constitution: Government and Decent Life. Oxford University Press, Oxford
Fawkes J (2017) Transformative Constitutionalism and the Global South. In: Bogdandy A V, Mac-Gregor E F, Antoniazzi M M, Piovesan F, Soley X (eds) Transformative Constitutionalism in Latin America: The Emergence of a New Ius Commune. Oxford University Press, Oxford
Fink M (2016) The Role of Dignity in Gay Rights Adjudication and Legislation: A Comparative Perspective. International Journal of Constitutional Law 14(1):26–53
Fried C (1978) Right and Wrong. Harvard University Press, Massachusetts
Gardbaum S (2003) The Horizontal Effect of Constitutional Rights. Michigan Law Review 201:387–459
Goldsworthy J (2006) Interpreting Constitutions: A Comparative Study. Oxford University Press, Oxford
Green L (2016) Law and the Role of a Judge. In: Ferzan K K, Morse S J (eds) Legal, Moral and Metaphysical Truths. Oxford University Press, Oxford
Grimm D (2007) Proportionality in German and Canadian Jurisprudence Constitutional Jurisprudence. The University of Toronto Law Journal 57(2):383–397
Grimm D (2016) Constitutionalism: Past, Present and Future. Oxford University Press, Oxford
Hailbronner M (2017) Transformative Constitutionalism: Not Only In The Global South. American Journal of Comparative Law 65(3):527–565
Harmsen R (2007) The European Court of Human Rights as a Constitutional Court: Definitional Debates and the Dynamics of Reform. In: Morison J, McEvoy K, Anthony G (eds) Judges, Transition and Human Rights. Oxford University Press, Oxford, pp 33–53
Hirschl R (2000) "Negative" Rights vs "Positive" Entitlements: A Comparative Study of Judicial Interpretations of Rights in an Emerging Neo-Liberal Economic Order. Human Rights Quarterly 22(4):1060–1098
Hobbes T (1968) Leviathan. Penguin Classics, London
Hohengarten W (1994) Same Sex Marriage and the Right to Privacy. Yale Law Journal 103
Hohfeld WN (1919) Fundamental Legal Conceptions as Applied in Judicial Reasoning and Other Legal Essays. Yale University Press, New Haven
Huat CB (2022) Liberal Order's Illiberal Prodigy: Singapore as a Non-Liberal Electoral Democratic State. In: Verhoeven H, Lieven A (eds) Beyond Liberal Order: States, Societies and Markets in the Global Indian Ocean. Oxford University Press, Oxford
Huq A (2018) What is Discriminatory Intent? Cornell Law Review 103(5):1211–1292
Hurd H, Moore M (2018) The Hohfeldian Analysis of Rights. The American Journal of Jurisprudence 63(2):295–354
Jackson V (2016) Positive Obligation, Positive Rights and Constitutional Amendment. In: Kahana T, Scolnicov A (eds) Boundaries of State, Boundaries of Rights: Human Rights, Private Actors and Positive Obligations. Cambridge University Press, Cambridge, pp 109–128
Kennedy D (1987) Form and Substance in Private Law Adjudication. Harvard Law Review 89:1685–1778
Kennedy D (1997) A Critique of Adjudication. Harvard University Press, Massachusetts
Klare K (1998) Legal Culture and Transformative Constitutionalism. South African Journal on Human Rights 14(1):146–188
Krishna Iyer VRJ (1978) Law and Social Change: An Indian Perspective. Punjab University Publication Bureau, Chandigarh
Krotoszynski Jr. RJ (2016) Privacy Revisited: A Global Perspective on the Right to be Left Alone. Oxford University Press, Oxford
Langa P (2006) Transformative Constitutionalism. Stellenbosch Law Review 17(3):351–360
Lau H (2017) Marriage Equality and Family Diversity: Comparative Perspectives from the United States and South Africa. Fordham Law Review 85(6):2615–2628
Lipkin R (1989) The Anatomy of Constitutional Revolutions. Nebraska Law Review 68:701–806
Lipkin R (2000) Constitutional Revolutions: Pragmatism and The Role of Judicial Review in American Constitutionalism. Duke University Press, Durham

MacKinnon C (1987) Feminism Unmodified. Harvard University Press, Cambridge, Massachusetts
MacKinnon C (2011) Substantive Equality: A Perspective. Minnesota Law Review 96(1):1–27
MacKinnon C (2019) Butterfly Politics. Harvard University Press, Massachusetts
MacKinnon C (2020) Equality. Daedalus 149(1):213–221
MacNaughton J (2001) Positive Rights in Constitutional Law. Journal of Constitutional Law 3(2):750–782
Mandal S (2009) 'Right to Privacy' in Naz Foundation: A Counter-Heteronormative Critique. NUJS Law Review 2(3):525–540
Mehta US (2010) Constitutionalism. In: Mehta P B, Jayal N G (eds) The Oxford Companion to Politics in India. Oxford University Press, Oxford, pp 15–27
Minow M (2022) Does the First Amendment Forbid, Permit or Require Government Support of New Industries? In: Jackson V, Dawood Y (eds) Constitutionalism and a Right to Effective Government? Cambridge University Press, Cambridge, pp 58–100
Moller K (2012) Proportionality: Challenging the Critics. International Journal of Constitutional Law 10(3):709–731
Murienik E (1994) A Bridge to Where? Introducing the Interim Bill of Rights. South African Journal of Human Rights 10:31–48
Murray M (2016) Obergefell v. Hodges and Nonmarriage Equality. California Law Review 104(5):1207–1258
Nayak N (2023) Constitutional Morality: An Indian Framework. American Journal of Comparative Law 71(2):354–387
Notes (2023) Romer Has It. Harvard Law Review 136:1936–1957
Pustorino P (2014) Same-Sex Couples Before the ECtHR: The Right to Marriage. In: Gallo D, Paladini L, Pustorino P (eds) Same Sex Couples before National, Supranational and International Jurisdictions. Springer, Berlin/Heidelberg
Rai S (2021) Courts, the Law, and LGBT Politics in India. In: Haider-Markel D (ed) The Oxford Encyclopedia of LGBT Politics and Policy. Oxford University Press, Oxford
Rao N (2013) Three Concepts of Dignity in Constitutional Law. Notre Dame Law Review 86(1):183–272
Rubenfeld J (1989) The Right to Privacy. Harvard Law Review 102(4):737–807
Saxena PP (2021) Family Law II, 4th edn. LexisNexis, India
Schauer F (2018) Positive Rights, Negative Rights and the Right to Know. In: Pozen D, Schudson M (eds) Troubling Transparency. Columbia University Press, New York, pp 34–51
Schlag P (2015) How to Do Things with Hohfeld. Law and Contemporary Problems 78:185–234
Schmitt C (2009) Constitutional Theory. In: Seitzer J (ed) Duke University Press, Durham
Schütze R (2020) Constitutionalism and the European Union. In: Barnard C, Peers S (eds) European Union Law. Oxford University Press, Oxford, pp 71–96
Shahid M (2017) The Right to Same-Sex Marriage: Assessing the European Court of Human Right's Consensus Based Analysis in Recent Judgements concerning Equal Marriage Rights. Erasmus Law Review 10(3):184–198
Siegel N (2014) Federalism as a Way Station: Windsor as an Exemplar of Doctrine in Motion. Journal of Legal Analysis 6(1):87–150
Singer JW (1982) The Legal Rights Debate in Analytical Jurisprudence: From Bentham to Hohfeld. Wisconsin Law Review 729:975–1059
Somek A (2014) The Cosmopolitan Constitution. Oxford University Press, Oxford
Soucek B (2017) Marriage, Morality and Federalism: The USA and Europe Compared. International Journal of Constitutional Law 15(4):1098–1118
Spieker L, Von Bogdandy A (2023) Transformative Constitutionalism in Luxembourg: How The Courts Can Support Democratic Transitions. Columbia Journal of European Law 29:65–92
Stacey R (2019) The Magnetism of Moral Reasoning and the Principle of Proportionality in Comparative Constitutional Adjudication. American Journal of Comparative Law 67(2):435–475
Strauss G (2018) What's Wrong with Obergefell? Cardozo Law Review 40(2):631
Sunstein C (1998) The Partial Constitution. Harvard University Press, Massachusetts

Suresh M (2011) Possession is 9/10th of the Body. In: Gupta A, Narrain A (eds) Law Like Love: Queer Perspectives on Law. Yoda Press, New Delhi, pp 378–392
Thio LA (2019) Singapore Relational Constitutionalism: The 'Living Institution' and the Project of Religious Harmony. Singapore Journal of Legal Studies 204–234
Tietel R (2000) Transitional Justice. Oxford University Press, Oxford
Tobler C (2014) Equality and Non-Discrimination under the ECHR and EU Law: A Comparison Focusing on Discrimination against LGBTI Persons. Zeitschrift für ausländisches öffentliches Recht und Völkerrecht 74(3):521–561
Tribe L (2004) Lawrence v. Texas: The Fundamental Right That Dare Not Speak its Name. Harvard Law Review 117(6):1893–1955
Tushnet M (1983) Following the Rules Laid Down: A Critique of Interpretivism and Neutral Principles. Harvard Law Review 96(4):781–827
Ulfstein G (2021) Transnational Constitutional Aspects of the European Court of Human Rights. Global Constitutionalism 10(1):151–174
Unger R M (1996) What Should Legal Analysis Become? Verso Books, New York
Vanita R (2005) Love's Rite: Same Sex Marriage in India and the West. Penguin Books, India
Vilhena O (2013) Some Concluding Thoughts on an Ideal Machinery and Method. In: Vilhena O, Baxi U, Viljoen F (eds) Transformative Constitutionalism: Comparing the Apex Courts of Brazil, India and South Africa. Pretoria University Law Press, Pretoria, pp 617–624
Waldron J (2009) Judges as Moral Reasoners. International Journal of Constitutional Law 7(1): 2–24
Watson A (1978) Comparative Law and Legal Change. Cambridge Law Journal 37(2):313–336
Wenar L (2005) The Nature of Rights. Philosophy & Public Affairs 33(3):223–253

Chapter 7
Gatekeeper Constitutionalism: Exploring the Role of the Indian Judiciary in Environmental Constitutionalism and International Law Integration

Eklavya Vasudev

Contents

Abstract This chapter offers a critical analysis of the Gatekeeper model within Indian constitutionalism. It focuses on the undiscerning manner in which the Indian Supreme Court integrates international law into domestic jurisprudence. While the model facilitates innovative legal exchanges and aligns with the Indian Constitution's global orientation, the focus of this analysis is on the challenges and risks associated with this integration. The Supreme Court's role as a "Gatekeeper" – balancing domestic constitutional needs with international legal principles, especially in environmental jurisprudence – is scrutinised. As a result of inconsistently adopting international norms, the judiciary may find itself taking on roles beyond its constitutional limits, leading to erratic legal shifts and ambiguities. The core argument of the chapter advocates for a more judicious and deliberate approach in exercising this gatekeeping function. By doing so, it aims to enhance the understanding of constitutional law's adaptability in the global legal landscape, while cautioning against the unchecked assimilation of international norms that might undermine constitutional integrity.

E. Vasudev (✉)
Public International Law and Human Rights, Friedrich-Alexander University Erlangen-Nuremberg, Erlangen, Germany
e-mail: eklavyavasudev@gmail.com

M. De Visser et al. (eds.), *European Yearbook of Constitutional Law 2024*, European Yearbook of Constitutional Law 6, https://doi.org/10.1007/978-94-6265-699-4_7

Keywords Constitutional Flexibility · Environmental Jurisprudence · Gatekeeper Model · International Law Integration · Judicial Discretion · Legal Innovation

7.1 Introduction

The transformation of the Indian Supreme Court ("the Court") in the post-Emergency era has been a topic of significant scholarly interest, particularly because of the context that led to this shift.[1] The Emergency, declared in India from 1975 to 1977, was a period marked by widespread political unrest and constitutional challenges. During this time, the government imposed strict censorship, suspended civil liberties, and altered the political landscape, leading to a crisis of democratic principles and human rights. This era marked a low point for the judiciary, which was perceived as ineffectual in safeguarding fundamental rights. In response to this period of constitutional crisis, the Court embarked on a subsequent journey of transformation, becoming more activist in its approach.[2] This shift was largely driven by a critical self-reflection regarding its subdued role during the Emergency, which highlighted its previous failures to uphold fundamental rights robustly. The post-Emergency era, therefore, saw the Court assertively redefining its guardianship of constitutional rights. It was propelled by an urgent need to restore public confidence in the judiciary and to reaffirm its commitment to justice and the rule of law by addressing issues of governance failures and human rights abuses.[3]

The post-Emergency era thus witnessed the Court taking bold steps to correct its past inadequacies by initiating innovations such as Public Interest Litigation (PIL) that allowed for greater judicial intervention in matters affecting the marginalised sections of society.[4] By easing the requirements of locus standi, the Court opened new avenues for addressing broader social and environmental injustices, thus significantly broadening the scope of legal redress available to the public.

Simultaneously with its newfound approach, the Court embarked on a significant shift towards integrating international law into its constitutional interpretations. This integration marked a pioneering phase, showcasing the Court's willingness to align domestic jurisprudence with global legal standards. However, this process was not without its challenges. Often carried out with limited rigor and insufficient oversight, the integration efforts sometimes pushed the boundaries of established frameworks, raising critical questions about the limits and appropriateness of such adaptations.

The role of the Court as a "gatekeeper" of international law facilitated a fluid incorporation of global principles into the Indian Constitutional context. In environmental jurisprudence, this gatekeeping model has been prominently utilised. While

---

[1] See, generally, Baxi 1980; Sathe 2002; Gill 2016.

[2] See Baxi 1980; Mate 2015, pp. 171–175.

[3] Mate 2015, p. 171.

[4] Report on the National Juridicare: Equal Justice- Social Justice. Indian Ministry of Law, Justice and Company Affairs (1977).

the model has succeeded in bringing international standards to the fore of national jurisprudence, it has also resulted in judgments that are sometimes unenforceable. These decisions have often created ambiguities in legal standards, which has led to confusion and inconsistency in the application of the law. Such outcomes raise questions about the effectiveness of this approach in fostering clear and actionable legal frameworks that are essential for effective governance.

To substantiate my argument, I have chosen to focus on environmental jurisprudence, as it serves as an effective constitutional *laboratory* for demonstrating the Indian Supreme Court's approach to incorporating international law. As highlighted by Iyengar et al., environmental law is distinctively complex due to its involvement of multiple stakeholders with divergent interests.[5] These cases provide a revealing context in which to observe how courts navigate the intricate balance between rights, economic considerations, justice, public interest, and ecological sustainability. Notably, environmental litigation often involves public interest issues, yet the "public" typically is not a direct party to these cases. This unique circumstance compels the courts to adopt the role of public guardians, deviating from their traditional stance as objective and neutral arbiters. Furthermore, environmental cases frequently expose overlaps between law violators and law enforcers, as evidenced by instances of the Executive's non-compliance or outright violations of environmental laws.[6] Such dynamics make environmental jurisprudence a particularly rich and appropriate field to explore the Supreme Court's gatekeeping role in the integration of international law into domestic jurisprudence.

In this chapter I first examine the Court's role as an arbitrary custodian of international law, a concept I call "Gatekeeper Constitutionalism". This examination will include a review of pivotal environmental law cases where the Court has applied international law to inspire its constitutional interpretations. Next, I examine the Indian constitutional framework to determine how it facilitates this form of constitutionalism. This is even though it is not explicitly mandated by the Indian Constitution. Finally, I outline the potential pitfalls and risks associated with such a gatekeeping practice. In my conclusion, I argue that while the gatekeeping model offers the potential for positive outcomes, a lack of judicial prudence can lead to significant challenges in implementation and legitimacy. Thus, although not inherently flawed, the gatekeeping model requires a careful and thoughtful approach.

7.2 The Indian Supreme Court's Gatekeeper Approach to Environmental Constitutionalism

During the 1980s, rights that were not explicitly stated in statutory laws were incorporated into constitutional mandates by India's judiciary. Building on the context of the post-Emergency period referred to earlier, this era marked the rise of PIL,

[5] Iyengar et al. 2019.

[6] Ibid., p. 2.

renowned for its inclusive, people-focused approach.[7] PIL revolutionized access to justice by introducing innovative judicial processes and remedies, leading to significant changes in legal procedures. These changes included expanding eligibility to file cases, adopting non-confrontational legal methods, and providing comprehensive remedies aligned with the broadened interpretation. Among the six fundamental rights of Indian citizens are the right to equality (Articles 14–18), the right to freedom (Articles 19–22), the right to avoid exploitation (Articles 23–24), the right to freedom of religion (Articles 25–28), the right to education and cultural access (Articles 29–31) and the right to constitutional remedies (Articles 32). A notable aspect of the rights expansion was the emphasis on the right to life, as stipulated in Article 21 of the Indian Constitution,[8] extending to encompass the right to a clean and healthy environment, including access to pollution-free water and air.[9]

Drawing on the analyses of Michael Anderson, Lavanya Rajamani and Geetanjoy Sahu, in this section I discuss the extensive efforts of the Court to enhance the right to a healthy environment. These efforts largely relied on integrating principles of international environmental law into Indian law.[10] The integration extended beyond established norms to embrace emerging principles, such as Inter-generational Equity,[11] the Precautionary Principle,[12] and the Polluter Pays[13] Principle.[14] Through a creative interpretation of constitutional provisions, the Court established the groundwork for a progressive environmental legal framework. It served as a pivotal connector, integrating international environmental principles into the domestic legal landscape. This created a novel model for environmental governance and legal interpretation in India.

While the Court has received commendation for its forward-thinking approach to environmental constitutionalism, there is also prominent criticism, particularly relevant to the current discussion, that focuses on two key aspects. Firstly, critics have underscored the Court's inability to provide a clear and precise definition of the environmental right.[15] This vagueness has raised concerns about the clarity and enforceability of such a right within the legal framework. Secondly, the Court's method of defining this right has been called into question due to its seemingly

---

[7] Gill 2016, p. 184.

[8] Art. 21 of the Constitution of India states: "No person shall be deprived of his life or personal liberty except according to the procedure established by law".

[9] Ibid.

[10] Rajamani 2007; Sahu 2008.

[11] Intergenerational equity refers to the concept of fairness or justice in the relationships between different generations, emphasising the ethical responsibility to preserve access to resources and a healthy environment for future generations.

[12] The precautionary principle is designed to safeguard public health and the environment against uncertain risks. It asserts that the lack of complete scientific certainty should not be a basis for delaying actions when there is a potential for serious or irreversible damage to public health or the environment.

[13] The polluter pays principle requires polluters to bear the costs associated with the environmental damage. This principle aims to incentivise pollution prevention, control and reduction costs.

[14] Rajamani 2007, pp. 280–281; Sahu 2010, p. 337.

[15] Rajamani 2007, p. 278.

haphazard application of international environmental law principles.[16] This approach has led to uncertainties about the consistency and coherence in integrating these global standards into the national legal context.

Despite numerous public interest environmental law cases over recent decades and frequent references to the environmental right in India, the challenge remains in precisely defining and thereby demarcating and solidifying this right, even at a theoretical level. Key questions persist about what specifically is being protected, why, and to what degree it includes procedural safeguards.[17] Various interpretations in landmark cases highlight this ambiguity.

For example, in the *Narmada Bachao Andolan* case,[18] the right was closely linked with the right to health. In contrast, the ruling *in Intellectuals Forum*[19] identified it as the right to environmental protection and conservation of natural resources. Meanwhile, in *Shantistar Builders*,[20] the right was characterized as a right to a decent environment. These varied characterisations illustrate a right that is not only imprecise but also presents considerable challenges in its interpretation, leaving substantial discretion to judges. While some may argue that ambiguity is an inherent part of the legal process, a more pressing concern emerges when the Court grounds these imprecise rights on contested principles of international environmental law.[21]

The principles of international environmental law that the Court relies on are notably varied in their development and legal status. Some principles represent emerging concepts that are still in the formative stages of recognition and acceptance within the global legal community. Others are part of "soft law" frameworks, which, while influential, do not possess the binding force of hard law and are instead adhered to on a voluntary or non-compulsory basis. Additionally, some principles are derived from non-binding treaties, which have been agreed upon by states but do not carry the same obligatory enforcement mechanisms as binding agreements. This eclectic reliance on a mixture of established, emerging, and non-binding international principles introduces significant complexities to the legal framework governing environmental rights in India. The diversity in the origins and statuses of these principles means that their integration into domestic law is not only challenging but also raises questions about their enforceability and consistency of their application.

For instance, in *Indian Council for Enviro-Legal Action v. Union of India*,[22] the Supreme Court invoked the polluter pays principle, drawing its authority from a passing reference to Article 130R (2) of the Treaty of Rome as discussed in an

---

[16] Ibid., p. 280.

[17] Ibid., p. 278.

[18] Supreme Court of India, *Narmada Bachao Andolan v. Union of India*, judgment of 18 October 2010, 10 SCC 664.

[19] Supreme Court of India, *Intellectuals Forum, Tirupathi v. State of AP*, judgment of 23 February 2006, 3 SCC 549, para 84.

[20] Supreme Court of India, *Shantistar Builders v. Narayan Khimala Totame and Others*, judgment of 31 January 1990, 1 SCC 520, para 9.

[21] See Sahu 2008; Rajamani 2016.

[22] Supreme Court of India, *Indian Council for Enviro Legal Action*, judgment of 13 February 1996, 3 SCC 212, para 67.

academic journal.[23] This legal action was initiated due to the environmental degradation affecting villagers in Bicchri, a village heavily impacted by nearby chemical plants. The Court integrated the principle into the provisions of the Environment Act, compelling the Central Government to act against factories discharging highly acidic waste.[24] The immediate outcome of this ruling shifted the financial burden of remediation from the government to the polluting industries. More significantly, in the long term, the decision associated the principle with a standard of absolute liability, a more stringent approach than the strict liability standard established by *Rylands v. Fletcher*.[25]

In a later case, *Vellore Citizens' Welfare Forum*,[26] the Court reiterated the polluter pays principle as a rule of customary international law and upheld the absolute liability regime established in the Indian Council for Enviro-Legal Action decision as essential to this principle. [27] However, as Anderson points out,[28] the doctrine of absolute liability is not a standard tenet [29] of customary international law but is rather specific to India, stemming from the 1986 Supreme Court decision in the *Oleum Gas Leak Case*. [30] Furthermore, the Court's interpretation that the polluter pays principle in Indian law not only mandates compensation to the victims but also covers the costs of environmental remediation significantly expands the scope of the principle compared to its usual applications in international law, which typically hold the polluter to a lesser standard of liability.[31]

The most significant example of the Court invoking international environment law principles is the Vellore Forums case referred to in the preceding paragraph.[32] In this case, the Vellore Citizens Welfare Forum filed a petition under Article 32 [33] of the Indian Constitution against approximately 900 tanneries and other leather industries in the state of Tamil Nadu. The petitioners alleged that these tanneries, using 170 types of toxic chemicals for chrome tanning and 35 litres of water per

---

[23] Ibid.

[24] Anderson 1998, p. 27.

[25] Ibid; UKHL *Rylands v. Fletcher* judgment of 17 July 1868, 1 LR 3 HL 330. This is a decision by the House of Lords which established a pivotal precedent in English tort law with the ruling that there is strict liability for any damage caused to another's land resulting from non-natural use of one's own land, particularly when it involves hazardous substances emanating from the property.

[26] Supreme Court of India, *Vellore Citizens' Welfare Forum v. Union of India*, judgment of 28 August 1996, 5 SCC 647.

[27] Supreme Court of India, *Indian Council for Enviro Legal Action*, judgment of 13 February 1996, 3 SCC 212, para 67.

[28] Anderson 1998, p. 27.

[29] See Sands 1995, pp. 213–217.

[30] Supreme Court of India, *M.C. Mehta v. Union of India*, judgment of December 20 1986, AIR 1987 SC 1086.

[31] Anderson 1998, p. 27; Birnie and Boyle 1992, p. 109.

[32] Supreme Court of India, *Vellore Citizens' Welfare Forum v. Union of India*, judgment of 28 August 1996, 5 SCC 647.

[33] Article 32 deals with the right to constitutional remedies, encompassing, among other things, the ability to petition the Supreme Court for the enforcement of fundamental rights.

kilogram of leather, were discharging large quantities of toxic effluents into the Palar River, a critical drinking water source. The petition highlighted that about 35,000 hectares of nearby agricultural land had become unusable due to this pollution. An independent survey by a non-governmental organization, found that 350 out of 467 wells used for drinking and irrigation were contaminated, causing significant distress to residents. A technical report from the Legal Aid and Advice Board of Tamil Nadu noted that these tanneries, constituting 80% of India's export-quality leather production, were significant contributors to foreign exchange earnings. The State Pollution Control Board had offered options to install common effluent treatment plants or individual pollution controls, aligned with Central Government Guidelines, but these measures proved ineffective. The central legal question then was whether the continued operation of these tanneries, contributing significantly to environmental degradation and affecting the lives of the river's surrounding communities, should be permitted.

In its ruling, the Court moved beyond a conventional perspective of conflict between development and ecology, adopting sustainable development as a key element in interpreting the Constitution. This approach permitted the continuation of tannery operations, conditional upon the payment of environmental fines and compensation for damages.

However, in incorporating sustainable development into Indian constitutionalism, the Court based its decision on the assertion that this principle was part of customary international law. It selectively extracted *salient features* of sustainable development from the Brundtland Report and other international documents, specifically adopting the precautionary principle and the polluter pays principle as its core elements. These principles were constitutionally embedded within Article 21[34] and Articles 47,[35] 48A,[36] and 51A(g) of the Constitution,[37] as well as in environmental legislation such as the Environment (Protection) Act, 1986.[38] It is notable that, apart from Article 21, the other constitutional references predominantly serve as guiding principles for state policy rather than enforceable duties. thus introducing complexities in directly applying broad international norms to the domestic legal context. Article 21, which guarantees the protection of life and personal liberty, is directly enforceable by the courts. This justiciable nature allows for judicial interventions that can directly enforce environmental standards as part of the fundamental rights. Conversely, other constitutional references, those encapsulated within the Directive Principles of State Policy (Articles 36 to 51), serve primarily as guiding principles. These principles

[34] Right to Life under the Indian Constitution.

[35] The Article addresses the obligation of the State to enhance nutrition levels and living standards, as well as to advance public health.

[36] The Article stipulates that it is the state's responsibility to strive towards the protection and improvement of the environment, and to preserve forests and wildlife.

[37] The Article mandates that every citizen of India has the duty to protect and enhance the natural environment, which includes forests, lakes, rivers, and wildlife, as well as to show compassion towards all living beings.

[38] Supreme Court of India, *Vellore Citizens' Welfare Forum v. Union of India*, judgment of 28 August 1996, 5 SCC 647, para 13.

are designed to inform and influence government policy and legislative action but do not confer enforceable rights upon individuals. For example, Article 48A directs the State to protect and improve the environment and to safeguard forests and wildlife, yet it does not provide a legal basis for individual enforcement in the courts. This dichotomy between enforceable rights and non-enforceable principles poses challenges in the direct application of broad international norms within the domestic legal framework. While Article 21 provides a clear pathway for integrating international environmental standards into Indian law, the Directive Principles, although influential in shaping state policy, do not mandate compliance with these standards in a legally binding manner. Therefore, the application of international norms through these principles can result in variable adherence, impacting the uniformity and effectiveness with which these norms are applied across different jurisdictions within India. This framework creates a scenario where the alignment of international environmental norms with domestic legislation remains contingent on the legislative and executive branches' commitment to these principles. Furthermore, there exists scholarly debate regarding the status of several international environment law principles as customary international law.[39]This ambitious incorporation of international environmental norms into domestic law also presents interpretative challenges. In this case, the Court's broad definition of the precautionary principle encountered practical difficulties in its application to the specific facts of the case. In defining the nebulous precautionary principle, the Court notably, and without elaboration, selected three key components to represent its meaning within the realm of domestic law.[40] These components were:

(a) Environmental initiatives – undertaken by the State Government and statutory bodies – should be proactive in anticipating, preventing, and addressing the causes of environmental harm.
(b) In situations where there is a risk of serious and irreversible damage, the absence of complete scientific certainty should not serve as a justification for deferring environmental protection measures.
(c) The responsibility to prove that an activity is environmentally harmless falls on the shoulders of the party undertaking the action, typically the developer or industrialist.

The Court failed to establish clear mechanisms for implementing these principles or for ascertaining individual liabilities, which has led to obstacles in the effective enforcement of compensation orders.[41] Additionally, the critical distinction between precaution and prevention, an essential element of environmental jurisprudence, was not adequately clarified.[42] Finally, the Court in this case affirmed what is often termed

---

[39] See Bodansky 1995. See also Rajamani 2016.

[40] Supreme Court of India, *Vellore Citizens' Welfare Forum v. Union of India*, judgment of 28 August 1996, 5 SCC 647, para 11.

[41] See Sahu 2010, p. 337.

[42] Rajamani 2007, p. 282.

as the strong form of the precautionary principle,[43] effectively reversing the burden of proof in cases of environmental damage. This approach may have resulted in consequences more detrimental than advantageous. Cass Sunstein posits that regulatory frameworks demanding proponents of an activity to prove its harmlessness set an insurmountable evidentiary threshold.[44] Further such stringent interpretation and application could inhibit innovation and creativity, potentially curtailing scientific and technological progress and leading to a state of regulatory stagnation.[45] Moreover, there are compelling economic arguments regarding the disproportionate costs associated with adhering to this stringent principle relative to its benefits, especially in a developing economy like India.

In a Constitutional framework that endeavours to assimilate international law, the current approach presents significant issues. The Court's method of integrating international principles into India's legal system is marked by a lack of comprehensive evaluation regarding their legal standing, relevance to specific Indian contexts, and a detailed analysis of potential costs and benefits. Furthermore, this form of judicial gatekeeping leads to an unexamined incorporation of these international principles into the fabric of constitutional law, thereby establishing a precedent that influences future cases. This trend is exemplified in the subsequent applications of the *Vellore* jurisprudence. Such applications have perpetuated the misapplication of these initially vague principles, which, once introduced by the Court, have become firmly entrenched in India's constitutional law.

The Supreme Court employed the three-limbed version of the Precautionary Principle from the Vellore Citizens case in the *Taj Trapezium Case*.[46] In this instance, the Court ordered numerous industries around the Taj Mahal to either relocate or adopt pollution abatement strategies to protect the monument from further decay. The same principle was applied to ban construction within one kilometre of two lakes near Delhi, [47] limit commercial shrimp farming on India's coastlines, [48] and require the relocation of 550 polluting tanneries in Calcutta. [49] These cases were not primarily concerned with scientific uncertainty but rather focused on preventive actions, with the normal prerequisites for demonstrating harm being waived. Anderson points out that the Court has used the precautionary principle strategically to sidestep conventional requirements for causation and proof, thus facilitating prompt interventions against industries deemed polluting in ecologically vulnerable

[43] See Sunstein 2003.

[44] Ibid.

[45] Rajamani 2007, p. 282.

[46] Anderson 1998, p. 27; Supreme Court of India *MC Mehta v. Union of India* (Taj Trapezium Case) 1997, 2 SCC 353.

[47] Anderson 1998, p. 28; Supreme Court of India *MC Mehta v. Union of India* (Badkhal & Surajkund Lakes Case) 1997, 3 SCC 715.

[48] Anderson 1998, p. 28; Supreme Court of India *S Jagannath v. Union of India* 1997, 2 SCC 87.

[49] Anderson 1998, p. 28; Supreme Court of India *MC Mehta v. Union of India* (Calcutta Tanneries Matter) 1997, 2 SCC 411.

zones.[50] Notably, these cases did not hinge on scientific uncertainty; instead, they predominantly involved preventive measures, with the usual requirements for proving damage being relaxed. As Anderson notes, the Court has leveraged the precautionary principle as a strategy to bypass traditional evidentiary and causation requirements, thus enabling swift action against industries perceived as polluting in environmentally sensitive areas.[51]

Similarly, in the *A.P. Pollution Control Board* case[52], the Court examined the suitability of allowing a hazardous industry to be established within 10 km of reservoirs supplying drinking water. The Court emphasized that this situation was a prime example of the application of the "precautionary principle", highlighting the potential risk of accidents in such close proximity to the reservoirs. The Court pointed out that the precautionary principle was about foreseeing possible environmental harm and taking steps to prevent it, or choosing the option that causes the least environmental damage, especially in situations of scientific uncertainty. Additionally, the Court observed that the burden of proof shifts to the party posing the potential hazard, referencing the *Vellore* case in this context. Although the Court attempted to determine the level of societal risk acceptable in relation to drinking water, the case again did not hinge on "scientific uncertainty". The uncertainty involved was the likelihood of an accident occurring, not the scientifically understood consequences of such an accident.[53] Therefore, this scenario more aptly demonstrates the application of the principle of prevention rather than precaution.

The examination of these pivotal cases provides a brief illustration of the Court's method of gatekeeping international law, characterized by its selective adoption of certain principles, along with an often-erratic application and lack of comprehensive explanation. However, to fully grasp how the court can integrate international law it would be necessary to understand the Constitutional framework facilitating this integration. In the following section, we will delve into how well the Court's gatekeeping strategy aligns with the broader constructs of India's Constitutional Framework.

---

[50] Anderson 1998, p. 28.

[51] Ibid.

[52] Supreme Court of India, *A.P. Pollution Control Board v. Prof. M.V. Nayudu (Retd.) and Others*, judgment of 27 January 1999, 2 SCC 718.

[53] Rajamani 2007, p. 283.

7.3 India's Constitutional Framework and International Law

7.3.1 The Constitutional Framework

The Constitution of India outlines a federal system in which power is distributed between the constituent States and the Union Government. Legislative authority is divided by subject matter, with the Union Parliament holding the power to legislate on any of the 97 topics listed under the "Union List", while the State Legislatures have authority over topics on the "State List". Both tiers of government can legislate on issues listed under the "Concurrent List".[54] The responsibility for foreign affairs, including interactions with the United Nations and other countries, is managed by the central Union Government.[55] The authority to negotiate treaties is exclusively held by the Union Government, The Constitution does not explicitly address treaty-making but treats it as an executive function. Article 53 assigns the Union's executive power to the President,[56] who relies on the advice of the Prime Minister and the Council of Ministers.[57] The processes of negotiating, signing, and ratifying treaties are considered executive functions. While the Council of Ministers must answer to the Lok Sabha, the lower house of Parliament, there is no requirement for Parliamentary endorsement in the treaty processes.[58]

On the other hand, Article 253 of the Constitution grants Parliament extensive authority to enact laws that implement treaties and international agreements, as well as decisions from international conferences, associations, or bodies, even if no formal treaty exists. However, any legislation passed under this Article must align with the Fundamental Rights outlined in the Constitution, serving as a potential limitation on Parliament's power to fulfil international treaty obligations.[59] Anderson argues that the Government of India considers its existing statutory framework, especially the broad powers granted by the Environment (Protection) Act of 1986, adequate to fulfil its obligations under international environmental treaties without the need for specific incorporating legislation. This viewpoint is supported by the fact that both the 1981

---

[54] The Seventh Schedule of the Indian Constitution details the distribution of powers and responsibilities between the Union and State legislatures. It comprises three distinct lists: the Union List, the State List, and the Concurrent List.

[55] Seventh Schedule of the Indian Constitution, List 1, Entries 10–16.

[56] Article 53 of the Indian Constitution vests the executive powers of the Union in the President, who exercises them directly or through subordinate officers, reserves command of the Defence Forces for the President, and specifies that this Article does not transfer state powers to the President or restrict Parliament from assigning functions to other authorities.

[57] Article 74 of the Indian Constitution provides for a Council of Ministers headed by the Prime Minister to aid and guide the President, who must act based on their advice, though he can request a reconsideration of this advice.

[58] Anderson 1998, p. 22.

[59] Anderson 1998, p. 22; Supreme Court of India, *Maganbhai Ishwarbhai Patel v. Union of India*, decision of 9 January 1969, AIR 1969 SC 783.

Air (Prevention and Control of Pollution) Act and the 1986 Environment (Protection) Act, while generally aligning with the spirit of the 1972 United Nations Conference on the Human Environment in Stockholm, do not comprehensively address all aspects of the Stockholm Declaration. Instead, these Acts focus on establishing detailed pollution permit systems that extend beyond the Declaration's directives. Furthermore, the unique structure of Indian federalism, where environmental issues primarily fall under state jurisdiction, complicates the enactment of national environmental legislation. Historical attempts to address environmental concerns through national legislation, like the Water (Prevention and Control of Pollution) Act of 1974, have faced significant delays due to the need for consensus and enabling resolutions from at least two state legislatures. By referencing the Stockholm Conference in the preambles of the Air and Environment Acts, the Parliament was able to legislate more promptly on state-controlled topics under the guise of implementing international agreements, illustrating a strategic use of international environmental discourse to navigate federal constraints.[60]

Moving on, the Indian Constitution's stance on International Law is primarily encapsulated in Article 51(c), which mandates:

> "The State shall foster respect for international law and treaty obligations in the dealings of organized peoples with one another; and encourage settlement of international disputes by arbitration."

The phrase "international law" in Article 51(c) encompasses all obligations arising from various sources of international law, including Customary International Law.[61] Conversely, "treaty obligations" refer to the commitments arising from international treaties. It is important to recognize that Article 51(c) is situated in Part IV of the Constitution, within the Directive Principles of State Policy. Although these Principles significantly influence governance and guide state actions, they are not enforceable in a court of law.[62] Moreover, the Indian Constitution does not provide a clear directive regarding the incorporation of international law into the domestic legal framework. There is an absence of an explicit mandate or prohibition for the judiciary in terms of integrating international law into their judicial decisions.[63]

The framework described reveals that India formally adopts a dualist[64] stance towards international law. In this system, the executive branch holds the power to enter into international agreements, while their domestic enactment necessitates approval by Parliament.

---

[60] Anderson 1998, pp. 22–23.

[61] Ranjan 2022, p. 5.

[62] Article 37 of the Indian Constitution, pertaining to Part IV, states that while the provisions in this Part are not enforceable by any court, the principles outlined are nonetheless essential for the country's governance. Furthermore, it is the duty of the State to implement these principles in the process of lawmaking.

[63] See Sehrawat 2021, p. 107. See also Jayawickrama 2005.

[64] In a dualist state, international law and domestic law are viewed as separate systems. International treaties require explicit legislative incorporation to become part of the domestic legal framework, despite being ratified internationally.

7.3.2 A Monist System in Practice

Constitutional Law Scholar, Aparna Chandra contends that, despite being a dualist system in theory, in practice, India operates more like a monist[65] state.[66] She points to a fundamental tension in the incorporation of international law within India's constitutional framework. In practice, Parliament has minimal control over integrating international norms, as the Executive often adopts these norms with limited or only retrospective Parliamentary oversight. Thus, the division of powers between the Executive and the Legislature, as conceptualized in dualist theories, does not hold true in practice in India. Additionally, judicial decisions allow courts to adopt international law norms directly, bypassing legislative domestication.[67]

The Constituent Assembly, which drafted the Constitution, debated the framework for integrating international law, ultimately granting Parliament the power to implement international obligations, even at the expense of the federal structure. This decision was influenced by limitations under the Government of India Act, 1935, which restricted the Federal Legislature's treaty implementation powers to matters outside provincial legislative competence unless with provincial consent. This restriction had hampered India's participation in International Labour Organization (ILO) conferences. To avoid such impediments and ensure that India could present a unified stance internationally and effectively implement international decisions, the Constituent Assembly endowed Parliament with overarching powers in Article 253. Additionally, the framers emphasized Parliamentary oversight in adopting international laws domestically, aiming to foster thorough debate, curb arbitrary Executive actions, protect state interests, and preserve the federal structure.[68]

However, in practice, the Executive has many opportunities for incorporating international law into domestic law without express Parliamentary approval, and without any, or with limited and ex-post, Parliamentary oversight. Further, when the Executive is granted wide discretion, or has ample rule-making powers, it can decide to ratify and domesticate international legal norms in the exercise of such powers, with no, or limited, parliamentary over-sight. For instance, the Environment (Protection) Act, 1986 invests the Central Government with the power "to take all such measures as it deems necessary or expedient for the purpose of protecting and improving the quality of the environment and preventing controlling and abating environmental pollution".[69] The Central Government has wide concomitant rule-making powers as well. In the exercise of this power, the Central Government has promulgated wide-ranging rules and often for incorporating international conventions into domestic

---

[65] Under a monist framework, international treaties and conventions automatically become part of a country's domestic legal system once they are ratified, without the need for any additional legislative action. This theory is based on the principle that there is a single, unified legal system in which international and national laws coexist harmoniously.

[66] See Chandra 2017.

[67] Ibid.

[68] Ibid; Constituent Assembly Debates 1948–1949.

[69] Section 3, Environment (Protection) Act 1986.

law.[70] Chandra notes that the Environment (Protection) Act mandates post-facto Parliamentary notification after the government has enacted rules, requiring these rules to be laid before Parliament for thirty days. However, for the ratification of international treaties, no prior Parliamentary approval is necessary, allowing the Executive to ratify significant treaties without public scrutiny or immediate Parliamentary oversight. This process can leave the country liable internationally, even if Parliament does not legislate in accordance with a treaty. Thus, ex-post control by Parliament over the Executive proves ineffective in ensuring accountability.

Furthermore, the dualist structure does not adequately allow for public debate or scrutiny before international obligations are assumed. Once assumed, many international norms are incorporated into domestic law through processes that bypass extensive Parliamentary oversight.[71] Despite calls for constitutional amendments to democratize the treaty-making process and legislative proposals aimed at restricting the Executive's power to bind the country to international obligations without Parliamentary consent, these efforts have not been successful.[72] Chandra also highlights that international lawmaking often centralizes power, shifting it away from states and affecting the federal balance envisioned in the Constitution.[73] Occasionally, preambles of Acts declare that legislation is being enacted to fulfil specific international obligations, primarily to justify Parliamentary competence over the matter. For instance, in the 1970s, environmental legislation often invoked Article 253 due to slow progress in state consultations.[74]

This background on the history and structure of the Indian Constitution serves to illustrate the inherent conflicts that arise in integrating international law among the three branches of government. The relationship between the executive and legislature is particularly strained by differing approaches to international law integration, which is further complicated by the judiciary's varied methods of incorporating treaty-based laws, non-ratified international treaties, and customary international law.

[70] Chandra 2017; Example: Hazardous Waste (Management, Handling and Transboundary Movement) Rules, as amended up to 2009 (incorporating obligations under the Basel Convention on the Control of Transboundary Movements of Hazardous Wastes and their Disposal, Basel, 1989).

[71] Similar concerns have been voiced by the National Commission to Review the Working of the Constitution 2002.

[72] See Dhavan 1997.

[73] Chandra 2017; Hartman 1967.

[74] Chandra 2017; Anderson 1998, p. 21.

7.3.3 Judicial Incorporation

In defining the judiciary's power to engage with international law, the Supreme Court has shifted from an initial position of transformation[75] to a position of incorporation.[76] Chandra notes that the shift from the transformation to the incorporation doctrine by the Indian Supreme Court was clearly manifested in the 1984 case, *Gramophone Company of India Ltd. v Birendra Bahadur Pandey*.[77] In this case, the Court chose to interpret a provision of the Indian Copyright Act in a way that aligned with India's international obligations. The Court's decision underscored that international law could be integrated into municipal law even without explicit legislative endorsement, provided there was no conflict with existing parliamentary acts.

This ruling signifies a fundamental change in the role of the legislature regarding international law. Previously, the internalization and domestic implementation of international law required explicit authorization from Parliament. However, following the *Gramophone Company* case, international law is deemed applicable within the domestic sphere unless explicitly contradicted by legislative action. This represents a pivotal shift: Parliament's role is transformed from enabling the incorporation of international law to potentially opposing it if necessary. Notably, the Court in the *Gramophone Company* case did not discuss the division of treaty-making powers between the Executive and the Legislature or the assumption that the legislature would typically internalize international law through legislation. Furthermore, the Court did not differentiate between self-executing and non-self-executing treaties. Its broad statement suggested that all international law could directly influence domestic law, situating international law within the domestic legal framework, albeit subordinate to contradictory statutory laws.[78]

The Supreme Court of India further developed its approach to international law in the 1996 *Vellore Citizens* case.[79] In this landmark decision, the Court extended the principles established for treaty-based law to customary international law. The Court referenced international environmental milestones from the Stockholm to the Rio declarations, citing significant documents such as the Brundtland Report and key conventions including the United Nations Framework Convention on Climate Change and the Convention on Biological Diversity. In its judgment, the Court declared that "Sustainable Development" had become a part of customary international law, acknowledging its role as a balance between environmental protection and developmental needs. Despite noting that the precise features of "Sustainable Development"

---

[75] Under the transformation doctrine, international obligations cannot be enforced domestically by municipal courts without accompanying legislation.

[76] The incorporation doctrine allows courts to directly enforce international law, provided there is no conflicting domestic law of superior authority.

[77] Chandra 2017; Supreme Court of India, *Gramophone Company of India Ltd. v. Birendra Bahadur Pandey*, decision of 21 February 1984, 2 SCC 534.

[78] Chandra 2017.

[79] Supreme Court of India, *Vellore Citizens' Welfare Forum v. Union of India*, judgment of 28 August 1996, 5 SCC 647.

were still being delineated by international law jurists, the Court embraced its core principles—namely, the Precautionary Principle and the Polluter Pays Principle—as integral elements of customary international law.

This decision was pivotal as it directly incorporated these principles into domestic law, stating that once accepted as part of customary international law, these principles could seamlessly be considered part of India's domestic legal framework, provided they did not conflict with existing statutory law and aligned with the Constitution of India. This approach underscored the Court's readiness to integrate international environmental standards directly into the national legal system without the need for explicit legislative enactment.

However, the Court's reasoning introduced a cautious note that somewhat contradicted its earlier bold affirmations of the doctrine of incorporation, which it had robustly supported in the *Gramophone case* of 1984. In *Vellore Citizens*, the Court qualified its endorsement of the incorporation doctrine, stating it was "almost an accepted proposition of law" that rules of Customary International Law which are not contrary to municipal law should be considered part of the domestic law. The use of "almost" introduces an element of ambiguity, suggesting a retreat from the earlier categorical acceptance in 1984, and raises questions about the full extent of the Court's commitment to the doctrine of incorporation at that point.[80] This subtle shift may reflect the Court's recognition of the complexities involved in aligning broad international principles with specific domestic statutes and constitutional provisions, or it may indicate judicial caution in overstepping legislative prerogatives.

Finally in reference to non-ratified treaties, Rajamani highlights an instance where the court favourably referenced international treaties, even those to which India is not a party.[81] In the relatively recent case of *G Sundarrajan v Union of India*,[82] the Court examined the public policy implications of establishing the Kudankulam nuclear power plant. While ruling that the plant's operation was in the larger public interest, the Court emphasized the necessity for stringent nuclear safety measures before the plant could commence operations. In this judgment, the Court took an interesting step by referring to several international treaties relevant to nuclear safety, including one that India had not ratified.[83] The Court extensively quoted from this unratified convention, acknowledging that although India was not a signatory, the treaty was significant for understanding global concerns regarding public safety. By doing so, the Court did not directly enforce the treaty's provisions but used it to frame its considerations and set safety benchmarks.

This analysis underscores that although the constitutional framework facilitates the incorporation of international law, there is a significant interaction between judicial activism and constitutional directives. This dynamic illustrates the possibilities and constraints inherent in adapting legal frameworks to meet global environmental challenges. The court's methodology in adopting international standards does provide

---

[80] See Anderson 1998, pp. 25–26.

[81] Rajamani 2016.

[82] Supreme Court of India, *G Sundarrajan v. Union of India*, decision of 6 May 2013, 7 SCC 705.

[83] IAEA 1997.

notable advantages, which I will examine in the subsequent section. However, I will highlight the key challenges that may negate these advantages.

7.4 Benefits, Challenges, and Possible Path Forward

In the age of globalization, the pervasiveness of international law is becoming increasingly apparent and unavoidable. The expansive and complex network of international law is illustrated by the vast array of treaties—multilateral, plurilateral, and bilateral—that cover a broad spectrum of regulatory areas.[84] Thus, it would help to understand the benefits of the Court's approach to dealing with international law, in addition to the challenges.

7.4.1 International Law Has Enriched Environmental Jurisprudence in India

The Indian Supreme Court's proactive approach has significantly advanced the country's constitutional environmental jurisprudence. It has consistently integrated international and foreign legal norms into its rulings, demonstrating active participation in global discussions on rights and values. Moreover, the Court's interpretation of the right to life has extended the scope of both environmental jurisprudence and human rights in India. Its directives to enforce environmental laws and hold violators accountable have enhanced the quality of life and curbed governmental overreach, establishing the Court as a pivotal protector of citizens' rights.[85]

Despite the challenges posed by a diverse and populous society, India has maintained a regime of constitutional liberty and robust judicial protection of human rights, highlighting the Supreme Court's essential role in this legal progress.[86]

As Lavanya Rajamani points out, despite criticisms:

> "…. the Indian Supreme Court has delivered a vast number of environmentally sensitive decisions, and it has shown itself willing to embrace innovative and progressive conceptual tools in the service of environmental protection."[87]

McCrudden's analysis emphasizes the role of international human rights law within national frameworks, introducing the concept of "comparative international human rights law".[88] This field examines how international law, particularly human rights law, is applied domestically. Core elements of McCrudden's framework—such

[84] Rajamani 2016.

[85] Sahu 2008, pp. 9–16.

[86] Rajamani 2007, p. 286; Galanter and Krishnan 2003.

[87] Rajamani 2007, p. 285.

[88] McCrudden 2015, p. 550.

as its foundation in international consensus, its focus on universal human rights, and its recognized legal status—equip domestic courts with a comprehensive set of standards. These standards enable courts and legal advocates to use international law effectively to address local issues or bypass restrictive domestic legal frameworks. The application of these norms can vary significantly across jurisdictions, resulting in diverse interpretations and implementations of human rights. These variations influence legal outcomes at the national level and provide a deeper understanding of how international norms operate within domestic legal systems, offering insights beyond what might be gleaned from studying international law or comparative human rights alone.

In India, the Supreme Court has adeptly utilized this framework. Neha Jain notes that the Court has strategically employed international law to advance domestic goals.[89] This process has been used to ensure a better quality of life and to curb lawlessness, leading Upendra Baxi to state that the Supreme Court of India has transformed into a Supreme Court of Indians.[90] However, this strategic use of international norms has also led to ambiguity, complicating the integration of these standards into the Indian legal context.

7.4.2 Challenges with the Court's Gatekeeping Approach

As previously discussed in Sect. 7.2, a significant challenge in integrating international environmental law principles into the Indian legal framework is the imprecision of these principles and the difficulties of adapting them to local conditions. For example, the application of the Polluter Pays principle by the Supreme Court in the *Indian Council for Enviro-Legal Action* case[91] did not yield the expected outcomes. The Court emphasized that the principle should be simple, practical, and suited to conditions in India. It ruled that in cases of hazardous or inherently dangerous activities, the polluter is absolutely liable for any loss caused, irrespective of whether reasonable care was taken. In this interpretation, the Polluter Pays principle extends liability not only to compensate victims but also to cover the costs of environmental restoration.

Despite its subsequent recognition as a key objective of government policy to control pollution, this principle has not been consistently followed or institutionalized, which has undermined its impact on environmental jurisprudence.[92] For instance, in the case, despite the Supreme Court's decision that compensation could be sought under the Environment Protection Act, the assessment and payment of compensation, along with remedial actions, remain unfulfilled. Similarly, in the case

[89] See Jain 2018.

[90] Baxi 2000.

[91] Supreme Court of India, *Indian Council for Enviro Legal Action*, judgment of 13 February 1996, 3 SCC 212, para 67.

[92] Sahu 2008, p. 10.

of *S. Jagannath*,[93] which dealt with the ecological damage caused by shrimp farming, the Court initially ordered the closure of offending firms and compensation based on the Polluter Pays principle. However, these directives were later stayed by the Court itself, and subsequent legislation effectively overturned these rulings. As a result, neither compensation nor environmental restoration has been adequately addressed. This inconsistency highlights the limitations of the Court's approach, particularly in controlling pollution from large enterprises, where the Polluter Pays principle has inadvertently allowed companies to simply pay for their pollution without adequate regulatory oversight to prevent ongoing environmental harm.[94]

The other challenge that an imprecise and inconsistent environmental right creates is that of a legal framework in flux. This is particularly true for stakeholders who rely on a stable legal framework to make informed decisions. Investors, environmental activists, and other concerned parties face considerable difficulties planning and executing their strategies when the boundaries of applicable international standards in Indian law are unclear and fluctuating.[95] These uncertainties can deter investors from investing in heavily regulated sectors or sectors with tight regulatory controls. Investors may perceive higher risks without a clear picture of future regulatory requirements, potentially reducing capital inflows or avoiding environmentally sensitive projects. Environmental activists and non-governmental organizations are also affected as they aim to hold businesses and the government accountable for ecological degradation. Uncertain legal standards make it challenging to advocate effectively for stronger environmental protections or enforce existing laws. This uncertainty can undermine advocacy efforts, as activists may struggle to pinpoint violations or advocate for specific legislative reforms when the legal framework itself is in a state of flux. In addition, inconsistent application of environmental standards complicates long-term compliance strategies for businesses and industries. Companies may face sudden changes in compliance requirements, leading to increased operational costs and difficulties with strategic planning. Thus, imprecision in defining and applying environmental rights hinders legal enforcement and compliance but also impacts economic and environmental policy planning across the board.

With regards to the legislature, the Court's use of international law has also presented challenges. Rajamani raises an important question in this context: Given that the environmental right in India, however defined, is actualized with reference to a mixture of well-established and emerging principles of international law, what should be the benchmarks for its realization? Should it be the statutes of domestic law or the broader framework of International Environmental Law?

There is also a notable challenge in how the Court navigates the interaction between international and domestic law, crucial for effectively aligning international norms with India's legal framework. Achieving conceptual clarity in the judicial application of international law calls for a nuanced understanding of several key aspects: the hierarchy of norms, the nature and sources of international law, the

---

93 Supreme Court of India *S Jagannath v. Union of India* 1997, 2 SCC 87.

94 Sahu 2008, p. 11.

95 Anderson 1998, p. 21.

distinctions between customary and treaty law, and the differentiation between hard and soft norms. This includes recognising the conditions under which state practices become customary international law, and the subtleties in treaty interpretation and obligation differentiation.

Ranjan et al highlight a critical query: whether the Court, in citing Article 51(c) along with Article 253 (which empowers Parliament to legislate on international law), can judicially incorporate international treaties into domestic law without parliamentary enactment.[96] This raises questions about the extent to which international treaties, consistent with Indian law, can be used to interpret and expand the scope of domestic laws like fundamental rights. Article 51(c) encourages the state to "foster respect for international law and treaty obligations", a directive that Rajamani and Ranjan interpret as a call for effort rather than a mandate for specific results.[97] Ranjan et al show that while this distinction may seem subtle, it carries significant practical implications. For instance, should the executive adopt measures to implement international treaties consistent with domestic laws even without specific legislative backing from Parliament? If we interpret the Supreme Court's stance to support the "direct effect" theory, then such executive actions would be justified. This was the position India took in the WTO Solar Panel case against the US, arguing that legislative action is only necessary when domestic legislation conflicts with an international agreement. [98] Nevertheless, the WTO Appellate Body rejected this argument, stating that using international law to interpret domestic laws does not equate to giving these international instruments direct effect in the Indian legal system.

Another pertinent question is whether the Court's jurisprudence suggests a classification of international treaties into those that are consistent with domestic law and those that are not. If so, can Article 51(c) be used to support such categorization? Likely not, since fostering respect for international law under Article 51(c) applies to all treaties India signs, not only those that align with domestic law.

In determining whether a norm has attained customary status, as seen in the Vellore Citizens' Welfare Forum case, the Court's inclination to equate soft law instruments with customary law, as critiqued by Rajamani, risks incorporating non-binding norms into Indian law.[99]

7.4.3 Potential Solutions

Although a detailed exploration of solutions falls outside this chapter's scope, some recommendations can be proposed for enhancing the Court's method of gatekeeping

---

[96] Ranjan et al. 2016.

[97] Ibid; Rajamani 2016.

[98] *India v. United States*, Appellate Body Report, WT/DS456/AB/R, ITL 148 (WTO 2016), 16 September 2016, World Trade Organization [WTO].

[99] Rajamani 2016; Supreme Court of India, *Intellectuals Forum, Tirupathi v. State of AP*, judgment of 23 February 2006, 3 SCC 549.

international law. First, the Court could establish a specialised committee on International Law to guide its integration of international norms, respecting constitutional boundaries. The Court forms committees routinely for a wide number of technical matters which come before it and the same could be used for a more nuanced understanding of International Law integration. Collaboration with the National Green Tribunal can also be beneficial in this regard since it is composed of both judicial members and expert scientific members who have a better understanding of how international environmental law principles can be better operationalised in the Indian Context. Second, prioritising treaty law over Customary Law could refine the Court's gatekeeping.[100] This approach would still need prudence but at least the Court would not be integrating international law based on assumptions of its customary status and would only be looking at law which has been internationally negotiated and agreed to. Third, the Court should aim for more rigorous reasoning in its judgments to ensure democratic legitimacy and to better adhere to constitutional limits, rather than relying on idealistic language and broad pronouncements. Often, the Court's decisions include extensive discussions on facts and lengthy obiter dicta, yet the actual reasoning is condensed into one or two pages. Detailed reasoning that clearly outlines the basis for the relevance of certain international environmental principles, their derivation, and their applicability within the Indian context might help to prevent constitutional overreach while advancing environmental constitutional jurisprudence.

7.5 Concluding Reflections: Navigating the Path of Constitutional Gatekeeping

In this exploration of Gatekeeper Constitutionalism, I have delved into the complex interplay between the Indian Supreme Court's integration of international law and its constitutional mandates, particularly in the realm of environmental jurisprudence. I have highlighted the innovative yet challenging role of the Court in shaping legal paradigms that align with global standards while adhering to domestic constitutional requirements. The Court's efforts to act as a gatekeeper have facilitated significant legal advances but have also exposed the judiciary to risks associated with inconsistent application and ambiguous legal standards. Moving forward, it is imperative that the judiciary adopts a more discerning and structured approach to integrating international norms. This would not only enhance the clarity and consistency of legal applications but also ensure that such integrations are aligned with India's constitutional framework and legislative intentions.

Acknowledgements I am grateful to Prof. Anna Katharina Mangold and Luisa Weyers for their insightful comments on an earlier draft of this chapter. All errors remain my own.

[100] See Sehrawat 2021, pp. 116–117.

Reference List

Anderson MR (1998) International Environmental Law in Indian Courts. Review of European Community & International Environmental Law 7(1):21–30

Baxi U (1980) The Indian Supreme Court and Politics. In: Mehr Chand Mahajan Memorial Law Lectures. Eastern Book Co, Lucknow

Baxi U (2000) The Avatars of Indian Judicial Activism: Explorations in the Geographies of [In] Justice. In: Verma K (ed) Fifty Years of Supreme Court of India: Its Grasp and Reach. Oxford University Press, New Delhi

Birnie PW, Boyle AE (1992) International Law & the Environment. Oxford University Press, Oxford

Bodansky D (1995) Customary (And Not So Customary) International Environmental Law. Indiana Journal of Global Legal Studies 3(1):105–119

Chandra A (2017) India and International Law: Formal Dualism, Functional Monism. Indian Journal of International Law 57:25–45

Constituent Assembly Debates (1948–1949) Constituent Assembly Debates, Vol. VII. Government of India, Lok Sabha Secretariat, New Delhi

Dhavan R (1997) Treaties and People: Reflections. Journal of Indian Law Institute 39:1–46

Galanter M, Krishnan J (2003) Debased Informalism: Lok Adalats and Legal Rights in Modern India. In: Heller T, Jensen E (eds) Beyond Common Knowledge: Empirical Approaches to the Rule of Law. Stanford University Press, Stanford

Gill GN (2016) Environmental Justice in India: The National Green Tribunal and Expert Members. Transnational Environmental Law 5:175–205

Hartman FL (1967) Federalism as a Limitation on the Treaty Power of the United States, West Germany, and India. Case Western Reserve Law Review 18:134

International Atomic Energy Agency (IAEA) (1997) Joint Convention on the Safety of Spent Fuel Management and on the Safety of Radioactive Waste Management. Adopted at Vienna on 5 September 1997; opened for signature 29 September 1997; entered into force 18 June 2001 (INFCIRC/546)

Iyengar S, Dolšak N, Prakash A (2019) Selectively Assertive: Interventions of India's Supreme Court to Enforce Environmental Laws. Sustainability 11(24)

Jain N (2018) The Democratizing Force of International Law: Human Rights Adjudication by the Indian Supreme Court. In: Roberts et al (eds) Comparative International Law, online edn. Oxford Academic, New York

Jayawickrama N (2005) The Role of Domestic Courts in Treaty Enforcement. In: Sloss D (ed) The Role of Domestic Courts in Treaty Enforcement: A Comparative Study. Cambridge University Press, pp 209–242

Mate M (2015) The Rise of Judicial Governance in the Supreme Court of India. Boston University International Law Journal 33:169

McCrudden C (2015) Why do national court judges refer to human rights treaties? A comparative international law analysis of CEDAW. American Journal of International Law 109(3):534–550

National Commission to Review the Working of the Constitution (2002) Report of the National Commission to Review the Working of the Constitution, Volume I and Volume II (Books 1–3). Government of India, Ministry of Law, Justice and Company Affairs

Rajamani L (2007) The Right to Environmental Protection in India: Many a Slip between the Cup and the Lip? Review of European Community & International Environmental Law 16:274–286

Rajamani L (2016) International Law and the Constitutional Schema. In: Khosla M, Choudhry S (eds) The Oxford Handbook of the Indian Constitution. Oxford University Press, Oxford, pp 143–162

Ranjan P (2022) The Supreme Court of India and International Law: A Topsy-Turvy Journey from Dualism to Monism. Liverpool Law Review 43:571–595

Ranjan A, Anmolan, Ahmad F (2016) Is the Supreme Court Confused About the Application of International Law? The Wire. Accessed 26 December 2023. https://thewire.in/law/supreme-court-international-law

Sahu G (2008) Implications of Indian Supreme Court's Innovations for Environmental Jurisprudence. Journal of Law, Environment and Development 4(1):3–19

Sahu G (2010) Implementation of Environmental Judgments in Context: A Comparative Analysis of Dahanu Thermal Power Plant Pollution Case in Maharashtra and Vellore Leather Industrial Pollution Case in Tamil Nadu. Journal of Law, Environment and Development 6(3):337–352

Sands P (1995) Principles of International Environmental Law. Manchester University Press, Manchester

Sathe SP (2002) Judicial Activism in India. Law in India Series. Oxford University Press, New Delhi/New York

Sehrawat V (2021) Implementation of International Law in Indian Legal System. Florida Journal of International Law 31(1)

Sunstein CR (2003) Beyond the Precautionary Principle. University of Pennsylvania Law Review 151:1003–1058

Chapter 8
Varieties of Constitutionalism and Religion: A Comparison of Greece, Israel and Lebanon

Maria Francesca Cavalcanti

Contents

Abstract Religion constitutes an essential element of human life for many reasons, forming the substratum of many communities' political orders. This commixture of the spiritual and secular spheres disappears with the consolidation of the state and the secularisation process that, in the conception of liberal democratic constitutionalism, results in the separation of church and state, as well as the recognition of religious freedoms. Nevertheless, for at least two decades, religion has progressively abandoned the private sphere to assume a prominent role in public life. This is particularly true of legal systems characterized by legal pluralism and the coexistence and competition between state and religious law. Given these premises, the paper aims to examine the relationship between the constitutional order and religion in three legal systems whose history and identity have been characterised by religious pluralism: Greece, Israel and Lebanon. At the constitutional level, these countries affirm the principle of laicity while simultaneously attributing an important institutional role to religion. The aim of this contribution is therefore to analyse how religion shapes constitutionalism in these countries and to explore the varieties of constitutionalism within liberal democratic paradigms exhibiting religious pluralism. Ultimately, it seeks to investigate if the relationship between the state and

M. F. Cavalcanti (✉)
Department of Public Law and Governance, School of Law, Tilburg University, Tilburg, The Netherlands
e-mail: m.f.cavalcanti@tilburguniversity.edu

M. De Visser et al. (eds.), *European Yearbook of Constitutional Law 2024*, European Yearbook of Constitutional Law 6, https://doi.org/10.1007/978-94-6265-699-4_8

religion typical of liberal-democratic constitutionalism, is capable of responding to the challenges posed by religious and legal pluralism.

Keywords Constitutionalism · Interculturalism · Law and religion · Legal Pluralism · Religious diversity · Religious minority

8.1 Varieties of Constitutionalism and Religion: Preliminary Remarks

Belonging to a religious community constitutes a fundamental aspect of the human experience, distinguished by the believer's commitment to a specific set of religious precepts. At the same time, religion encompasses an institutional perspective referencing a set of symbols, beliefs, and crystallized practices within a visible social institution that accompanies personal and religiously oriented behaviours.[1] In this context, religion pre-dates the state and constitutes the foundational basis for the political structure of communities. This intermingling of the spiritual and secular spheres undergoes historical dissolution with the advent of the modern state and the concurrent process of secularization.[2]

The debate on secularism within liberal democratic constitutionalism is traditionally conducted following a binary model: for the state to be genuinely neutral, it must be nothing other than secular. Consequently, while the private choices of each individual may be guided by religious motivation, public choices, including the entire decision-making process from which they derive, must be grounded in neutral principles that are shareable by the generality of citizens, regardless of their religious affiliation.[3] From the notion that rational neutrality is the sole language universally shareable by all citizens arises the imperative to keep the state separate from religion. This imperative is justified by the fact that each religious denomination carries with it a distinct system of values, potentially conflicting with those of others. Secularism, therefore, serves to defuse such potential social and religious conflicts. By creating this distinct division between secular public space and private religious domain, western constitutionalism has attempted to confine religious ritual to a narrow sphere, devoid of direct political influence in the affairs of the modern state.[4]

Despite secularism being inherent in constitutionalism, their relationship is not easy to define. The challenge arises from the varying degrees of intensity that the separation of state and religion can assume in different constitutional settings. Regardless of the long process of secularization that has characterized most contemporary legal systems, the cultural, religious and political history of a country tends to have a lasting

[1] Pannikar 2015, p. 155.

[2] Lübbe 2003, p. 23.

[3] Ferrari 2019, p. 16.

[4] Asad 1993, pp. 27–29.

impact on the conception of faith and social norms in general. This influence is also rooted in legal culture, which is difficult to ignore even in the most secularized or secularizing societies. Even in these cases, religious imprinting continues to influence, more or less consciously, the legal rules produced by secularized institutions.[5]

No less significant is the fact that the secular model typical of liberal democratic constitutionalism carries with it a strong religious echo. In addition to the well-known influence of Christianity on western constitutionalism,[6] it should be noted that among the constitutions that adhere to this model, some openly distance themselves from the religious factor, others embrace it, and still others could be described as agnostic by accepting only certain aspects of it. Nevertheless, no constitution remains indifferent to religion. In this all-encompassing perspective, law systematically conceives religion in terms recognizable within the constitutional framework.[7]

Even in cases where the state succeeds in finding its foundation solely in itself, a choice must still be made regarding the type of secular state it wishes to embrace: a neutral state that allows the free expression of any religious expression, tending to be indifferent to the phenomenon; or a state that values the religious dimension and encourages its development. The construction of the secular state proves to be more challenging than one might imagine.

While maintaining as milestone a certain degree of separation between state and religion, the model presents a significant number of variations that have been the subject of multiple historical, legal and political studies.[8]

8.2 Constitutionalism and Religion in a Modern Context

In his taxonomy of different contemporary approaches to the relationship between state and religion, Ran Hirschl has identified eight possible variations: 1) the atheist state; 2) assertive secularism; 3) separation as state neutrality toward religion; 4) the weak religious establishment; 5) formal separation with *de facto* pre-eminence of one denomination; 6) separation alongside multicultural accommodation; 7) religious jurisdictional enclaves; 8) the strong establishment-religion as a constitutionally enshrined source of legislation.[9] With regard to the secularist model, Michel Rosenfeld identifies five alternatives: 1) the militant secularist model; 2) the agnostic secularist model; 3) the confessional secular model; 4) the official state religion with institutionalized tolerance for minority religion model; 5) the millet-based model. These models in turn have significant variations.[10]

---

[5] Norris and Inglehart 2004, p. 33.

[6] Hulme 1986, p. 84; Zagrebelsky 2014, pp. 247–268.

[7] Berger 2015, pp. 24–28.

[8] Just to mention a few examples: Martinez Tórron 1994; Mancini 2020; Perl 2008; Ahdar and Leigh 2005; Kuru 2009.

[9] Hirschl 2011, pp. 422–437.

[10] Rosenfeld 2013, pp. 29–37.

In other settings, the relationship between the state and religion can be further nuanced by referencing constitutional norms that deal with a specific legacy of religion and morality, or with a state-endorsed religion alongside the protection of the rights of religious minorities. Therefore, it is evident that, in contemporary reality, the framework of factors influencing relations between the state and religion is the result of a combination of highly complex political, ideological, social, economic and institutional elements.[11]

The qualification of the state concerning its relationship with religion derives from the observation of empirical and contingent traits that characterize the relationship between religious society and civil society. These relations are endowed with such dynamism as to suggest that their classification should be as ductile as possible.[12] While acknowledging the difficulty of any effort to classify the state according to its relationship with religion, it is, nevertheless, possible to assert that constitutional systems, to belong to the model of liberal democratic constitutionalism, must include some form of secularisation. Consequently, despite its possible variations, this model requires at least three basic elements: a) a certain degree of separation and independence of state institutions from the religious factor, b) the guarantee of religious freedom and equality, c) a neutrality that does not necessarily translate into indifference to the religious factor. It perhaps would be simpler to establish the elements under which it is plausible to exclude the possibility of classifying the state within the model of liberal democratic constitutionalism: a) subordination of state institutions to the religious factor or complete overlap of these two elements; b) a consequent low if not non-existent degree of religious freedom guarantees and recognition of religious pluralism.

Having established these minimum elements, it is necessary to consider how, in recent years, the relationship between state and religion has been undergoing a rapid evolution even in secular states. Religion has emerged at the centre of public debate with a new force capable of mobilizing collective identities that claim their own space in the public sphere, undermining the model described so far. The religious factor, with its cross-border, transnational and solidaristic bases, challenges contemporary constitutionalism, for the most part still marked by the Westphalian model, offering an alternative to the constitutional framework based on territory and nationhood.[13]

The global dimension of religion thus represents an element of instability within the social order as well as a challenge to the monopolistic power of the state in the Weberian sense. Moreover, religious denomination, understood as *nomoi groups,*[14] are endowed with rules and principles capable of coherently welding together to form a normative system. Religious norms are heterogeneous but capable of tracing the identity of the community and its members and regulating various aspects of their lives. Consequently, religious communities aspire to exercise a certain degree

---

[11] Halmai 2015, pp. 10–27.

[12] Pegoraro 2012, pp. 1–34.

[13] Hirschl and Shachar 2018, pp. 426– 449.

[14] Shachar 2001, p. 88.

of autonomy in the public sphere, especially concerning elements that define the religious identity of individuals.

This becomes particularly pronounced in those legal systems characterised by legal pluralism and the coexistence or competition between state law and religious law. This is especially so in the context of pluralist societies that the religious factor becomes a significant actor, capable of speaking the language of collective identities.[15]

The cultural and religious pluralism of contemporary societies represents a source of tension for the principle of neutrality, which develops in close correlation with the dominant religion, reflects the religious demands of the majority and limits itself to ensuring equal religious freedom for all individuals.[16] A religious monism that time and demographic phenomena have undermined. The effective protection of religious minorities requires more than the formal recognition of equal freedom, mere tolerance and the prohibition of discrimination, leading the state to explore alternative paths.

The interplay between state and religion in multicultural societies is evident in the fact that judges are increasingly confronted with the conceptual limits of accommodating spiritual demands made by members of religious minorities.[17] This occurs primarily with regard to legislators' reluctance to accept as binding or even recognisable any potentially competing legal system, originating in religious or cultural sources.[18] The accommodation of minority cultural and religious demands is a critical issue for the secular state model to which contemporary constitutional orders can't remain indifferent.

Given the framework described, it seems useful to inquire: a) whether the process of secularisation that characterised the modern state is irreversible or whether, instead, we are witnessing a phase of post-secularism, in which religion represents a political resource; b) whether the model of secularism typical of liberal democratic constitutionalism represents the most suitable tool to govern the pluralisation and the publicization of religion that characterising contemporary societies.

In an attempt to address these questions, the constitutional systems of Greece, Israel and Lebanon will be analysed. These three jurisdictions govern highly pluralistic societies, whose history has left a particularly marked religious imprint on their legal culture. The study of the constitutional model of these three cases will be conducted through the analysis of the three fundamental elements of the relationship between state and religion typical of liberal democratic constitutionalism: the degree of separation between institutions and religion, the guarantee of religious freedom, and the level of neutrality. These elements will be analysed in terms of the principle of secularism, the influence of the religious factor in their sources of law, the existence and role of religious jurisdiction and their relationship with civil jurisdiction, as well as the role of religion at the institutional level. The analysis of these three cases is

---

[15] Cavalcanti 2023, p. 112.

[16] Nieuwenhuis 2012, pp. 153–174.

[17] Rinella 2020, pp. 74–120.

[18] Benhabib 2002, p. 170.

useful for reflecting on the ability of secularism to guarantee the legal framework needed to achieve a balance between pluralism and the fundamental principles of the legal system. Or rather, whether liberal democratic constitutionalism should open to new paradigms of the relationship between law and religion.

8.3 Personal Federalism and Religious Jurisdiction Enclaves

Greece, Israel and Lebanon, represent three examples of legal systems that, while affirming the principle of secularism at the constitutional level, at the same time attribute an important institutional role to religion. The relationship between state and religion in these three legal orders has shaped their constitutionalism, expressing three different variations on the paradigm of liberal democratic constitutionalism. What characterises these three jurisdictions in their relationship with the religious element is the implementation, to varying degrees, of the system known as personal federalism.[19]

The idea that culturally, traditionally and religiously diverse peoples can coexist in a virtuous manner is generally traced back to the western political and religious tradition, since the Latin tradition of *ius gentium* and the medieval Holy Roman Empire. However, there are other significant experiences in this regard.

Personal federalism represents one of the alternative forms of governance of religious plurality in the prism of liberal democratic constitutionalism, according to a model especially prevalent in the Global South. Personal federalism represents a form of political organisation in which the personalist principle prevails over the territorial one. In accordance with this model, a community of individuals, defined by ethnic, religious, linguistic, or historical characteristics, is recognized by the state as the holder of specific rights and self-governance functions, precisely due to these identity elements. These communities are granted the power to regulate certain matters, typically family relations and personal status, deemed central to the collective community identity, through a normative framework of religious or traditional origin, distinct and alternative to that applied by the state legal system.The exercise of powers of self-government requires the recognition by the state of community institutions endowed with sufficient political autonomy to exercise them. An autonomy that implies the broadest possible protection from state interference.

The model of personal federalism, although it can coexist with that of territorial federalism, disregards the need for the different communities to be linked to a specific territory or to have clear spatial roots.[20] Their identity is, in fact, founded on elements that relate personally to the members of the group, such as those pertaining to religious faith. This allows the state to recognize rights for community members regardless of where they are located, merely because they belong to that social group. At the

[19] Gaudreault-DesBiens 2010, pp. 159–180.

[20] Ibid., pp. 159–180.

same time, the autonomy they enjoy requires acknowledgment by the state in whose territory they are physically located.

This model of religious community governance is generally adopted by those legal systems that are facing the peculiarities and needs of particularly religiously, culturally and linguistically fragmented societies. These are societies characterised by cultural and political *cleavages*, as well as the need to ensure full participation in the public sphere for all communities. This model emphasises the sharing of power between the state and religious communities by attempting to establish a clear separation between issues of communitarian and non-communitarian interest, through the definition of conflict rules applicable in the event of overlapping between the different competing legal systems.[21]

The oldest and most emblematic example of the application of the personal federalism model is represented by the millet system used by the Ottoman Empire to govern an immense space inhabited by a population characterised by strong ethnic, linguistic and religious pluralism. Ottoman rulers understood that such diversity could not be assimilated, and given the vast territorial expanse of the Empire, there was no sufficiently effective way to grant these groups rights based on a stable connection to the territory.[22] Will Kymlicka has identified the Ottoman structure as a hyper-communitarian model of tolerance based not on individual rights but on collective rights.[23] As a result, the Ottoman approach can be viewed as a form of tolerance based on the recognition and respect of the other, with barriers that were far from impermeable, leading to reciprocal contamination among minorities and between these groups and the majority, although the general disadvantageous position of non-Muslim communities cannot be ignored.

The Ottoman Millet system, intended as a structural framework of religious groups endowed with broad autonomy, gradually changed from the 19th century onwards, when the Empire initiated a series of structural reforms aimed at countering the progressive international decline and the independence aspirations of religious groups. Despite this progressive transformation in a secular sense, at the fall of the Empire, the European powers that received the mandate to administer those territories reverted to applying the traditional and original structure of the millet system.[24]

This system involved the control of the administration of colonial territories through pre-existing local authorities, allowing important aspects of individuals' lives to continue to be governed by traditional and religious norms.

In this context, the recognition of religious jurisdictions corresponded to a policy of balancing impositions and concessions, aimed at strengthening the dominant position of the colonial regime. This was a logic, therefore, quite different from the one that today should move democratic governments that govern pluralist societies and wish to recognise the different communities a space to live in harmony with their own value, cultural and legal universe of origin. Nevertheless, this hybrid system

[21] Gannagè 2001, p. 239.

[22] Barkey and Gaurilis 2016, pp. 24–42.

[23] Kymlicka 2001, pp. 91–119.

[24] Gerring et al 2011, pp. 377–433.

between state law and religious law was maintained even after the end of colonial regimes.

Some of the new nation-states that, in the areas formerly ruled by the Ottoman Empire, govern highly pluralistic societies maintained, to varying degrees, a legal regime based on the personality principle.

It is a model based on a selective accommodation of religion in certain areas of law. The law generally applied is secular, however a certain degree of autonomy is granted to religious communities, mainly in matters of personal status and education, according to a pattern of religious jurisdictional enclaves.[25] A model of Neo Millet[26] adopted, although with different conditions and through profoundly different historical and political processes, by Greece, Israel and Lebanon.

8.3.1 Constitutionalism and Religion in Greece: Prevalent Religion and Neo Millet

The history of Greece is characterised by an intense relationship with the religious factor that has influenced the constitutional order. The connection between the Greek Orthodox confession and Greek institutions remains profound, to the extent that state and church can be considered traditionally connected. This bond stems from the role religion played in the definition of the Hellenic national identity, developed in opposition to the historical antagonists of the Greek people: initially the Ottoman Empire and later Turkey.[27] Even in contemporary Greece, religion continues to represent a fundamental element in the definition of national identity, determining, together with language and the heritage of ancient Hellas, the membership of the Hellenic nation.[28]

Article 3 of the 1975 Constitution expressly regulates the relationship between the state and the Greek Orthodox Church, stating that: a) the Greek Orthodox Church is the prevailing religion; b) the Church of Greece is inseparably united doctrinally with the Ecumenical Patriarchate of Constantinople and with all the Orthodox Churches; c) the Church of Greece is self-governing and autocephalous.

Furthermore, any reform concerning the relations between the state and religious denominations, as well as any legislation related to religious freedom, must be debated and voted upon by Parliament in plenary session (Art. 72).

According to the majority doctrine, the nature and significance of defining the Orthodox Church as the predominant religion by Article 3 of the Constitution are limited to the simple proclamation that Greeks are, in their majority, Orthodox Christians. This expression would hence be merely descriptive and not properly normative. Supporting this interpretation would be the real will of the constitutional legislator,

---

[25] Hirschl 2011, pp. 422–437.

[26] Rowe 2007, pp. 329–350; Tsitselikis 2007, pp. 354–372.

[27] Clogg 2021, pp. 46–97.

[28] Tsitselikis 2008, p. 27.

expressed in the deliberations that led to the approval of the 1975 Constitution and which saw all the political forces united in describing the relationship between State and religion in terms of separation.[29]

One of the most controversial issues about the relationship between the state and the Greek Orthodox Church concerns the most recent constitutional reform of 2019. On 14 February 2019, the outgoing Parliament voted on the constitutional amendments to be submitted for revision to the new Parliament that would result from the elections in July. Among the proposals was to amend Article 3 of the Constitution to explicitly establish the religious neutrality of the state. Nevertheless, the final text of the constitutional reform did not include the described proposal, leaving the constitutional system of relations with the Greek Orthodox Church intact.[30]

Despite the proclamation of the Greek Orthodox religion as the prevailing one, the Greek constitutional system appears, therefore, characterised by the element of separation between state and religion typical of liberal democratic constitutionalism. The role and influence of the Greek Orthodox confession on state institutions appears to be closely linked to the majority culture and tradition. There is no doubt that there is a deep connection between state institutions and the prevailing confession: for example, the opening of parliamentary work is officiated by the Orthodox Archbishop every year and the President of the Republic is required to take the oath in the Christian form. However, the implications of this recognition do not impact public life to the extent of causing a complete overlap between institutions and religion. This connection is no less apparent than in other systems that belong to the tradition of liberal democratic constitutionalism, which recognise a state or prevailing religion, such as Great Britain and the Scandinavian countries.

Regarding the relationship between the state and religious denominations other than the Greek Orthodox Church, the Greek system is characterised by a principle of cooperation similar to that of Great Britain, Denmark and Sweden. The right of association for religious purposes and the right of self-government of religious communities, represents one of the expressions of religious freedom (Article 13) in its collective dimension.[31] Law 590/1977 recognises the Jewish and Islamic communities as legal persons under public law, as well as the Greek Orthodox Church. All other known religious denominations can obtain recognition as legal persons under private law. In this regard, Law 4301/2014, amended by Article 39 of Law 4589/2019, introduced for the first time in the Greek legal system the term 'religious community' to denote the union of a sufficient number of individuals belonging to the same known religious denomination. Such religious communities may acquire legal personality under private law by registration in the special public register of religious legal persons of the territorially competent court.[32]

---

[29] Papageorgiou 2021, p. 63; *contra* Papastathis 1996, pp. 816–850.

[30] Gemi 2021, p. 92.

[31] European Court of Human Rights, *Canea Catholic Church v. Greece*, judgment of 16 December 1997, 25528/94.

[32] For a more in-depth discussion of the topic, see Papageorgiou 2021, p. 34.

As for the individual dimension of religious freedom, Article 13 of the Constitution in its first paragraph, which cannot be amended (Article 110), establishes the inviolability of freedom of conscience and freedom of worship. These freedoms find further expression in the right to free religious thought, in the freedom to change religious belief or to have no religious belief at all, in the freedom of individual and collective worship, which can be exercised privately and in public if it does not constitute proselytism. Religious freedom is also expressed in the principle of equality and religious non-discrimination. This freedom, in accordance with the model of liberal democratic constitutionalism, is not absolute but is susceptible to restrictions as long as they are proportionate and in accordance with the constitutional order.

Certain elements of the Greek constitutional system related to the guarantee of religious freedom have often led to doubts as to whether the system complies with the principles enshrined in the European Convention on Human Rights. The prohibition of proselytism has been considered by the Strasbourg Court as a tool that circumvents the principles safeguarding religious freedom and stifles the pluralism typical of a democratic society.[33] It imposes stringent, if not prohibitive, conditions on the exercise of a belief different from the Greek Orthodox one.[34]

The deep connection between the Greek Orthodox religion and the construction of the Greek national identity also influenced the model for governing cultural and religious pluralism.[35] At the dawn of its gained independence, the borders of the Greek state encompassed a territory inhabited by diverse communities in terms of ethnicity, language, and religious belief. Within this context, Greek national identity has historically been constructed in opposition to other religious denominations, notably the Muslim community, due to its historical and ideological ties with Turkey. While this perception has gradually evolved over time, it still echoes today as a traditional ideological belief that has influenced the protection of religious minorities. This is observed in the recognized status granted to the Islamic minority in Thrace.

The legal status of the Islamic minority of Thrace is regulated by the Treaty of Sèvres of 1920 and the Treaty of Lausanne of 1923, which, together with the national legislation enacted in execution of these agreements, constitute a form of Neo Millet.[36] As envisaged by the Ottoman model, the religious minority of Thrace enjoys extensive autonomy and powers of self-government due to its religious identity. The cornerstone of the regulation concerning the Thrace's historical minority's status lies in the potential application of Sharia law in matters of personal status, family

[33] Constitution 1975, art. 13; Law 1672/1939, art. 2.

[34] European Court of Human Rights, *Kokkinakis v. Greece*, judgment of 22 August 1988, 14307/88; ECHR *Sofianopoulos v. Greece*, judgement of 12 December 2002, 1988/02 1997/02 1977/02; ECHR *Larissis and others v. Greece*, judgement of 24 February 1988, 23372/94; ECHR *Manoukassi and others v. Greece*, judgement of 26 September 1996, 18748/91; ECHR *Pentidis and others v. Greece*, judgement of 9 June 1997.

[35] Fokas 2012, p. 403.

[36] Tsitselikis 2013, p. 288.

relations[37] and inheritance,[38] through the religious jurisdiction of the mufti, who act as judges.

Law 4964/2022 codified the regulation of the office of the mufti in order to rationalise the position of the Islamic minority within the Greek legal system. The law defines the mufti's offices as decentralised public services, subject to the Ministry of Education and Religious Affairs.[39] The Islamic Courts of Thrace, therefore, represent a state court rather than a community institution. Greek Islamic jurisdiction is configured as a special religious-based jurisdiction, personal, territorial and concurrent with civil jurisdiction. It can only be activated on a voluntary basis and is applicable solely to Greek citizens of Islamic faith belonging to the historical minority of Thrace.

Excluded from this special treatment are other ancient Islamic communities, as well as members of the so-called New Islam,[40] which includes Muslims who arrived in Greece through the migration flows starting in the 1990s. The distinct approach adopted by the legal system towards the more recent Islamic communities reflects a prevailing territorial model that, although predominant in liberal democratic constitutionalism, in this case does not seem entirely consistent with the principle of equality.[41]

Until the reforms between 2019 and 2022, the legal system was silent on the exclusive or voluntary nature of this special jurisdiction. Civil courts have consistently denied the possibility for members of the minority the option to turn to secular courts for matters subject to Islamic jurisdiction.[42] The European Courts of Human Rights, in resolving the Molla Sali v Greece case, recently affirmed that the protection of religious freedom does not require contracting states to create a special legal framework and differentiated legal status for minority religious communities. However, if granted, the enjoyment of special religious rights must not entail discrimination. Preventing a member of the religious minority from voluntarily opting for the application of ordinary law constitutes discriminatory treatment, a violation of the minority protection system, and of the right to self-determination.[43] The Law 4511/2018 amended the regulation in this regard by stipulating that matters falling under the jurisdiction of muftis are governed by ordinary civil law. Subjection of these matters to Sharia and its related religious jurisdiction is only allowed in case of a mutually agreed upon agreement between the parties.[44]

---

[37] Law 147/1914, art. 4.

[38] Law 1920/1991, art. 5.

[39] Law 4964/2022, art. 146–148.

[40] Tsitselikis 2012, p. 9.

[41] Mehdi et al 2008, p. 216.

[42] Areios Pagos (Supreme Civil and Criminal Court of Greece) 231/1932, 105/1937, 14/1938, 322/1960, 738/1967, 1723/1980, 1041/2000, 2113/2009, 321/1960, 1097/2007, 2113/2009, 1497/2013, 1370/2014.

[43] European Court of Human Rights, *Molla Sali v. Greece* judgment of 19 December 2018, 20452/14.

[44] Legge 4964/2022, art. 146 co. 10.

Despite the amendments and progress made to enhance the system, there are still lingering concerns, especially regarding the compatibility of muftis' interpretation of Sharia with the Greek legal system, the accommodation of community-based law within a uniform legal context, and the actual protection of the most vulnerable members of the community who are often influenced in their decisions by undue social pressures.[45] These discrepancies can be resolved either by abolishing the system, an undesirable solution in terms of a pluralist society, or by orienting the interpretation of Sharia law in a direction that is compatible with the core principles of the Greek legal system. It must, however, be emphasised that the alignment of Islamic law with these standards must not mean a total elimination of its fundamental characteristics. This would lead to the opposite and undesirable result of the hegemony of the dominant legal system over a minority legal system. The reforms of the system are still too recent to assess their real effectiveness. However, it is desirable that such interventions continue in the direction of genuine protection, rather than exclusion, of the minority, as well as the recognition of the collective religious rights of other Muslim citizens.

The particular significance of religion in the Greek constitutional system and the prevailing character of the Greek Orthodox Church, outline the features of a system that represents a substantial variation from typical model of the relationship between the state and religion in liberal democratic constitutionalism. Greece belongs, in fact, to that category of states capable of reconciling the presence of a prevailing religion with the religious freedom of all citizens and all religious denominations, ensuring the separation between state institutions and religion. At the same time, the legal system takes religious pluralism into account and is characterised by a phenomenon of heterointegration, consisting of an integration of the state legal system through recourse to alternative legal systems and sources of law to the dominant one. This phenomenon manifests itself through the inclusion of religious precepts in the legal system, already discernible at constitutional level.

8.3.2 Constitutionalism and Religion in the Jewish and Democratic State of Israel

The religious factor plays an essential role in the Israeli legal system, contributing to shaping one of the fundamental characteristics of this country: the religious, ethnic, cultural, and linguistic heterogeneity of its population, which leads to an almost constant social and political conflict.[46]

Ideally comparing the Israeli legal system with that of other Middle Eastern countries, the degree of involvement between state and religion appears among the lowest

---

[45] Tsitselikis 2023, p. 2.

[46] Lapidoth 1998, p. 441.

in this geographical area. However, when compared with constitutional democracies elsewhere in the world, this involvement seems more pronounced.[47]

The Israeli constitutional system outlines a secular state, whose laws are adopted by the parliament elected by the people and in which the application of religious law depends exclusively on the will of the state legislature.[48] Israel does not have a formal constitution. Therefore, the analysis of the relationship between the state and the religious factor must turn to the Declaration of Establishment of the State of Israel of 14 May 1948, and the 14 Basic Laws: what can be defined as a constantly evolving multi-textual constitution.

The essential role of religion in the Israeli order is underlined by the 1948 Declaration of Establishment of the state of Israel, which defines the state of Israel as a Jewish as well as a democratic state. This definition is also referred to in Art. 1 of the Basic Law Human Dignity and Freedom of 1992 and Art. 7 of the Basic Law on the Knesset of 1984. The fundamental question regarding the relationship between the legal system and the religious factor is whether these two characteristics can be combined. The exact meaning of defining Israel as a Jewish state has never been expressly clarified by the legislature and is still particularly controversial. According to the draft of a formal constitution proposed by a special parliamentary committee in 2006, the term 'Jewish state' would denote the state in which the Jewish people exercise their right to self-determination.[49] The fundamental values of the state coincide with those of the Jewish religion and culture, influencing its legal culture, but must be understood in a general and abstract manner.[50]

According to a different perspective, the definition of the Jewish state would entail the recognition of the Jewish religion as the state religion.[51] Another interpretation suggests that the Jewish character of the state would obligate the courts to interpret the principles of the Basic Law in accordance with Jewish religious law.[52] Given the lack of clear indications from the constitutional legislature, the most reasonable approach would seem to be the interpretive one, establishing a case-by-case balance between the two characteristics of the state.[53] Despite the absence of the proclamation of a state religion, it is possible, however, to assert that the Jewish confession can be considered substantially prevalent. The Israeli legal system operates in continuity with the history and tradition of the Jewish people. Consider, for instance, the Law of Return of 1950 and the Flag and Emblem Law of 1949, which adopted the Tallit, the Menorah and the Hatikva as symbols of the state and its national anthem. Moreover, Jewish religious law takes on legal value and social force, to the point that the Legal

[47] Madley 2015, p. 209.

[48] Lernen 2017, p. 421.

[49] Constitution, Law and Justice Committee of the Sixteenth Knesset, Proposal for a Constitution, 13 February 2006.

[50] Barak 1995, p. 17.

[51] Alon 1993, pp. 668–670.

[52] Lapidoth 1998, p. 443.

[53] Steinberg 2001, p. 93.

Foundation Act of 1980 identifies the principles of Jewish tradition as complementary sources of law.

Considering this, although the Jewish confession is the determining element of Israeli legal culture, there is no evident overlap between state institutions and the religious factor. The state maintains a relationship of separation, albeit not entirely distinct. In fact, state and religion, rather than being firmly separated, seem to interact on a symbolic, institutional and legislative level, without merging. This relationship is characterised by the implementation of a system of personal federalism that involves all citizens of the state.

In accordance with Article 83 of the Palestinian Order in Council,[54] adopted by the British government in 1922, the Israeli legal system has maintained the system of self-government for religious communities, recognising the application of religious law in personal status matters, through the jurisdiction of religious courts. In this way, religious law is integrated into the system as a complementary source of law, applied by religious jurisdiction within the limits set by the state.[55]

The religious jurisdiction of the Jewish, Islamic, Christian, and Druze denominations constitutes a special jurisdiction based on religious and personal grounds, concurrent with civil jurisdiction in personal status matters, and exclusive in matters of marriage and divorce.

Rabbinical, Muslim and Druze courts are part of the state's judicial apparatus. Rabbinical courts are supervised by the Chief Rabbinate of Israel, which is the supreme Jewish religious body in Israel. As for historical and political reasons, the Orthodox stream of Judaism holds the control of the Rabbinate, *dayanim* follow the Orthodox interpretation of Jewish law. Druze and Islamic courts are subject to the Ministry of Justice. Christian courts instead are not part of the state's institutional apparatus. They are granted the status of autonomous institutions, and they are free to devise their own structure and procedural norms. They also retain full control over the appointment of judges.[56] It follows that Canon law judges, unlike judges presiding over Rabbinical, Islamic and Druze courts, are not state officials.[57]

To have legally binding effect within the legal system, decisions made by religious courts must be enforced by civil courts. However, civil courts reserve the right to refuse enforcement if the decisions exceed jurisdictional limits or violate principles of natural justice.[58] Despite adopting a generally non-interference attitude in the internal activities of religious communities, the Israeli legal system has not remained indifferent to the potential discriminatory effects of religious law. Parliament has passed a series of laws to safeguard gender equality, which the religious courts

---

[54] Palestine Order in Council 1922, art. 83; Religious Communities (Organisation) Ordinance 1926.

[55] Rabbinical Court Jurisdiction (Marriage and Divorce) Law 7/1953; Druze Religious Courts Law 17/1962; Palestine Order in Council 1922 (see n. 54 above), art. 52.

[56] Karayanni 2021, p. 126.

[57] Sezgin 2010, pp. 631–654.

[58] Palestine Order in Council 1922 (see n. 54 above), art. 55.

are required to adhere.[59] Additionally, the Supreme Court has affirmed that it is mandatory for religious courts to enforce Basic Laws that guarantee fundamental rights and freedoms.[60]

From 1948 to the present day, the scope of minority groups in religious matters has gradually been restricted.[61] However, the retention of exclusive religious jurisdiction over marriage and divorce weakens pluralism, necessitating religious affiliation. To this end, the religious membership of Israeli citizens is recorded by the Ministry of the Interior and reflected in personal documents.

This legal framework has raised doubt on the full recognition of religious freedom by the Israeli legal system. The affirmation of religious freedom, originally recognised by the Palestine Order in Council of 1922 and reaffirmed by the 1948 Declaration of Establishment of the state of Israel and the 1992 Basic Law Human Dignity and Liberty, has been then further clarified by the Supreme Court.[62]

The Court reiterated that religious freedom is one of the cardinal principles of the legal system.Consequently, every legislative act must be interpreted in light of this fundamental freedom.[63] At the same time, religious freedom is not absolute but subject to balancing with other rights and interests.[64] The joint application of the principle of equality and religious freedom protects the religious pluralism that characterises Israeli society, as well as the identity and tradition of the different religious communities.[65] Every individual is free to convert and change his or her religious affiliation. However, for conversion to have legal consequences in the legal system, the consent of the religious communities involved is required and the conversion must be communicated to the Ministry of the Interior.[66]

Israel's attitude towards the majority religion and the adoption of a neo-millet structure are based on a communitarian paradigm which constructs citizenship along ethno-religious lines. The ethno-religious communities recognised by Israel's public

[59] Women's Equal Rights Law 1950; Capacity and Guardianship Law 5722/1962; Succession Law 5725/1965; Spouse Property Relation Law 5733/1973; Financial Relationship between Spouses Law 5733/1973; Financial Relationship between Spouses Law 1973; Prevention of Violence in the Family Law 5751/1991.

[60] HCJ 6892/93; HCJ 3077/1995; HCJ 3856/2013.

[61] Family Court Law 1995; Family Law Court 2001.

[62] Medina 2006, p. 148.

[63] Israeli Supreme Court *Faithful of the Temple Mount v. Commander of Police in the Jerusalem Area*, judgement of 18 May 1984, H.C. 292/83 38 (2) P.D. 449.

[64] Israeli Supreme Court *Yossipoff v. Attorney General*, judgment of 29 March 1951, Cr.A. 112/50 5 P.D. 481.

[65] Israeli Supreme Court *El-Al Israel Airlines Ltd v. Danielevitz*, judgment of 30 November 1994, 48 (5) PD 749, 759, HC 721/94.

[66] Israeli Supreme Court *Pesachu Goldstein v. Minister of Interior*, judgment 30 November 1993, H.C. 1031/93 51 (4) P.D. 661.

authorities are generally regarded as homogenous entities.[67] However, this oversimplified archetype of homogeneous groups[68] hardly mirrors the reality. Most importantly, it poses serious challenges to non-Jewish minorities living in the country as well as non-Orthodox Jewish people in their daily life. As Israel's adoption of a *millet*-like system makes religious affiliation legally relevant on some crucial matters of personal status, people whose religious affiliation is contested – such as the non-Orthodox Jews – are often left in a limping legal status that jeopardizes their constitutionally protected rights: the rights to freedom of religion and from religion, the right to marry and to family life, the right to be equal before the law and to non-discrimination in the access to public religious services, as well as children and women's rights.[69]

Given the described legal framework, it is possible to affirm the existence of religious freedom in the Israeli legal system. However, it is necessary to distinguish between religious freedom as an individual right and as a collective right. The legal system recognises the religious freedom of the various religious denominations which, organised in autonomous confessional communities, enjoy the right of non-interference by the state. In this sense, the state obliges citizens to submit to religious regulations based on their community affiliation. Individuals, therefore, enjoy full religious freedom as members of a community. In the case of the Israeli legal system too, it is possible to find a system of relations between state and religion that, while based on the model of liberal democratic constitutionalism, represents a substantial variant of it. Although the Jewish denomination shapes the legal culture of the country and religious precepts are integrated into the legal system within the limits set by the state, there is no institutional overlap between state and religion.

8.3.3 Constitutionalism and Religion in the Lebanese Mosaic of Religious Diversity

Lebanese society is characterised by a multiplicity of ethno-religious communities whose socio-political balances have left a marked imprint on its history. From the 16th century onwards, Lebanon became part of the Ottoman Empire and later fell under French domination, which began as an occupation in 1864 and was formalised into a Mandate after World War I. The French Mandate kept alive the confessional pluralism of the Lebanese people. The French Mandate kept alive the confessional pluralism that, after independence in 1946, continued to characterise the Lebanese legal system.

The Lebanese Constitution of 1926, promulgated under the French Mandate and reformed in 1990 under the Taëf Agreement, outlined a secular, democratic state, based on the constitutional principle of the separation of powers and respect for

67 Parrilli 2021, pp. 61–77.

68 Palermo 2013, pp. 31–33.

69 Parrilli 2021, p. 68.

political and civil liberties. At the same time, the legal system is defined by a strong religious pluralism that is reflected in the exercise of state powers. This, however, does not result in a complete overlap between institutions and the religious factor.

This intersection of religion, law and politics, defined as confessionalism by Article 95 of the Constitution, identifies religious identity as the ordering principle of political representation and the legal system. Consequently, the organisational structure of the state can only be understood by considering the particular relationship between state and religion.[70] The Lebanese Constitution, despite proclaiming the country's Arab identity, does not proclaim Islam, or any other religion, as the state or prevailing religion. Instead, the constitutional system outlines a multi-religious system, marked by the presence of 19 recognised religious communities[71] within a pluralistic society. All religious communities are granted legal personality and extensive prerogatives.[72] The different religious communities, endowed with administrative and jurisdictional autonomy, each apply different rules to the personal status of their members, according to the interpretation provided by their respective religious courts.[73]

Article 9 of the Constitution guarantees religious freedom as absolute freedom, as well as respect for the personal status and religious interests of the population. The provision also guarantees the equality of all religious communities and the state's respect for their specificities. The constitutional provision establishes a community secularism with the aim of fostering tolerance, ensuring confessional pluralism and guaranteeing religious peace.[74] This religious peace is expressed through the affirmation of the autonomy of religious communities and the obligation of non-interference by the state.[75]

The first element through which the autonomy granted to religious communities is expressed is that of exclusive legislative power in matters of personal status: in matters of family law, personal status and inheritance, Lebanese citizens are subject to the religious law of the religious denomination they belong to. The Constitution grants religious communities the right to bring an action before the Constitutional Council to challenge state regulations that are detrimental to personal statutes and community religious interests (Art. 19).[76] The constitutional provision of this exclusive legislative competence in favour of religious communities establishes a confessional legal reserve on personal status, and the consequent absence of state regulation on this matter. Religious communities have their own tribunals to adjudicate not only

---

[70] Corim 1992, p. 32.

[71] Di Peri 2012, p. 235.

[72] Caprara 2018, pp. 703–728.

[73] *Arrêté* L/R n.60 del 1936, art. 2. There are fifteen denominational laws on personal status applied on Lebanese territory for eighteen religious communities. Some Christian communities share the same discipline.

[74] Caprara 2015, p. 9.

[75] *Arrêté* 60/L.R., 1936; *Arrêté* 146/L.R., 1938.

[76] Gannagé 2013, p. 72.

matters of a spiritual nature but also those (civil) pertaining to the personal status of their respective members.

The legislator defines the tribunals of non-Muslim communities as spiritual or ecclesiastical,[77] while within Muslim communities, it distinguishes between the *chariya* tribunals of Sunni and Shiite communities, and the *mazhabiya* tribunals of the Druze community.[78] Non-Muslim communities, unlike Muslim communities, possess their own judicial organization independent of the state, with the result that their respective tribunals report exclusively to the religious authorities of each community.[79] It is therefore the confessional authority that appoints the judges in charge of the individual judicial offices and pays their salaries from its own resources.

The confessional courts are granted with an exclusive jurisdiction over disputes concerning personal status involving members of the relevant community. This competence derives from the express wish of the state[80] to defer to the confessional authorities in matters of personal status.

It must therefore be taken into account that it is the state that recognises and legitimises the powers of communities in matters of personal status and the state has the power to control, limit or abolish them.[81] Religious jurisdiction in the Lebanese legal system is established *ratione personae* and *ratione materiae.* All matters that are not subject by law to religious jurisdiction are subject to state jurisdiction and law.[82]

For Islamic communities, religious jurisdiction *ratione materiae* is broader than that of the religious courts of other communities. Thus, for example, the concept of family law and personal status takes on a different extension for Islamic law and for the law of Christian communities. Under Ottoman rule, members of Christian communities were subject to the confessional discipline of personal status regarding marriage, filiation, adoption, divorce and nullity of marriage, with the exclusion of the patrimonial effects of marriage and succession subject to imperial law. This arrangement was also maintained by the Lebanese legal system. Article 17 of the Law of 16 July 1962 indicates the 21 matters subject to the jurisdiction of the Islamic courts, which also extends to the property effects of marriage and divorce, as well as successions. There is thus a relatively unique situation in the Lebanese legal system: the personal status of Muslims extends to all aspects of family law and succession, whereas for Christian communities these matters are regulated by civil law and, more specifically, by the Law on Succession of Non-Muslims of 23 June 1959.

---

[77] Law 2 April 1951, art. 33.

[78] The regulation of the spiritual tribunals was entrusted to the laws of 2 April 1951, and 23 June 1959; that of the *chariya* tribunals to decree-law 141 of 4 November 1942, and the law of 16 June 1962; and that of the *mazhabiya* tribunals to the law of 24 February 1948, and decree No. 3473 of 5 March 1960.

[79] Caprara 2018, p. 710.

[80] Moukazel Héchaime 2010, pp. 121–164.

[81] Najm 2004, p. 131.

[82] For the Christian and Jewish communities, the reference is the Law of 2 April 1951; for the Sunni and Jafarite communities, it is the Law of 16 July 1962; for the Druze community, it is the Law of 24 February 1962. For a more in-depth study, see Bilani 1985, p. 268.

It should, however, be pointed out that numerous provisions of civil law regulate matters that indirectly influence the regulation of the personal status of members of confessional communities, such as, for example, donations, capacity to act and guardianship, creating a continuous interaction between civil and confessional law. In addition, the enforcement of community court rulings is subject to the civil courts. The civil courts and, more specifically, the Court of Cassation are also responsible for resolving conflicts of jurisdiction between civil and religious courts as well as between the courts of different communities. The Court also ensures that the fundamental rights of the parties and public order are respected, although this review cannot go into the substance of the dispute, nor can it concern the interpretation of Community law.[83]

Community membership is determined at birth, based on paternal religious affiliation[84] until at least the age of majority.[85] This system has inevitable repercussions on the exercise of subjective rights by Lebanese citizens, who must necessarily belong to a religious community in order to apply personal, political and civil status.[86] Since the 1950s, civil society appeals, and legislative proposals aimed at unifying and secularising Lebanese family law have multiplied. However, the strong opposition of the community's religious leadership has, so far, led to the failure of any secularisation attempt of the personal status.

The Lebanese system based on community and confessional affiliation is complemented by Article 95 of the Constitution, which, on the one hand places community representation within the institutions and, on the other establishes a community privilege for access to public employment. In line with the need to defuse possible ethno-religious conflicts that have characterised the history of this country, the Constitution establishes a confessional structure of the National Assembly. Electoral laws have, therefore, always ensured a community-based distribution of seats, according to a mechanism of reserved quotas proportionate to the size of the community in each electoral district.[87]

Although the Preamble of the Constitution announces the abolition of political confessionalism, and Article 95 establishes the elimination of political sectarianism, the Lebanese political framework has remained in practice that outlined by the National Pact of 1943. The Pact, a gentlemen's agreement between the political forces that led Lebanon to independence, establishes a confessional division of the highest public offices: the Presidency of the Republic is entrusted to the Christian-Maronite community, the Prime Minister to the Muslim-Sunnite community and the Presidency of the National Assembly to the Muslim-Shiite community.

---

[83] Code of Civil Procedure, art. 95 c. 3.

[84] Law of 7 December 1951.

[85] Any change in personal status and religious affiliation follows specific procedures and is subject to registration (Law of 2 April 1951, sect. 15; Law of 16 July 1962, sects. 61–62).

[86] Nammour 2007, p. 51.

[87] Corm 2012, p. 10.

Just as with normative confessionalism in matter of personal status, political confessionalism presupposes that every citizen has a religious affiliation and is represented based on this. Added to this is the substantial impossibility of playing a political role except under the aegis of a religious community.[88] Due to this triple normative, jurisdictional and political confessionalism, the structure of this state appears federal, but with a personal rather than territorial basis. Moreover, the presence and institutionalisation of religious pluralism represents the raison d'être of the Lebanese nation. If, on the one hand, the institutionalisation of confessionalism has represented the only possible way to ensure peaceful coexistence between different religious communities,[89] on the other hand, the exclusivity of the community system represents the weak point of the constitutional order, especially in terms of guaranteeing religious freedom in its individual dimension and the protection of minorities within communities.

The success of any reform of Lebanese inter-community law cannot be separated from the identification of a civil regulation of personal status and an opening of the community system that ensures a better balance between collective and individual rights.

Compared to the model of relations between the state and religion typical of liberal democratic constitutionalism, the Lebanese case represents an extreme variation from that of Greece and Israel. The legal system recognises full freedom and equality for all religious denominations, assuming a system of state non-interference by and maximization of community autonomy, embodying what could be called inter-community secularism.

The guarantee of equidistance between all religious denominations, in the Lebanese historical, political and social context, however, leads to a profound interposition of religion in the relationship between institutions and citizens, with a consequent imbalance between individual and collective rights.

8.4 Varieties of Constitutionalism and Religion: Concluding Remarks

Over the past 20 years, the binary model of conceiving the relationship between the state and religion, typical of liberal democratic constitutionalism has been increasingly challenged. In particular, what is being challenged is the claim that western secularism is a universal principle in its meaning and purpose.[90] The ideal of institutional neutrality as constitutional standard of the relationship with the religious factor encounters multiple challenges in its practical implementation in contemporary pluralistic societies. The classical secular model has its roots in Christian history and tradition but cannot be considered a universal category. Instead, it needs to be

[88] El Hage 2009, p. 806.

[89] Harris 2009, p. 9.

[90] Ferrari 2019, p. 6.

contextualised as a product of a specific culture and history: the European one. In other parts of the world, the objectives pursued by the secular state are achieved through different legal mechanism, based on different conceptions of secularism, leading, in some of its extreme variations, to the implementation of religious personal laws.[91]

More recently, the challenges of a rigid consideration of the secular model have become apparent also in European states. The issue that western constitutionalism faces today is no longer only whether its secularism is a universal model exportable to the rest of the world. The real problem is whether this model is still useful in effectively managing the relationship between state and religion in pluralist societies, defusing possible religious and cultural conflicts. Compared to the genesis of secularism in liberal democratic constitutionalism, the religious landscape, especially in Europe, has changed radically. Religious diversity is growing, and religion is taking on an increasingly pervasive role in the public sphere.[92]

Given the elements of complexity highlighted above and the peculiar historical, cultural and political characteristics of each country, it appears difficult, if not impossible, to identify a single solution to the challenges posed to constitutionalism by an ever-increasing and sometimes unprecedented religious pluralism. Taking all these elements into due consideration, the approach to religion in the constitutional system of Greece, Israel and Lebanon, although full of limitations, represents a variation on the model of classical secularism that may be of some utility.

Assuming the classical secularism model of liberal democratic constitutionalism as the *tertium comparationis*, it is possible to consider Greece, Lebanon, and Israel as states with a differentiated religious factor interposition. In all three constitutional systems, there is, indeed, a certain degree of separation between the state and religion. More precisely, although religion plays a fundamental role in shaping the legal framework, there is no subordination to religion or complete overlap between institutions and religion. Given this basic separation, compared to the classical secularism model, the religious factor assumes an explicit role in the legal system and interposes itself in the relationship between rulers and the ruled. However, the impact of religion is variable and manifests itself in three different degrees or levels.

Drawing an ideal line that takes as its starting point the *tertium comparationis*, at the first level we would find Greece with a moderate religious intervention; followed by the Israeli deep religious intervention and, at the end of the line we would find the pervasive religious intervention typical of Lebanon. Contrary to the typical system of liberal democratic constitutionalism, based on the full and exclusive sovereignty of the state in legislative and jurisdictional matters, these three cases are characterised by the recognition of a community privilege expressed by the legislative and jurisdictional autonomy of religious communities. An autonomy that moves within the limits established by the state which, through the law, delegates, without abdicating, these powers to religious communities, according to different levels of extension.

---

[91] Asad 2003, p. 14.

[92] On this progressive transformation, see Ferrari 2008, pp. 103–112.

In the Greek legal system, this privilege leads to the affirmation of an alternative religious jurisdiction to that of the state, giving the members of the Islamic minority of Thrace the possibility to choose whether to regulate certain aspects of their lives according to the precepts of community religious law. The system, however, carries with it an implicit and potential discrimination, as it does not extend to all minority religious communities and does not provide adequate means of protection for minorities within minority. In the cases of Israel and Lebanon, the system is taken to extremes, producing an exclusive jurisdiction that imposes religious affiliation on all citizens, without the possibility of turning to state law in matters of marriage and divorce (Israel) or personal status (Lebanon). The exclusivity of the system is its weak point, leading to a total absence of dialogue among communities and between communities and the state, with negative effects on the resilience of the system guaranteeing fundamental rights. In the Lebanese case, moreover, community privilege also extends to political representation.

In all three cases, this community privilege leads to a phenomenon of normative integration, consisting of the integration of alternative religious and cultural systems and sources of law into the state legal system. Religious law thus assumes the role of a complementary source of law, accentuating the legal pluralism of the legal system. In all three cases, the plurality of normative sources is characterised by a thread of consistency that derives from the institutionalisation of religious communities. It should also be noted how this legal pluralism and community autonomy, or privilege finds its source of legitimacy in the legal system that establishes its extension and boundaries.

As for the guarantee of religious freedom, this fundamental principle appears enshrined in all three constitutions examined. However, compared to the model of liberal democratic constitutionalism, it is more relevant in its collective than in its individual dimension. The individual appears, in fact, capable of fully exercising his religious freedom as a member of a community. In a different manner, therefore, from the model of liberal democratic constitutionalism in which the individual dimension of freedom prevails over the collective one. This element is also expressed according to three different levels of intensity in the three legal systems.

The main issue in this case concerns the often mistaken assumption of the existence of a free choice regarding religious affiliation. This assumption does not consider elements such as social, community, or even familial pressure. The only guarantee for a proper balance between individual rights and collective rights, therefore, seems to be the recognition of a civil discipline of personal status and of the right of each individual to leave their original community, to belong to multiple communities, or to none. The model of the secular state with a differentiated religious intervention, despite the highlighted criticisms, can nevertheless serve as a useful starting point for rethinking the governance of religious diversity.

From what has been highlighted so far, we can draw two considerations: 1) The model of the secular state, typical of liberal democratic constitutionalism, is not based on universal principles but is the result of specific, often unique, historical, political, economic, and cultural characteristics. Consequently, there are different types of secular states, whose common denominator can be identified in a certain degree of secularism, understood as separation or non-overlap between state institutions and the religious factor, a guarantee of religious freedom and equality, a sufficient level of neutrality; 2) Neutrality if understood as mere tolerance, indifference, exclusion or contempt for religion cannot be an effective legal instrument to govern the new plurality of contemporary societies.

Starting from constitutional experiences far removed from the typically European one, such as those of Greece, Israel and Lebanon, it is possible to identify an alternative that is more intelligible to religious communities that address different legal cultures, without betraying the fundamental principles of liberal democratic constitutionalism.

Drawing inspiration from systems belonging to legal cultures different from the European Christian one, what I would like to define as *intercultural accommodation* may represent a possible solution to accommodate religious diversity. This form of accommodation requires a transition of the legal system from monism to legal pluralism, in search of new forms of coexistence that go beyond the legal categories typical of western constitutionalism. The reference point is the concept of the intercultural state that, overcoming the multicultural paradigm, focuses on the relationship and negotiation between distinct values and traditions, breaking the hegemonic pattern of one dominant culture and others subordinate.[93]

There are several cultural configurations in heterogeneous societies, which have a set of symbols, beliefs and values that constitute an identity and that can enter into negotiation with others with the aim to solve social conflicts. Intercultural theory can recognize the conflict of different worldviews, which are often antagonistic, and tries to rebuild a system able to incorporate ontological values of different legal cultures.

Applied to religious diversity, this form of accommodation requires a transformation of the approach to religion that favours the community dimension. In this sense, intercultural accommodation requires the state to grant certain spaces of autonomy for minority religious communities, to value the collective dimension of religious freedom and to recognise specific normative protections for religious minorities that go beyond mere tolerance. The limit of accommodation remains respect for the fundamental principles of the legal system and the guarantee for members of the community to freely choose which value system(s) they adhere to.

Concurrently, the principle of equality must be redefined to ensure not just equal treatment, but also the right to diversity. This reflects the multicultural dilemma that echoes in the debate between individual and collective rights.

In the context of a multicultural society, the presence of minorities whose identity is rooted in faith compels democratic systems to reconsider the role of state neutrality towards religion, and to seek solutions for the inclusion and protection of differences.

This leads to the need to explore forms and mechanisms that enable a positive interaction between value systems oriented towards religion and legal frameworks, capable of overcoming the prejudice of their absolute incompatibility and accommodating their differences. In this context, the protective system offered by religious

---

[93] For a definition of the concept of interculturalism, see Bagni 2017, pp. 137–190; Walsh 2009, p. 41.

freedom, that is predominantly focused on individual aspects, seems insufficient to address the needs of collective identity that are particularly expressed by religious minorities. In the absence of specific protection for minorities that goes beyond the confines of religious freedom, it is necessary to explore new modes of dialogue which, in strictly legal terms, means drawing on the tools provided by law to bridge deeply different normative and value systems.

The participation of religious communities in the public space is the first condition of intercultural dialogue. In this participation, minority religious communities can take two paths: a) to participate in determining the political choices and normative content of laws; b) to invoke derogations and exceptions when applying norms that they have not helped to design.

The first path defines the places for dialogue by creating favourable conditions for it, the second risks deepening the exclusion that democratic constitutionalism is supposed to fight.

Reference List

Ahdar R, Leigh I (2005) Religious Freedom in the Liberal State. Oxford University Press, Oxford

Alon M (1993) Constitution by Legislation: The Values of a Jewish and Democratic State in Light of Basic Law: Human Dignity and Personal Freedom. Iunei Mishpat 17:659-670

Asad T (1993) Genealogies of Religion: Discipline and Reasons of Power in Christianity and Islam. The Johns Hopkins University Press, Baltimore/London

Asad T (2003) Formation of the Secular: Christianity, Islam, Modernity. Stanford University Press, Stanford

Bagni S (2017) Lo Stato interculturale: primi tentativi di costruzione prescrittiva della categoria [The Intercultural State: First Attempts at Prescriptive Construction of the Category]. In: Bagni S, Figueroa Mejía G A, Pavani G (eds) La ciencia del derecho constitucional comparado [The science of comparative constitutional law], II. Tirant Lo Blanch, Mexico, pp 137-190

Barak A (1995) La revolution constitutionnelle: la protection des droits fondamentaux [The Constitutional Revolution: The Protection of Fundamental Rights]. Pouvoirs 72:17-32

Barkey L, Gaurilis G (2016) The Ottoman Millet System: Non-Territorial Autonomy and Its Contemporary Legacy. Ethnopolitics 15:24-42

Benhabib S (2002) The Claims of Culture: Equality and Diversity in the Global Era. Princeton University Press, Princeton

Berger BL (2015) Law's Religion: Religious Difference and the Claims of Constitutionalism. University of Toronto Press, Toronto

Bilani B (1985) Personal Status. In: El-Gemayel A (ed) The Lebanese Legal System. International Law Institute and Georgetown University, Washington, pp 267-285

Caprara L (2015) L'autonomia normativa e giurisdizionale delle confessioni religiose nel sistema degli statuti personali in Libano [The normative and jurisdictional autonomy of religious confessions in the system of personal statuses in Lebanon]. Jus 3:1-40

Caprara L (2018) Il Confessionalismo Giudiziario Libanese [Lebanese Judicial Confessionalism]. Il Diritto Ecclesiastico 3:703-728

Cavalcanti MF (2023) Giurisdizioni alternative e Legal Pluralism: le Minoranze Islamiche negli Ordinamenti Costituzionali occidentali [Alternative jurisdiction and legal pluralism: Islamic minorities in Western legal systems]. Editoriale Scientifica, Naples

Clogg R (2021) A concise History of Greece. Cambridge University Press, Cambridge

Corim G (1992) Laïcité et confessionalisme au Liban [Secularism and confessionalism in Lebanon]. Confluences 1:28-42
Corm G (2012) Le Libain Contemporain [The Contemporary Lebanese]. Edition La Découvert, Paris
Di Peri R (2012) Costruzione identitaria e democrazia locale in Libano [Identity Building and Local Democracy in Lebanon]. Meridiana 1:231-256
El Hage N (2009) Le pluralisme juridique au Liban [Legal pluralism in Lebanon]. Revue juridique et politique des États francophones 4:720-806
Ferrari S (2008) State Regulation of Religion in the European Democracies: The Decline of the Old Pattern. In: Motzkin G, Fischer Y (eds) Religion and Democracy in Contemporary Europe. Alliance Publishing Trust, London, pp 103-112
Ferrari S (2019) The Secular State in a Declining Europe: Beyond the End of the European Universal Dream. Journal of Law, Religion and State 7:13-30
Fokas E (2012) Eastern orthodoxy and Western secularization in contemporary Europe (with special reference to the case of Greece). Religion, State and Society 40:395-414
Gannagè P (2001) Le pluralisme des statuts personnels dans les Etats multicommunitaires: Droit libanaise et Droit proche-orientaux [The pluralism of personal statuses in multicommunity states: Lebanese law and Middle Eastern law]. Bruylant, Brussels
Gannagé P (2013) L'accès des communautés légalement reconnues au Conseil constitutionnel. Conseil constitutionnel [Access of legally recognized communities to the Constitutional Council. Constitutional Council]. Annuaire 1:69-80
Gaudreault-DesBiens J F (2010) Religious Court, Personal Federalism and Legal Transplant. In: Adhar R, Aroney N (eds) Shariah in the West. Oxford University Press, Oxford, pp 159-180
Gemi E (2021) The "prevailing religion" and the governance of diversity. In: Triandafyllidou A, Magazzini T (eds) Routledge Handbook on the Governance of Religious Diversity. Routledge, London/New York, pp 88-98
Gerring J, Ziblatt D, Van Gorp J, Arévalo J (2011) An Institutional Theory of Direct and Indirect Rule. World Politics, 63:377-433
Halmai G (2015) Religion and Constitutionalism. State-Church Relation and Religious Freedom. MTA Working Paper No.2015/05:1-83
Harris W (2009) Reflections on Lebanon. In: B Rubin (ed) Lebanon: liberation, conflict, and crisis. Palgrave MacMillan, New York, pp 9-23
Hirschl R (2010) Constitutional Theocracy. Harvard University Press, Cambridge/London
Hirschl R (2011) Comparative Constitutional Law and Religion. In: Ginsburg T, Dixon R (eds) Comparative Constitutional Law. Edward Elgar, Northampton, pp 422-440
Hirschl R, Shachar A (2018) Competing Orders? The Challenge of Religion to Modern Constitutionalism. The University of Chicago Law Review 85:425-455
Hulme P (1986) Colonial Encounters. Methuen, New York
Karayanni M (2021) A Multicultural entrapment. Religion and State among the Palestinian-Arabs in Israel. Cambridge University Press, Cambridge
Kymlicka W (2001) The Politics in Vernacular. Nationalism, Multiculturalism, Citizenship. Oxford University Press, Oxford
Kuru AT (2009) Secularism and State Policies towards Religion: The United States, France and Turkey. Cambridge University Press, New York
Lapidoth L (1998) Freedom of Religion and Conscience in Israel. Catholic University Law Review 2:441-465
Lernen N (2017) Religion and the Secular State in Israel, International Centre for Law and Religion Studies Annual Report
Lübbe H (2003) Säkularisierung eines ideen politischen Begriffs [Secularization of an ideological political concept]. Verlag Karl Alber, Baden-Baden
Madley J (2015) Constitutional Models and the Protection of Religious Freedom. In: Ferrari S (ed) Routledge Handbook of Law and Religion. Routledge, New York, pp 209-227
Mancini S (2020) Constitution and Religion. Edward Elgar Publishing, Cheltenham

Martinez Tórron J (1994) Separatismo y cooperación en los acuerdos del Estado con la minorias religiosas [Separatism and cooperation in state agreements with religious minorities]. Editorial Comares, Granada
Medina B (2006) Enhancing Freedom of Religion Through Public Provision of Religious Services: the Israeli Experience. Israel Law Review 39:127-157
Mehdi R, Petersen H, Woodman GR, Sand ER (2008) Law and Religion in Multicultural Society. DJOF, Copenhagen
Moukazel Héchaime A (2010) Actualités du statut personel des communautés musulmanes au Liban [News on the personal status of Muslim communities in Lebanon]. Droit et Cultures 1:121-164
Najm MC (2004) Pour uné legislation civil unifiée de la famille au Liban [For a unified civil family legislation in Lebanon]. Travaux et jours 74:131–171
Nammour J (2007) Les identités au Liban, entre complexité et perplexité [Identities in Lebanon, between complexity and perplexity]. Cités 1:51-72
Nieuwenhuis AJ (2012) State and religion, a multidimensional relationship: Some comparative law remarks. International Journal of Constitutional Law 10:153-174
Norris P, Inglehart R (2004) Religion and Politics Worldwide. Cambridge University Press, New York
Palermo F (2013) Current and Future Challenges for International Minority Protection. In: European Yearbook of Minority Issues. Brill, Leiden/Boston
Pannikar R (2015) Religion and Religion. Orbis Books, New York
Papageorgiou C (2021) Religion and Law in Greece. Wolters Kluwer, Alphen aan den Rijn
Papastathis CK (1996) The Hellenic Republic and the Prevailing Religion. BYU Law Review 4:816-850
Parrilli A (2021) "Non-Western" Secularism: The Case of Religious Citizenship in Israel and Turkey. Comparative Law Review 11:62-77
Pegoraro L (2012) Empezando por Cádiz: las clasificaciones dúctiles en el Derecho constitucionales comparado [Starting from Cadiz: flexible classifications in comparative constitutional law]. Revista Latino-americana de Estudos Constitucionais 13:1-34
Perl L (2008) Theocracy. Political Systems of the World. Marshall Cavendish, New York
Rinella A (2020) La Shari'a in Occidente [Sharia in the West]. Giurisdizioni e diritto islamico: Regno Unito, Canada e Stati Uniti d'America [Jurisdictions and Islamic Law: United Kingdom, Canada and United States of America]. Il Mulino, Bologna
Rosenfeld M (2013) Constitution and Secularism: a Western Account. In: Berman B J, Bhargava R, Laliberté A (eds) Secular State and Religious Diversity. UBC Press, Toronto, pp 21-40
Rowe PS (2007) Neo Millet System and transnational Religious Movements: The Humayun Decrees and Church Construction in Egypt. Journal of Church and State 49:329-350
Sezgin Y (2010) The Israeli Millet system: Examining Legal Pluralism through lenses of nation building and human rights. Israel Law Review 2:631-654
Shachar A (2001) Multicultural Jurisdiction: cultural differences and women's rights. Cambridge University Press, Cambridge
Steinberg GM (2001) Interpretations of Jewish Tradition in Democracy, Land and Peace. Journal of Church and State 43:93-114
Tsitselikis K (2007) The Pending Modernisation of Islam in Greece: From Millet to Minority Status. Südosteuropa 4:354-372
Tsitselikis K (2008) Minority Mobilisation in Greece and Litigation in Strasbourg. International Journal of Minority and Group Rights 15:27-42
Tsitselikis K (2012) Old and New Islam and Greece from Historical Minorities to Immigrant Newcomers. Brill-Nijhoff, Leiden
Tsitselikis K (2013) A Surviving Treaty: The Lausanne Minority Protection in Greece and Turkey. In: Henrad K (ed) The Interrelation between the Right to Identity of Minorities and their socio-economic Participation. Brill, Leiden, pp 287-313
Tsitselikis K (2023) ENTAN policy paper No. 12 (March 2023). ISSN 2671-3896. https://entan.org/wp-content/uploads/2023/02/Entan-Policy-Paper-No.-12_final.pdf

Walsh C (2009) Interculturalidad, Estado, Sociedad: Luchas (de)colonials de nuestra época [Interculturality, State, Society: (De)colonial struggles of our time]. Abya-Yala, Quito
Zagrebelsky G (2014) One Among Many? The Catholic Church Between Universalism and Pluralism. In: Mancini S, Rosenfeld M (eds) Constitutional Secularism in an Age of Religious Revival. Oxford University Press, Oxford, pp 247-268

Chapter 9
Is the *Ius Constitutionale Commune* in Latin America Missing the Point?

Sergio Verdugo

Contents

Abstract Latin America offers a rich and diverse history for discussing what ideas are and should be considered associated with constitutionalism. A particularly influential type is the *ius constitutionale commune* (ICCLA). Championed by a group of scholars and judges, the ICCLA seeks to identify and promote a version of constitutionalism that emphasizes the protection of human rights understood from an egalitarian perspective, offering a transformative regional project that emphasizes the (final) authority of the Inter-American Court of Human Rights (IACtHR). Critics have questioned the possibilities of this normative project, challenged its liberal European-centred inspiration, objected that it promotes the judicialization of politics while weakening more compelling versions of democracy, and claimed that it could undermine alternative projects rooted in the idea of constitutional pluralism. This chapter argues that the ICCLA provides a means (the judicialization of human rights issues) poorly suited to advance its egalitarian goals fully. Even though some proponents of the ICCLA are aware of this limitation, they have done little to correct it.

S. Verdugo (✉)
Law School, IE University, Madrid, Spain
e-mail: sverdugo@faculty.ie.edu

M. De Visser et al. (eds.), *European Yearbook of Constitutional Law 2024*, European Yearbook of Constitutional Law 6, https://doi.org/10.1007/978-94-6265-699-4_9

Some of their ideas can even deepen the problem by distracting from the real causes that prevent social rights expansions and promoting constitutional arrangements that undermine the goal of producing a more responsive political process.

Keywords American Convention on Human Rights · Constitutionalism · International Human Rights Law · *Ius Constitutionale Commune* · Latin America · Social Rights · Theories of Constitutionalism

9.1 Introduction

Latin America is a diverse region with some common features and with regional projects that can be traced back to the plans of Simón Bolívar and the Logia Lautarina. Most Latin American countries follow a variation of the presidential regime, and there are several regional agreements, including an inter-American human rights system. Different territories have a colonial past and are populated by indigenous peoples who have been marginalized or neglected. The European civil law tradition (with variations) has been (and remains) dominant in the domestic legal systems, the Catholic Church has been particularly influential, and many countries have had dictatorships in the 20th century. Even though some countries like Uruguay and Costa Rica rank well in democratic and rule of law indicators, there is a widespread perception that Latin America is a region of political instability, fragile institutions, and widespread populism. This perception is influenced by biases or specific examples that hardly represent the entire region. Still, there may be some truth if one looks into specific dimensions, such as the relatively brief endurance of many Latin American constitutions. Many times, though, the differences existing in Latin America are not duly accounted for. Latin America has multiple languages (including indigenous languages), countries have different identities, and sometimes there are territorial and political conflicts. There are also relevant differences in Latin American political systems. Some countries are federal—Mexico, Argentina, Brazil—and others are unitary. Some countries have a dominant party regime—e.g., Venezuela, Nicaragua, Cuba—and some are ruled by populists with authoritarian inclinations—e.g., Mexico, El Salvador—while others have competitive democracies that rotate power frequently, despite episodes of democratic regression or major political crises—e.g., Brazil, Colombia. Centrist presidents are rare, and politicians presented as social democrats are sometimes members of corrupt governments—e.g., Peronismo in Argentina and the PRI regime in Mexico. National Congresses can be weak compared with the executive branch, but sometimes they can act strongly and turn down governments—e.g., Ecuador, Perú, and Paraguay.

European and North American ideas, such as popular sovereignty, bills of rights, the rule of law, a written constitution, and presidentialism, partly shaped the Latin American political landscape and its 19th-century constitutional documents, which were also influenced by the ideas of local intellectuals such as Juan Bautista Alberdi in Argentina and Diego Portales in Chile. These ideas have also accompanied colonization processes and combined with significant historical developments, such as the revolutionary 1917 Mexican Constitution, or the 19th-century constitutions of Colombia and Venezuela, which experimented with unprecedented types of judicial review mechanisms.[1] Different types of constitutional ideas have flourished. European intellectuals such as Hans Kelsen and the Nazi scholar Carl Schmitt have been influential,[2] as well as more contemporary thinkers. Some movements have tried to resist these influences and advance a decolonial constitutional project partly inspired by Indigenous beliefs and partly by European intellectuals,[3] even though all constitutional projects have adapted at least some foreign element, such as a bill of rights and judicial review.

In this context, a group of scholars and judges, partly inspired by European ideas such as the French block of constitutionality doctrine and the *Ius Publicum Europaeum*—ideas mediated by local judicial doctrines such as those of the Colombian Constitutional Court—have promoted a version of constitutionalism: the *ius constitutionale commune* (ICCLA).[4] The ICCLA is typically presented as a progressive set of constitutional ideas that seeks to advance a transformative project emphasizing human rights protections, sees rights as principles that should be advanced judicially, and promotes the development of strategic litigation[5]—which is already influential in the inter-American system.[6] The ICCLA gives a central role to the IACtHR, and seeks to identify a common regional approach to overcoming the history of violence and inequality in Latin America.[7] Proponents of the ICCLA are typically criticized for selecting "positive" cases of convergence as examples of the *ius commune* but neglecting the negative cases.[8] (To be sure, critics of the ICCLA are perhaps vulnerable to the opposite criticism: they emphasize the negative examples while downplaying the positive cases.).[9] Responding to these types of criticisms, ICCLA advocates typically claim that there is a *potential* for the *ius commune,* and appeal to the way the domestic constitutional frameworks have opened themselves to accept international human rights instruments as a sort of regional superior law.[10] (Critics of the ICCLA could claim the opposite: that there is a potential for backlash, regardless of what the constitutional texts say.).

---

[1] Colón-Ríos 2014.

[2] See, e.g., Ramírez Cleves 2024; Colón-Ríos 2011.

[3] See, e.g., the influence of de Sousa Santos 2014.

[4] See generally von Bogdandy 2015b; von Bogdandy 2015a; von Bogdandy et al. 2017b; von Bogdandy et al. 2017a; Mac-Gregor 2017; Morales Antoniazzi and Saavedra Alessandri 2017; Piovesan 2017; Herrera 2021.

[5] Von Bogdandy 2015a, p. 110; García Ramírez 2017, p. 313.

[6] Soley 2017, pp. 352–353.

[7] Von Bogdandy 2015a, p. 110. Also, von Bogdandy 2015b, pp. 9–10.

[8] Werneck Arguelhes 2019, p. 372.

[9] I thank Jorge Contesse for pointing this out to me.

[10] Von Bogdandy 2015b, p. 11; Morales Antoniazzi and Saavedra Alessandri 2017, pp. 258–260; Piovesan 2017, pp. 62–63; Góngora-Mera 2017, pp. 237–238; García Ramírez 2017, pp. 316–318; Góngora-Mera 2017, pp. 237–238; Herrera 2021, p. 1402.

Unlike the European model(s), the ICCLA does not seek economic and political integration.[11] To foster solutions to the problems it seeks to solve, the ICCLA is particularly interested in the enforcement of social rights[12] and in defending the power of the IACtHR, which has gradually opened itself to protect social rights while overcoming the human rights instruments' limited language on the matter.[13] The ICCLA prescriptions often align with the approaches taken by the IACtHR, for example, by claiming that local judges should also become inter-American judges.[14] Due to its ambitious goals—even if gradual and incremental[15]—and strong conception of rights and judicial power, the ICCLA fits with a variation of liberal constitutionalism that Mark Tushnet has called "maximalist".[16] As with all maximalist definitions of constitutionalism,[17] the ICCLA does not reflect exactly any real-world regime but offers an essentially normative project.

Despite its essentially normative nature, it might be useful to distinguish (1) descriptive, (2) normative, and (3) interpretative dimensions the ICCLA still possesses: From (1) a descriptive perspective, it argues that there is a common legal framework that different jurisdictions are discovering or advancing to. When common human rights standards are achieved, they are part of the *ius commune*. From (2) a normative approach, the ICCLA endorses progressive values, accepts a (contested) version of democracy that gives a prominent role to judges, and rejects authoritarian regimes, conservative interpretations of human rights law, and also democratic ideas that are sceptical of judicial review. That way, it offers a nuanced approach to popular sovereignty, it distrusts representative institutions, it is sceptical of constitutional pluralism, and it advocates for legal convergence. From (3) an interpretative perspective, the ICCLA seeks to reconstruct the best judicial practices that can be identified in the region. The jurisprudence of the IACtHR and the Colombian Constitutional Court have become essential examples of this interpretative dimension.[18] For those reasons, it is sometimes difficult to distinguish criticisms against the IACtHR from criticisms against the ICCLA.

As I will explain later, despite its growing influence in the region, scholars such as Alejandro Rodiles and Ana Micaela Alterio[19] have formulated criticisms against the ICCLA. At the political level, the resistance that some countries in the region have shown against the IACtHR[20] —including withdrawals or threats to withdraw[21]—has

[11] Von Bogdandy 2015b, p. 15; von Bogdandy 2015a, p. 112.

[12] See, e.g., von Bogdandy 2015a, p. 111.

[13] Piovesan 2017, pp. 58–60; Burgorgue-Larsen 2017, pp. 384–385.

[14] Dulitzky 2015a, p. 103.

[15] Von Bogdandy 2015b, p. 20.

[16] Tushnet 2020, p. 101.

[17] Ibid., p. 106.

[18] Von Bogdandy 2015a, p. 111; von Bogdandy et al. 2017b, p. 37; Góngora-Mera 2017, pp. 246–247, 251.

[19] Rodiles 2018; Alterio 2018.

[20] See Huneeus 2011; Contesse 2019.

[21] Soley and Steininger 2018.

the potential to weaken the impact of the ICCLA project. This chapter will claim that the ICCLA offers a method—the regional and domestic judicialization of human rights issues—that is poorly suited to advance its goals. As I will show, even though some ICCLA advocates are aware of this problem, they have done little to correct it and have promoted solutions that distract from discussing more promising routes, even at the cost of undermining those routes.

Section 9.2 explains how the ICCLA fits (or not) with other variations of constitutionalism in the region. Section 9.3 engages and expands on existing criticisms. Section 9.4 develops the chapter's central argument and illustrates how an emphasis on the judicialization of human rights may prove counterproductive for the ICCLA's egalitarian goals. My purpose here is not to suggest that the ICCLA should be necessarily abandoned nor to formulate a criticism against the IACtHR. To be sure, the IACtHR is central to the ICCLA's project and has been relatively receptive to—at least—parts of that project. Nevertheless, my argument targets the ICCLA as an intellectual movement promoting a type of constitutionalism and not the IACtHR understood as a court that can pursue valuable goals. The idea is to suggest that a nuanced approach to constitutionalism in the region should also deepen the institutional mechanisms necessary for advancing solutions to the region's problems and explain how a robust version of the ICCLA can undermine that aim. This is a task that the IACtHR can contribute to in a rather limited way. A version of constitutionalism that advocates for solutions outside of the scope of the IACtHR's jurisdiction becomes necessary if one is to take seriously the transformative goals of the ICCLA.

9.2 Latin American Constitutionalism(s) and the Rise of the ICCLA

Latin America's early constitutions were influenced by many schools of thought that Roberto Gargarella classifies as radicalism, liberalism, and conservatism.[22] Even though versions of these schools of thought can be identified today in contemporary constitutional structures, new constitutional ideas seem particularly relevant. The Chilean 1980 Constitution and the failed 1980 Uruguayan constitutional proposal are examples of an authoritarian form of constitutionalism that combined nationalistic values, conservative principles, and natural law ideas.[23] In Chile, the Constitution highly distrusted the party regime and was connected to the doctrine of national security, an undemocratic approach to how the military should protect the institutions against external threats such as Marxism.[24] To a lesser degree, perhaps one could also include Fujimori's Constitution in Peru, enacted in 1993 after a self-coup.

[22] Gargarella 2010; Gargarella 2013a. For a more contemporary (though partial) mapping of the constitutional schools of thought, see the helpful article by Coddou Mc Manus 2021.

[23] On the failed Uruguayan constitutional proposal, see Katz 2023.

[24] See Barros 2002.

They combined authoritarian and plebiscitary elements with mainstream constitutional arrangements, such as judicial review and bills of rights.[25] The existence of an "authoritarian" form of constitutionalism is contested from a normative perspective,[26] even though it has been widely recognized that authoritarian regimes frequently find it helpful for their own goals to use the mechanisms associated with constitutionalism.[27] From a normative perspective, a thin version of authoritarian constitutionalism is still possible if one accepts that limits to political power can also exist in authoritarian regimes.[28]

The Venezuelan 1999 Constitution, followed by Ecuador (2008) and Bolivia (2009), are also examples of plebiscitary forms of hyper-presidentialism that embraced elements of radical constitutionalism. Some people call them "Neobolivarian" constitutional experiments or examples of the "New Latin American Constitutionalism".[29] The New Latin American Constitutionalism is a set of constitutional ideas drawing inspiration from a group of Latin American left-wing movements that combine agendas of decolonization, socialism, human rights, a scepticism against mainstream political parties and traditional channels of political representation, a rejection of market-driven ideas connected to Europe and the US, and an approach to a radical form of democracy centred on a strong executive branch capable of connecting directly with the peoples.[30] The Neobolivarian constitutional experiments have authoritarian elements (Venezuela is the most extreme example,[31] and, perhaps, also Nicaragua). They were justified by dubious versions of the constituent power theory[32] that emphasized the descriptive and symbolic ideas of political representation in the hands of a single *caudillo*,[33] and they were made in ways that were functional to political leaders trying to establish dominant party regimes. They tried to reboot their states using egalitarian and Indigenous narratives, responded to populist agendas that tried to replace ruling elites, and recognized an extensive list of rights. They ended up establishing constitutional frameworks that some connect to constitutional abuses.[34] The New Latin American Constitutionalism does not pass a liberal

[25] For a mainstream version of constitutionalism, see Loughlin 2022, pp. 38–50.

[26] On the idea of the possibilities of an authoritarian constitutionalism, see Tushnet 2014; Tushnet 2015.

[27] See generally Ginsburg and Simpser 2014.

[28] This is the central argument of Barros 2002.

[29] See, e.g., King 2013; Couso 2014.

[30] Important examples are the political agendas that existed during the constitution-making processes of Ecuador and Bolivia. See, e.g., Pisarello 2014.

[31] Landau 2018.

[32] Compare Hughes 2019; Verdugo 2023.

[33] Díaz de Valdés and Verdugo 2019.

[34] On Venezuela and Colombia, see, e.g., Landau 2013a. In Latin America, the term "abusive constitutionalism" is important but contested because it arguably downplays relevant functions that Latin American constitutions can also play. See González-Jacome 2017.

democratic test, and its transformative aims have come at the cost of weakening judicial independence and the political parties of the opposition, harming the competitiveness of the democratic system, and advocacy for executive branch aggrandizement that weakens the separation of powers.[35]

Latin America also witnessed transformative experiments that were not aimed at harming principles such as rotation in power and judicial independence. Under the institutional framework of the Colombian (1991) and Brazilian (1988) constitutions, for example, and despite their problems, we can find empowered courts capable of limiting the authority of powerful executive branches and dynamic party systems able of providing for genuine electoral competition.[36] Despite episodes of constitutional abuses and democratic erosion,[37] both transformative experiences in Colombia and Brazil have arguably succeeded in advancing social rights demands such as healthcare,[38] even if those advancements have been modest.

Along with the constitutional and political projects described above, Latin America has received the influence of a more contemporary school of thought called "Neoconstitutionalism". Even if controversial and resisted by some scholars,[39] Neoconstitutionalism has helped to make the criticism against legal formalism and narratives of judicial apoliticism more visible.[40] Neoconstitutionalism rejects textualism and emphasizes the need to treat rights as principles. It favours judicial methodologies such as the proportionality test and rights balancing, promotes forms of judicial activism, and helps justify creative legal interpretations leading to judicial decisions that can change the meaning of the law. Even though one can find a remote influence in the work of European (and, to a lesser extent, North American) scholars such as Ronald Dworkin, Robert Alexy, Peter Häberle, and Luigi Ferrajoli,[41] Neoconstitutionalism has spread quickly in the region. The Mexican Supreme Court and the Colombian Constitutional Court offer paramount examples of how neoconstitutional ideas have accompanied the expansion of judicial power.[42]

On the other side of the spectrum, we find scholars who reject judicial activism,[43] often explicitly criticizing the ideas promoted by neoconstitutionalists.[44] They typically offer a procedural or deliberative version of the democratic regime. An example can be found in the work of the Argentinian scholar Roberto Gargarella, who suggests

---

[35] This problem is, of course, not unique to the New Latin American Constitutionalism. Guillermo O'Donnell had identified the issue and named it "delegative democracy" years before the idea of New Latin American Constitutionalism arose. See O'Donnell 1994.

[36] See, e.g., Katz 2020; Barroso 2016.

[37] In the case of Colombia, see, e.g., Bernal 2013. In the case of Brazil, see, e.g., Meyer 2021.

[38] See, e.g., Nunes 2010; Cardoso 2021.

[39] See, e.g., Aldunate 2010; Núñez 2010; Alterio 2018, p. 10.

[40] Hilbink 2007.

[41] Rodiles 2018.

[42] See, e.g., Alterio 2019; Landau 2012; Landau 2014.

[43] See, e.g., García and Verdugo 2013.

[44] See, e.g., Atria 2016.

the search for poles of citizens' participation,[45] while showing scepticism against the possibilities of achieving genuine and legitimate transformations via courts, including the IACtHR.[46]

In this context, a space for a democratic defence of judicial power and fostering the regional human rights framework using a transformative narrative was open for the ICCLA to fill. That's how a group of organized scholars and judges started to promote the ICCLA in the workshops of the Max Planck Institute in Heidelberg, attracting several Latin American scholars who then generated a network that has been pushing for the ICCLA with relative success.[47] Even if it does not have unanimous support and has been resisted on some levels, the ICCLA has been particularly attractive for centre-left and progressive intellectuals seeking to advance transformations without accepting the authoritarian and populist inclinations of competing left-wing agendas.

Unlike the New Latin American Constitutionalism—which is consistent with authoritarian and populist elements, as explained before—the ICCLA is committed to liberal democracy and rejects the plebiscitary mechanisms that are so popular in the region. It offers a gradual and incremental transformative agenda[48] that does not believe in forms of instantaneous democracies.[49] It also rejects full authoritarianism and conservatism and is inconsistent with approaches that merely focus on the procedural aspects of democracy. The idea is to offer a variation of constitutionalism that seeks the protagonism of judges and makes them engage with human rights understood as principles[50]—which makes Neoconstitutionalism particularly helpful for them—while advocating for the identification of a regional common legal approach that describes and promotes openness to international law, a comparative mindset, the merging of domestic constitutional law with human rights treaties, the binding authority of the jurisprudence of the IACtHR, and the promotion of values—i.e., democracy, human rights, and the rule of law—even though the emphasis is on the idea of human rights.[51] The ICCLA has often been presented along with other transformative constitutional projects in the global south that also embrace the role of judges in advancing those social transformations.[52] The primary difference is how the ICCLA seeks to use the regional human rights framework centred on the work of regional and local judges, which makes the ICCLA hardly compatible with other approaches to transformative constitutionalism emphasizing procedural aspects of

---

[45] Gargarella 2022b.

[46] Gargarella 2021.

[47] See generally von Bogdandy 2015b, pp. 5–6; Rodiles 2018; Herrera 2021, pp. 1387–1388; Contesse 2022, p. 316; García-Huidobro and Guidi 2021, pp. 1298–1302; Coddou Mc Manus 2021, pp. 7–8.

[48] Herrera 2021, p. 1402.

[49] On the idea of an instantaneous democracy, see Kuo 2019.

[50] Von Bogdandy 2015a, p. 109. Also, von Bogdandy 2015b, pp. 6–7.

[51] Von Bogdandy 2015b, pp. 16–17.

[52] See generally Bonilla Maldonado 2013; Vilhena et al. 2013; von Bogdandy et al. 2017a.

democratic regimes and requiring a more modest judicial function.[53] The main areas of concern for the ICCLA are violence, exclusion, and substantive inequality, which are common problems in the region.[54] The main tools of the ICCLA to solve these problems are the recognition and enforcement of human rights—including social rights—at the regional and domestic levels.[55] Judicial activism, legal networks, and strategic actors representing social movements pushing for litigation became crucial for the ICCLA's success.

The reception of the ICCLA in the region has been strengthened by constitutional doctrines such as the block of constitutionality—which, in the Latin American version, advocates for broadening the scope of domestic constitutional rights using international instruments—and the control of conventionality.[56] The latter is a doctrine that arguably lacks a textual ground in the American Convention of Human Rights,[57] and it was first explicitly announced in the *Almonacid* case by the IACtHR.[58] The control of conventionality doctrine contends that the IACtHR's interpretations are the final interpretations of the regional human rights treaties in both the judicial decisions and (arguably) its advisory opinions.[59] All states and domestic judges should follow those interpretations even if they were not a party in the cases that led to the IACtHR decisions.[60] Local judges are supposed to follow the IACtHR's interpretations in *ex officio* ways—i.e., operating without the need for a specific request,[61] though they should be sensitive to the appropriate domestic procedures.[62] All judges—and arguably every administrative officer of any state agency[63]—are inter-American agents capable of using the power of judicial review

53 See an excellent example of this alternative position to transformative constitutionalism in Fowkes 2024.

54 Piovesan 2017, pp. 50–51; Soley 2017, pp. 348–350.

55 Von Bogdandy 2015b, p. 19; Piovesan 2017, pp. 58–60.

56 Von Bogdandy 2015a, p. 113; Góngora-Mera 2017.

57 Compare Sagüés 2010, p. 120; Fuentes Torrijo and Pérez Farías 2018, pp. 130–131. Also, Morales Antoniazzi and Saavedra Alessandri 2017.

58 Inter-American Court of Human Rights, *Almonacid-Arellano v. Chile*, judgement of 26 September 2006, (Preliminary Objections, Merits, Reparations and Costs) (ser. C) No 154.

59 Sagüés 2010, p. 125; Ferrer Mac-Gregor 2015, p. 98; García Ramírez 2017, p. 307.

60 Sagüés 2010, p. 125. According to the *Barrios Altos* decision, a widely cited amnesty law case before the *Almonacid* decision, judges are expected to deprive the laws inconsistent with the American Convention of legal effects. Inter-American Court of Human Rights *Barrios Altos v. Peru*, judgement of 14 March 2001, (Merits) (ser. C) No 75; Inter-American Court of Human Rights *Barrios Altos v. Peru*, judgement of 3 September 2001, (Interpretation of the Judgment of the Merits) (ser. C) No 83.

61 Ferrer Mac-Gregor 2015, p. 95; Dulitzky 2015a, p. 102.

62 Compare Sagüés 2010, pp. 121–122; Ferrer Mac-Gregor 2015, p. 95; Carozza and González 2017, p. 439.

63 See a discussion in García-Huidobro and Guidi 2021, p. 1300.

to enforce the IACtHR's interpretations at the domestic level.[64] A vertical dialogue should happen between the IACtHR and the domestic judiciaries.[65]

With both the block of constitutionality and the control of conventionality doctrines, combined with the tools of Neoconstitutionalism, the ICCLA finds a fertile ground to claim that there is, in fact, important common norms in Latin America—or a powerful potential to find those common norms—and to argue that the jurisprudence of the IACtHR is, and should be, at the core of that endeavour. Some scholars have gone beyond this and even argued—without necessarily endorsing—that the IACtHR has become a regional constitutional court.[66]

9.3 The Objections against the ICCLA

9.3.1 How Do Democratic Approaches to Constitutionalism Impact the ICCLA Project?

The ICCLA is a type of liberal constitutionalism project because it recognizes some of the core aspects of liberalism: judicial review, a bill of rights, constrained governments, separation of powers, and a rejection of extremely centralized political power, to name a few. The main twist that it adds is its regional approach and the human rights emphasis. As Tushnet has argued, whether liberal constitutionalism is superior will largely depend on our normative views regarding the available alternatives.[67] The ICCLA can be associated with "judicial constitutionalism" or "legal constitutionalism", which by no means have unanimous support in the region. As Alberto Coddou has shown, other types of constitutionalism schools of thought in the region undermine the feasibility of finding the "common" norms that the ICCLA promotes.[68] Underlying these conceptions, there is the controversy on how democracy should be conceived, and the same liberal ideas risk overlooking critical communitarian and indigenous perspectives that can resist the individualistic and rights-oriented nature of the ICCLA.[69]

The debate about different approaches to democracy can explain why scholars like Roberto Gargarella and Ana Micaela Alterio have challenged the ICCLA based on alternative conceptions of democratic theory. While Gargarella has largely emphasized a procedural approach that can fit with his idea of a "conversation among

[64] See, e.g., García Ramírez 2017, pp. 319–320.

[65] Ferrer Mac-Gregor 2015, p. 99.

[66] See, e.g., Dulitzky 2015b; Contesse 2022, pp. 315–316.

[67] Tushnet 2016.

[68] Coddou Mc Manus 2021.

[69] On how the ICCLA may produce tensions in this regard, see Alterio 2018, pp. 6–7; Alterio and Giménez 2018, pp. 119–120. Also, see how the tension between the autonomy of indigenous communities and liberal ideas can occur in Aguilar Riverat 2013.

equals",[70] Alterio promotes a version of constitutionalism that can be more easily associated with views of popular constitutionalism that are highly sceptical of judicial supremacy.[71] In her view, the fact that the ICCLA requires the judicialization of politics is sufficient reason to reject it.[72] Connected to this, the argument goes, the court-centric aspect of the ICCLA is part of a legal type of constitutionalism that neglects the need to embrace the political means that can secure the advancement of genuine social transformations.[73] Thus, it is understandable that scholars like Alterio and Gargarella are also critical of doctrines such as the control of conventionality. Because the ICCLA, in the end, rests in the final and binding authority of the IACtHR, alternative accounts based on the consequential nature of majority rule, political deliberation, and citizens' participation, can be considered incompatible with the ICCLA project. Along with this, other versions of how to organize a constitutional democracy, such as weak judicial review,[74] the commonwealth model of review,[75] political constitutionalism,[76] the evolutionary type of constitutionalism that Signe Larsen identifies in northern Europe,[77] popular constitutionalism,[78] or a procedural approach to constitutionalism connected to Ely-type of ideas,[79] can be inconsistent with the ICCLA.

Proponents of the ICCLA can respond to these criticisms using a pragmatic argument. They can claim, for example, that political constitutionalism is ideal but, as Waldron has recognized in his criticism against judicial review, challenging the power of constitutional review based on the idea of judicial supremacy requires a context of sufficient respect for rights and a well-functioning democratic regime.[80] Proponents of the ICCLA can claim that, if these conditions are not met[81]—as in some countries in Latin America—, then we should embrace the ICCLA until those conditions exist. In other words, because Latin America is a region that contains many flawed democracies, vulnerable institutions, and fragile political regimes, with political cultures that are not completely democratic—the argument goes—the ICCLA can offer a temporary path to get there.[82] This was a strong argument in the context of the region's authoritarian and post-authoritarian fragile regimes. Nevertheless,

[70] Gargarella 2021; Gargarella 2022b.

[71] Alterio 2018.

[72] Ibid., 4.

[73] Alterio and Giménez 2018, pp. 118–119. See a defence of the court-centric approach in Herrera 2021, pp. 1407–1409.

[74] Tushnet 2008; Tushnet 2011.

[75] Gardbaum 2013; Gardbaum 2011; Choudhry 2013.

[76] Bellamy 2008; Bellamy 2011.

[77] Larsen 2021, pp. 488–494.

[78] Kramer 2004; Post and Siegel 2004; Tushnet 2006. For a Latin American approach, see Alterio and Niembro Ortega 2013.

[79] Gardbaum 2020. See a discussion on Latin America in Verdugo 2021.

[80] Waldron 2006.

[81] See, e.g., Soley 2017, p. 349.

[82] See also González Bertomeu 2011; Roa 2019.

following the same logic, the better the democratic conditions of the specific countries are, the weaker the need for an ICCLA project becomes. This assumes that we accept the conditions that Waldron has identified, even though those conditions may appear rare from a global perspective.

However, this type of defence of the ICCLA project appears to overestimate the similarities among Latin American countries. Why do we need a common regional project if some countries are more democratic than others? The claim also underestimates the problems in other parts of the world by assuming that political constitutionalism is justified in jurisdictions like the UK despite flawed political processes[83] and critical human rights issues.[84]

9.3.2 *The Shortcoming of the Inter-American Judicial Dialogue*

Some ICCLA scholars have advocated for a type of regional judicial dialogue that can boost a conversation among domestic and regional judges,[85] and claimed that such a dialogue exists both *vertically* and *horizontally*.[86] By a vertical dialogue, they mean a jurisprudence from local judges that cite or follow the IACtHR. By a horizontal dialogue, they refer to cases in which the IACtHR uses domestic case law to justify its rulings. In order to argue that judicial dialogue helps legitimize the ICCLA project, the ICCLA proponents find it helpful to cite examples from the IACtHR judicial decisions and procedures to show how the inter-American human rights regime can support the dialogic narrative. They have highlighted that the IACtHR has held its sessions in different parts of Latin America,[87] organized conferences, cited decisions of domestic judges, and some domestic courts also cite the rulings of the IACtHR.[88]

Nevertheless, the above observations have limited normative appeal for the following reasons:

First, the dialogue, even if it exists, only operates at the level of non-elected and non-accountable institutions—elected judges are rare, but they do exist, as in Bolivia, but their democratic nature is contested.[89] Even though some scholars have claimed that courts themselves can develop democratic and participatory instances in their procedures, as Jorge Roa has claimed in the case of Colombia,[90] the participatory mechanisms associated with courts have a strong selection bias and do not resemble

[83] See, e.g., the criticisms against the Brexit referendum in Weale 2018.

[84] See, e.g., Ronald Dworkin's outdated but still helpful argument for a bill of rights in Britain in Dworkin 1990.

[85] See, e.g., García Ramírez 2017, 313–314.

[86] See an important example in the work of Ferrer Mac-Gregor 2017, pp. 322–327.

[87] Von Bogdandy 2015b, p. 31.

[88] Maués et al. 2021.

[89] See a discussion in Driscoll and Nelson 2012; Driscoll and Nelson 2015; Verdugo 2019.

[90] Roa Roa 2020.

a genuine exercise of equal political rights. Also, the potential of those types of instances has to be genuinely inclusive and achieve measurable results, which is a challenging and perhaps an unfeasible task. Even in Colombia, effective judicial responses to social rights demands cannot replace a responsive political process. The issue is not only about how the dialogue works but the fact that the dialogue is not grounded in respectful attitudes to democratic processes.[91] The idea of dialogue cannot be supported by a democratic justification based on elections and majority rule. There is a way in which the democratic justification can be attached to epistemic and deliberative virtues that judges can provide, but this is a more limited way to justify it.

Second, the idea of dialogue assumes a horizontal type of conversation in which judges from all over the region contribute to discovering the best possible interpretations of human rights issues and promoting convergence in a bottom-up way. This might be particularly valuable when assuming that several judicial authorities can interpret the same human rights instruments and those rights have contested meanings.[92] The role of the IACtHR would be to recognize the best practices, give deference to local judges in some cases, and decide that the jurisprudence that was born at the domestic level can sometimes prevail over regional approaches, even to the point of overruling previous IACtHR case-law.[93] Every judicial actor should then be available to study each other's case law and try to persuade each other in principled and non-cynical ways. The problem with this idealized approach to judicial dialogue is that it is untrue,[94] and unfeasible if one is to take seriously the core elements of the ICCLA project. The current dialogue s not horizontal and bottom-up but vertical and top-down.[95] True, the IACtHR cites some decisions taken at the domestic level, but it does so in selective and non-principled ways,[96] often to confirm or give additional reasons to support the interpretations of the IACtHR[97] or to educate the region on the views that the IACtHR considers appropriate. The judicial decisions of local judges have not produced a significant impact on the IACtHR's doctrines.[98]

The control of conventionality doctrine has helped the IACtHR to build a narrative in which judicial supremacy is centralized at the level of the IACtHR, and if all domestic judges are also inter-American judges, it is only because they must follow the IACtHR's interpretations. The ICCLA proponents may reply by suggesting that they are not advocating for the type of dialogue that we can see in the IACtHR today but for a more idealized and horizontal version—although I am not aware of ICCLA proponents that have criticized the IACtHR's rulings on these grounds. It should come as no surprise because the version of the control of conventionality that they

[91] Gargarella 2015, p. 119.

[92] See Celis Vela 2023.

[93] Compare Dulitzky 2015a; Contesse 2017b; Carozza and González 2017.

[94] Compare Herrera 2021, pp. 1412–1413; Coddou Mc Manus 2021, p. 8.

[95] Rodiles 2018.

[96] Dulitzky 2015a, p. 103.

[97] See Dulitzky 2015b.

[98] See a helpful discussion of the evidence in Gonzalez-Ocantos and Sandholtz 2021.

typically defend is in direct tension with horizontal forms of dialogue. It is more likely that it led to a monologue.

Third, the judicial dialogue argument is less persuasive when the IACtHR shows less deference to political processes that have met important democratic qualities. The lack of criticisms from ICCLA advocates against these types of decisions and the fact that those decisions appear relevant for identifying the human rights convergence that the ICCLA proponents promote makes the objections against the IACtHR's case law relevant to the ICCLA project. The example of the IACtHR decision in the *Gelman* case has boosted these types of criticisms. In *Gelman*, the IACtHR found that Uruguay had violated human rights during the dictatorship and declared that the amnesty law preventing the prosecution of those crimes violated binding human rights instruments.[99] Even though this decision appeared consistent with the IACtHR's jurisprudence on amnesty laws, the case of Uruguay could have been considered different because of the democratic legitimacy of the amnesty law in that country. Indeed, and following Roberto Gargarella's argument, the court treated the Uruguayan case as if it had no differences with other amnesty laws in the region, including self-amnesty laws that lacked citizens' approval.[100] The issue is that the amnesty law in Uruguay was enacted "within the context of full civil and political liberty (…)" and after two popular votes accepting it, an issue that the IACtHR itself explicitly recognized and dismissed.[101] The IACtHR treated the democratic processes as merely "formal matters that have little to do with the substantive validity of a law".[102]

Again, ICCLA proponents may respond that they don't need to agree with the IACtHR in this case and can promote an alternative approach that is more respectful of democratic processes. Nevertheless, some ICCLA proponents have used the *Gelman* case as evidence of a regional human rights convergence in the cases of amnesty laws,[103] to show how the IACtHR can remove obstacles to "memory and action",[104] or even to show that a type of judicial dialogue has been possible due to the interaction between the rulings of the IACtHR and the decisions of the Uruguayan Supreme Court.[105] Thus, instead of incorporating the criticisms and modifying or accommodating their approaches, ICCLA proponents have strengthened their distrust of democratic processes and advocated for a court-centric perspective that prefers to advance a progressive and substantive approach to rights rather than discussing procedural approaches following an Ely-type of discussion.

---

[99] Inter-American Court of Human Rights *Gelman v. Uruguay*, judgement of 24 February 2011, (Merits and Reparations) (ser. C) No 221.

[100] See, e.g., Gargarella 2015.

[101] Ibid., 117.

[102] Ibid.

[103] Ferrer Mac-Gregor 2014; von Bogdandy 2017, pp. 33, 46; Morales Antoniazzi and Saavedra Alessandri 2017, p. 266.

[104] García Ramírez 2017, p. 310.

[105] Parra Vera 2017, pp. 370–372.

9.3.3 On Constitutional Pluralism and the Margin of Appreciation

The IACtHR does not embrace a doctrine of margin of appreciation as its European counterpart does,[106] despite the fact that some ICCLA proponents recognize that a standard of deference could be valuable.[107] To be sure, some scholars have identified specific cases in which the IACtHR defers to the interpretations given by local authorities.[108] Still, those cases are exceptional, or they only confirm the previous views that the IACtHR has defended—which are rarely criticized by ICCLA proponents. If a margin of appreciation doctrine exists, it is limited and controversial.[109] This issue has raised essential debates in the region. Scholars have invited the IACtHR to follow a version of the margin of appreciation doctrine elaborated by the European Court of Human Rights[110] or ground it in a version of the principle of subsidiarity[111] without much success.

Typically, advocates of a strong IACtHR claim that the situation in Latin America differs from that of the Council of Europe. The IACtHR became important due to its jurisprudence in addressing human rights violations committed during brutal dictatorships. Thus, it has offered many decisions dealing with extreme situations in which a strong judicial approach was required. That way, for example, the IACtHR was able to build a robust jurisprudence engaging with amnesty laws and human rights reparations. The problem is that the IACtHR could have developed a more democratic jurisprudence even in some of those cases—such as in the *Gelman* case cited above—and the IACtHR did not abandon those strong approaches when dealing with other types of questions, especially because Latin America has abandoned the phase of dictatorships,[112] at least to a certain extent.

Of course, important exceptions or new forms of authoritarianism exist, even if they differ from the dictatorships that prevailed in the 1970s and 1980s. Human rights abuses in places like El Salvador and Venezuela—even if Venezuela had denounced the Convention—appear to be growing in scale. Nevertheless, a number of countries in the region rank well in democratic quality indicators, even more than countries belonging to the Council of Europe,[113] which frequently celebrate competitive elections with sufficiently impartial electoral processes. The IACtHR is busy engaging with more classical human rights disputes, such as reproductive rights. Whether there is a clear trend or emerging consensus in Latin America about these issues remains

---

106 Burgorgue-Larsen 2017, pp. 406–407; Follesdal 2017, p. 362.

107 Herrera 2021, p. 1409.

108 Contreras 2014; Contreras 2012.

109 See Morales Antoniazzi and Saavedra Alessandri 2017, p. 261.

110 Follesdal 2017.

111 Bertelsen 2021.

112 Alterio 2018, p. 12.

113 Follesdal 2017, p. 369.

unclear. The rotation in power between right-wing and left-wing presidents in countries like Colombia, Brazil, Argentina, Ecuador, Perú, and Chile suggests that, at least at the political level, a clear trend may be difficult to identify in many issues. Nevertheless, even in that context, the IACtHR has not abandoned its strong approach to deciding cases, and the ICCLA proponents have not advanced a theory on how the decisions of the IACtHR should impact diverse jurisdictions differently. The IACtHR typically offers vertical interpretations or selects the domestic jurisprudence that it considers appropriate to ground a top-down approach to interpreting human rights. The existence of a sort of living instrument doctrine (to use the European term), which understands human rights in a dynamic and evolving way, even at the cost of abandoning literal approaches to the text, has boosted additional criticisms and resistance, not only from authoritarian agendas but also from mainstream conservative agendas that are popular enough sometimes to win elections. None of those approaches seem to fit on the agenda of the ICCLA.

The case of women's reproductive rights is a good example. Even though Article 4.1 of the American Convention on Human Rights does not settle the question of when the life of the human individual starts to be protected, its language was carefully written to try to make the American Convention consistent with countries and governments that largely disagreed.[114] Many politically relevant conservative approaches that existed at the time of the Convention's ratification remain popular in some settings. Nevertheless, instead of articulating a doctrine trying to balance the issues at stake, in *Artavia-Murillo v. Costa Rica,* the IACtHR offered a progressive approach that appears incompatible with significant pro-life views that are prevailing in some countries in the region[115] and that has operated following a "top-down attitude in its relationship with the states party to the ACHR".[116] Although Costa Rica argued that there was no regional consensus on the matter in that case, the IACtHR still decided to address the case with "the same requirement of an actual proportionality test"[117] using an "evolutionary interpretation" of the Convention.[118] Of course, this does not say whether the IACtHR had the wrong or the correct interpretation of Article 4 in a context where opposing interpretations were plausible.[119] The point is helpful because it illustrates how the IACtHR uses a strong approach that advances the type of legal constitutionalism idea that ICCLA scholars promote and advances a progressive agenda that is attractive to them. They could respond by suggesting that the issue of reproductive rights of women should not be subject to contingent majorities that are unlikely to protect them and claim that judicial activism is justified in such cases. The point is that these types of defences can only be grounded in

---

[114] See a discussion, from a conservative perspective, in Paúl 2012.

[115] Inter-American Court of Human Rights *Artavia Murillo et al (in vitro fertilization) v. Costa Rica*, judgement of 28 November 2012, (Preliminary Objections, Merits, Reparations and Costs) (ser. C) No 257.

[116] Carozza and González 2017, p. 441.

[117] Follesdal 2017, p. 369.

[118] Piovesan 2017, p. 61.

[119] Compare opposite approaches in Paúl Díaz 2013; Brena Sesma 2014.

philosophical approaches about the role of courts that have been broadly questioned in the literature.

The problem might deepen if the control of conventionality doctrine—which ICCLA proponents typically cite and defend—is taken seriously. In that case, and despite controversial interpretations suggesting that decisions of the IACtHR cannot be imposed on states that were not a party to the processes, the IACtHR's role as the final interpreter of the American Convention should lead us to conclude that the interpretation must be imposed to all domestic judges and local politicians of the inter-American system, even in those states where pro-life or relatively moderate majorities have prevailed politically after inclusive, deliberative, and democratic processes have taken place.

A good example is the case of Chile, a historically conservative country that recently, thanks to former President Bachelet, could pass a law to allow abortion only in specific and exceptional circumstances. From a pro-choice perspective, the Chilean abortion law is still too conservative. But for Chile, it was a remarkable victory for the rights of women, as it responded to changing perceptions on reproductive rights, a political process that was responsive to those perceptions, and democratically elected politicians that discussed it extensively and could advance their views even in the context of a Constitutional Court that not many years before had declared the unconstitutionality of the morning-after pill.[120] That same Constitutional Court accepted the bill's constitutionality after extensive and inclusive hearings that involved presenting and contrasting arguments from all sides.[121] The Chilean process leading to the approval of the limited and moderate abortion bill was democratically and deliberatively rich, representing the median voter, and done after years of public debate—even to the point that today, conservative politicians reject the possibility of striking it down.[122] Nevertheless, suppose one takes the conventionality control doctrine seriously. In that case, the democratic qualities that can serve to support and justify the abortion law in Chile should be meaningless or of little weight. Arguably, the bill may be interpreted against the IACtHR's reading of Article 4 in the *Artavia Murillo*'s case. The case was about an IVF ban, but the reasoning was arguably broader. According to a wide reading of the judgment, the reasoning may appear incompatible with domestic legislation restricting women's private life and their autonomy to make decisions regarding their sexual and reproductive health. If this interpretation is accurate—an issue that can be contested, to be sure—constitutional judges in Chile may, in principle, be obliged to invalidate Bachelet's law for still forbidding abortion in the more general cases and protecting the unborn if no specific cause is invoked. And not only judges are obliged to do this, but also legislators should be obliged to repeal the abortion statute. Domestic judges have not yet challenged the abortion bill, and no cases have arrived at the Commission nor to the IACtHR asking to revise Bachelet's law. Perhaps pro-choice activists following the type of strategic litigation that the ICCLA project promotes are aware that trying

[120] Muñoz León 2014.

[121] Constitutional Court of Chile Decision No 3729, 28 August 2017.

[122] On the politics of the approval process of the bill, see Escoffier and Vivaldi 2023.

to repeal Bachelet's law may trigger a backlash and prefer not to intervene. If that is the case, they may be doomed to live with the paradox of defending the control of conventionality control doctrine while tolerating the existence of approaches inconsistent with the IACtHR's jurisprudence. Perhaps it is only a matter of time before another IACtHR case is triggered.

Another example is the issue of same-sex marriage, where the IACtHR released an advisory opinion claiming that all states should recognize same-sex marriage[123]—a stronger approach than the one taken by the European Court of Human Rights in the *Fedotova* case, which only requires the possibility of legal recognition for same-sex couples.[124] In the IACtHR case, Judge Eduardo Vio released a dissenting opinion, complaining that the IACtHR recognized but found it irrelevant that only 6 out of the 23 states had approved same-sex marriage,[125] even though some states have later stated that they have implemented the advisory opinion.[126] If the *Fedotova* case triggers legitimacy concerns for the European Court of Human Rights in the context of an emerging consensus and a weaker standard of protection,[127] one can only imagine the legitimacy concerns that can challenge the IACtHR in the same-sex marriage case.

The IACtHR is then living in a context of constitutional pluralism inconsistent with the ICCLA narrative of seeking (or being close to achieving) consensus. As ICCLA proponents must say that they reject constitutional pluralism—or limit their claims to defend a weak version of constitutional pluralism—the ICCLA can end up harming the "very notion of international law". The search for any state's consent has been frequently neglected while the IACtHR has developed the control of conventionality doctrine to achieve "regional homogeneity",[128] a fact that has been recognized even by the ICCLA advocates.[129]

9.3.4 An Inevitable Pluralism?

Even if the IACtHR intervened in many cases to try to settle a regional standard, countries that can accept the existence of a common standard, in theory, could still implement it in different ways. Defenders of the ICCLA could argue that examples of

---

123 Inter-American Court of Human Rights *Gender Identity, Equality, and Non-Discrimination of Same-Sex Couples*, Advisory Opinion 24/17 of 9 January 2018 (ser A).

124 European Court of Human Rights *Fedotova and others v. Russia*, judgement of 17 January 2023 (Merits and Just Satisfaction), European Court of Human Rights, 40792/10, 30538/14, 43439/14; Inter-American Court of Human Right *Almonacid-Arellano v. Chile*, judgement of 26 September 2006, (Preliminary Objections, Merits, Reparations and Costs) (ser. C) No 154.

125 Contesse 2021, pp. 1256.

126 Contesse 2024.

127 Palazzo 2023.

128 Rodiles 2018. These arguments partly follow Frishman and Benvenisti 2016.

129 See, e.g., Sagüés 2010, p. 119.

how regional standards can be applied in diverse ways across the region do not undermine the existence of such a standard. Nevertheless, sometimes the question is not about diverse possibilities of implementation, but about whether those possibilities exist in the first place. As often happens with social rights enforcement, sometimes domestic regulations are necessary, but implausible. Inter-American and domestic judges may lack the tools and the authority (sometimes with good reasons) to enforce those standards, even in ways that try to adapt them to local jurisdictions.

A good example is *Baena Ricardo*, a case cited by ICCLA proponents to illustrate social rights protection[130] or compliance with the IACtHR's rulings in cooperative but authoritative ways.[131] The example is appropriate—and not the cherry-picking of a negative case—precisely because it is a case positively used by some ICCLA proponents. In *Baena Ricardo*, Panama's legislative assembly had enacted a statute to remove many public employees after those employees had protested against the government and were suspected of having participated in a failed coup attempt while giving the executive branch the power to determine the types of antidemocratic actions that warranted that punishment. The IACtHR established that the statute had violated the principles of legality and due process and established an inter-American standard relevant to labour law and administrative law: removing a public employee as a form of punishment is valid as long as the process follows a rule-of-law standard, and that the employee is given due process and appropriate guarantees.[132] In short, the power to remove officers as a sanction was severely limited.

Many years after this decision was released, it is possible to identify different ways to understand and implement this inter-American obligation. In their research on Mexico, Chile, and Argentina, Luis Eugenio-García Huidobro and Sebastián Guidi have shown that, after twenty years, the *Baena Ricardo* standard has failed and that the transformative goals of the ruling were largely undermined by the existence of diverse domestic institutional responses that either ignored the standard, or that applied it in contested ways.[133] The problems were not necessarily the judges, as these cases require administrative and legislative regulations that judges are unlikely to successfully push for. In Argentina, the problem was associated with the lack of a serious attempt to enact and implement regulations.[134] In Chile, the Supreme Court resisted the *Baena Ricardo* standard, Chilean public employees remain subject to a precarious labour regime, and legislators have not implemented it.[135] In Mexico, public employees remain particularly vulnerable regarding the populist policies of its current President.[136]

---

[130] Piovesan 2017, p. 60.

[131] Burgorgue-Larsen 2017, p. 396.

[132] Inter-American Court of Human Rights *Baena Ricardo et al v. Panamá*, judgement of 2 February 2001 (Merits, Reparations and Costs) (ser. C) No. 72.

[133] García-Huidobro and Guidi 2021.

[134] Ibid., p. 1308.

[135] Ibid., pp. 1310–1312.

[136] Ibid., pp. 1314–1315.

Even if some domestic judges in those countries may try to enforce something like the *Baena Ricardo* standard, the lack of appropriate regulations makes it hard—if not impossible—for the ICCLA project to succeed in this subject matter. This is no minor issue for the ICCLA, as the rights of employees and other social rights are at the core of the egalitarian demands that motivated its existence in the first place. ICCLA proponents may respond by suggesting stronger ways in which judges can intervene and point out the gradual nature of the political project involving the ICCLA. Nevertheless, suppose those responses are to be taken seriously. In that case, the democratic cost of judicial power will elevate considerably, making the ICCLA project more vulnerable to the criticisms I identified in previous sections.

Instead, advocates of the ICCLA may concede the point but argue that the *Baena Ricardo* case is an exception. Thus, they could say that a negative example such as *Baena Ricardo* does not falsify their hypothesis. Methodologically, this criticism might be correct. Nevertheless, as it will be clearer from the sections below, the number of social rights cases in the jurisprudence of the IACtHR is too small, their content too contested, and the decisions too recent to provide a more comprehensive picture of social rights enforcement in the region. This is a methodological problem for both the ICCLA advocates and their critics. In this context, discussing landmark cases like *Baena Ricardo* is valuable for understanding the ICCLA project and its current prospects.

9.4 Towards a Non-IACtHR-centred Idea of Constitutionalism?

Responding to the objections explained in the section above, the ICCLA proponents could claim that their project is not about the current existence of common standards but of the *potential* for those standards to exist[137]—even if, after twenty years, there is no prospect for that potential to be realized—as in the case of *Baena Ricardo*. The idea, the argument goes, is to use that potential via strategic litigation and the judicialization of politics. Still, cases like *Baena Ricardo*—where the strategic litigation happened, and the reforms got judicialized—show that those approaches are insufficient. The ICCLA seems to be aiming at the wrong target. The formal openness of a domestic constitutional regime may even become irrelevant, partly because the focus on rights has neglected the institutional questions necessary to advance policies capable of making political reforms at the domestic level. Any idea of constitutionalism that aims to advance relevant social reforms should not give a central role to the IACtHR, as the IACtHR has limited tools to incentivize and enforce such reforms. A focus outside the IACtHR becomes necessary.

Here, the proponents of the ICCLA face a difficult conundrum. If they accept the challenge and decide that the ICCLA should also involve a sort of policy-based approach offering institutional responses at the local level with common standards,

---

[137] See note 9.

the IACtHR and other regional organs might become too powerful, and the democratic objection against the ICCLA will only grow. The growing strength of a democratic objection can make it difficult for democratic and liberal intellectuals and judges to continue to endorse the ICCLA idea, at least explicitly. On the contrary, if the ICCLA proponents decide not to engage in that debate, they will face difficult questions about the feasibility of their normative project. We should then wonder whether the ICCLA and the IACtHR could be better off just by moderating their views, developing a nuanced doctrine of margin of appreciation, and becoming more respectful of democratic processes taking place at the local level. Nevertheless, if they decide to take this path, they will need to recognize the limited possibilities of the ICCLA and leave space for the development of rival approaches to the type of (legal) constitutionalism they have been advocating for.

As I will show in the next subsections, the ICCLA problems do not end here. By avoiding entering into institutional questions like those of *Baena Ricardo* and *Gelman*, the ICCLA also threatens to defeat its egalitarian purposes by preventing the existence of competing views of constitutionalism that can give a more effective response to those egalitarian promises.

9.4.1 How Can the ICCLA Undermine Its Own Goals?

The ICCLA proponents claim to care about the region's domestic institutional frameworks, have explicitly rejected authoritarian institutional arrangements and hyper-presidential regimes, claim that policies must accompany judicial actions, and advocate for independent institutions and separation of powers. For example, one of their most influential scholars illustrates these points by emphasizing the importance of independent electoral institutions and courts.[138] The IACtHR has also engaged with helpful institutional questions, although rarely, such as the advisory opinion in which the IACtHR established the regional standards for regulating presidential term limits.[139] Even though the ICCLA proponents can celebrate these types of decisions and claim that their views are now incorporated into the canon of the *ius commune*[140]—and we can undoubtedly celebrate its pertinence due to President Bukele's agenda in circumventing the constitutional rules of El Salvador to be re-elected[141]—it is important to stress that these institutional questions rarely address how the political process can be more responsive to the protection of social rights. Most of the IACtHR's jurisprudence, and most of the work of the ICCLA proponents, focus on substantive discussions about rights.

---

[138] Von Bogdandy 2015b, p. 22; von Bogdandy 2015a, p. 112.

[139] Inter-American Court of Human Rights *Presidential Reelection without Term Limits in the Context of the Inter-American Human Rights System* Advisory Opinion OC-28/21 of 7 June 2021.

[140] See, e.g., Binder and Morales Antoniazzi 2021.

[141] The Economist 2023.

Questions about reparations for human rights violations, amnesty laws, freedom of speech cases, women's rights, indigenous peoples' rights, and the like, tend to dominate the contemporary agenda of the IACtHR. This is not surprising, as the ICCLA and the IACtHR have developed court-centric constitutional ideas based on substantive human rights issues, and those ideas tend to prevail over procedural aspects of democracy, as illustrated by the *Gelman* case cited above. In that case, the IACtHR cared little about the existence of deep deliberation and the occurrence of electoral processes taking place in democratic and competitive conditions, allowing free voters to decide to uphold the amnesty regulation in Uruguay. Unlike the amnesty case, say, in Peru, which was self-imposed after a coup in non-democratic conditions, the case of Uruguay took place in a functioning democracy where all relevant considerations were subject to serious deliberation and debate. But for the IACtHR—and the ICCLA proponents citing that decision—the Uruguayan amnesty was no different from the Peruvian amnesty. That is one way in which an exclusive focus on substantive human rights issues can undermine the possibilities of identifying structural problems in political regimes. But there are other ways in which this can happen.

I will show two examples that illustrate how leading ICCLA proponents have developed claims that distract from the question of how to elevate the democratic standards of the countries they engage with. This approach neglects more consequential questions regarding how to effectively advance the types of social reforms that will meet the egalitarian goals the ICCLA project aims to pursue. It might also lead to the suggestion of counterproductive solutions.

These cases involve social rights demands. Sure, one could claim that the American Convention on Human Rights provides weak protection for social rights in the first place, and securing social rights protections would be too much to ask. Even though I find that point persuasive, that has not stopped ICCLA advocates from promoting their protection and even valuing the gradual case law of the IACtHR on the matter.[142]

9.4.2 Cherry-Picking Examples from Non-Democratic Constitutional Projects

An influential ICCLA proponent used the constitutions of Ecuador and Bolivia as examples of how the constitutional frameworks of both countries have opened themselves to give the regional human rights framework a special place in their legal systems,[143] even though both constitutions were the product of the Latin American New Constitutionalism that the ICCLA is supposed to reject. The ICCLA is against plebiscitary presidentialism and arguably also against hyper-presidentialism.[144] It

[142] See, e.g., Piovesan 2017, pp. 58–60.

[143] Von Bogdandy 2015b, pp. 28–29; von Bogdandy 2017, p. 41. The author does not do the same in a later work. See von Bogdandy et al. 2017a, b, pp. 18–20.

[144] Compare von Bogdandy 2015b, p. 20; Valadés 2017.

is also against mechanisms that undermine the independence of the judiciary and other fourth-branch institutions.[145] Still, the Ecuadorian and the Bolivian constitutions have been enacted as part of political projects that have aimed to establish a dominant party regime,[146] and the rights agendas associated with their projects have tried to legitimize those undemocratic political projects. In the case of Ecuador, the recognition of rights was the result of a political "bribe" that the Rafael Correa administration was seeking in exchange for the political entrenchment of his supporting coalition.[147] The purpose was to legitimize the regime's populist plans, including nullifying the opposition. Correa had previously established a constituent assembly and controlled the Constitutional Court to make sure to shut down the Congress.[148] How can the Constitution of Ecuador be a good example? Cherry-picking on the norms that advance part of the goals of the ICCLA (the norms that embrace the regional human rights framework) comes at a high cost because it assumes that the openness of the Ecuadorian Constitution was helpful for the liberal project that the ICCLA was advancing when, in fact, it was functional to achieving a problematic outcome. Instead of discussing whether the Constitution established independent institutions, accountable representatives, and responsive political processes, the focus was on rights protections.

In the case of Bolivia, the Constitution was enacted in a violent and complicated constitution-making process that aimed at perpetuating President Evo Morales's political project after the existing constitutional court was dismantled.[149] The new constitutional court had a problematic composition driven by an electoral system incapable of securing its independence,[150] and the human rights narrative helped remove Morales's term limits.[151] The Bolivian Constitutional Court embraced the human rights framework and offered a dubious interpretation of the American Convention of Human Rights—this decision came before the IACtHR's advisory opinion on this matter—to not only remove the term limits but also to justify the rejection of the decision made by Bolivian voters—a majority of Bolivian voters had decided in a referendum that Evo Morales could not pass an amendment to remove the term limits. As in the case of Ecuador, cherry-picking the norms of the Bolivian Constitution that serve the agenda of the ICCLA risks overlooking and an agenda of democratic erosion that other parts of the ICCLA's ideas are supposed to reject. By neglecting this and focusing exclusively on the human rights dimension, the ICCLA ends up—perhaps contrary to its own purposes–prioritizing the rights agenda over the democratic and institutional concerns. That way, it appears that the ICCLA does not escape Gargarella's well-known criticism claiming that constitutionalism in Latin America has focused mainly on rights issues while neglecting what

[145] Von Bogdandy 2015b, p. 22.

[146] See Conaghan 2011; Conaghan 2016; Mendoza-Botelho 2016; Wolff 2012; Landau 2013b.

[147] Dixon 2018.

[148] Venegas Maingón and Hernández Muñoz 2019.

[149] See Castagnola and Pérez-Liñán 2011; Verdugo 2019.

[150] Driscoll and Nelson 2012; Driscoll and Nelson 2015.

[151] Verdugo 2019; Landau and Dixon 2020.

he calls the "engine room" of constitutionalism,[152] which can also be problematic regarding the inter-American human rights system.[153]

9.4.3 *How Does a Human rights-centric Approach Neglect the (Real) Protection of Rights?*

Another example focuses on the failed Chilean constitution-making process of 2022. A recent editorial uses the failed constitutional proposal as an example of a progressive project that was generous in rights, particularly social rights. The editorial argued that the proposal was "built on the conviction that deep inequality is one, perhaps even the main, cause for many Latin American ills. This conviction is categorically manifest in the Proposal. It places great emphasis on substantive equality (…)" and aims at aligning "Chile with the Latin American transformative constitutionalism (…)".[154] By making this argument, the editorial did not refer to the fact that the proposal also tried to strengthen the presidential regime (which the ICCAL seems to dislike), and did not mention that the constitution-making process was an attempt that politicians tried to pursue partly to circumvent the need to respond to the popular demands claiming for social reforms. Instead of compromising on the social reforms Chileans demanded, politicians opened a constitution-making process to recognize social rights and kick the problem to future legislators. That is why some commentators have used the Chilean case as an example of "social rights scapegoating",[155] while others have argued that the Chilean Constitutional Convention was an example of "utopian constitutionalism".[156] In this context, how can celebrating the Chilean constitutional proposal provide an effective defence of the goals of the ICCAL?

It is possible that proponents of the ICCLA agreed with the proposal due to the context in which the constitution-making process was initiated. The Chilean constitution-making process was possible because of the October 2019 protests, which made social rights demands more visible.[157] The political parties achieved a bipartisan agreement to open the constitutional replacement process. This attempt to institutionally channel social demands while keeping the government in power was intended to avoid the experiences of the New Latin American Constitutionalism processes and ensure that the Pinochet constitutional model could be abandoned.[158] As the ICCLA is both a democratic alternative to the New Latin American Constitutionalism and a rejection of conservative constitutional schools of thought, perhaps the goals were apparently aligned.

---

[152] Gargarella 2013a; Gargarella 2013b.

[153] Gargarella 2017, p. 233.

[154] Von Bogdandy 2023.

[155] Chilton et al. 2023.

[156] Landau and Dixon 2023b; Landau and Dixon 2023a.

[157] On the reasons parties had to open the process, see Escudero 2022.

[158] On the goals of the process, see Verdugo and Prieto 2021.

Nevertheless, at that time, the lack of political responsiveness to social rights demands was more connected to the political process's flaws than the constitutional text's language.[159] The combination of a presidential regime and a multiparty system, short, non-renewable presidential terms, a Congress elected with proportional rule, an electoral timetable that prevents disciplined political alliances beyond the elections, and the lack of incentives for legislative collaboration, are critical problems that explain how the political process hasn't been responsive enough to significant social demands. True, some scholars complained against the language the Constitution uses regarding social rights[160] and the veto power of the Constitutional Court, which, during the second Bachelet administration, put speedbumps on legislative initiatives such as the creation of the consumer protection agency and the educational agenda that Bachelet was promoting.[161] Nevertheless, courts in Chile have long engaged in forms of judicial activism for both the progressive and the conservative sides. The Supreme Court has proven to be particularly helpful for social rights expansions,[162] although with the typical limitations of social rights enforcement. Passing policies that judges cannot provide for, is necessary to advance true solutions. The actual problem was (and is) the design of the political process and the party system.

Unfortunately, the constitutional proposal that the editorial praises was generous regarding social rights but weak regarding the reforms to the institutional framework. Despite the editorial's celebration of an "inclusive constitutional process" that channelled "true popular energy" to the proposal and that had "sterling democratic legitimacy" while also showing that "the Rights Revolution is alive and kicking,"[163] Chileans strongly rejected the proposal. In truth, the Convention's process was controversial due to the assembly's socially inclusive but politically unbalanced composition.[164] It did not matter that the proposal included an extensive list of rights, embraced the regional human rights framework, and advanced a political project that was supported by many left-wing global scholars who were either impressed by the rights catalogue[165] or were enthusiastic about leaving a constitution that was born in a dictatorship.[166] The editorial celebrated the proposal because of its generous social rights recognitions, though it also complained that it did not seem to offer sufficient judicial mechanisms to enforce the rights it tried to recognize. Despite the fact that the proposal lacked a governance model for the country that could secure the establishment of a responsive political process capable of enacting social reforms responsive

---

159 See Dixon and Verdugo 2021.

160 See, e.g., Arenas Catalán 2021.

161 Atria 2013; Atria et al. 2017.

162 See, e.g., Henríquez Viñas 2010; Bassa Mercado and Aste Leiva 2015.

163 Von Bogdandy 2023. Certainly, von Bogdandy is explicitly aware that neglecting the conservative members of the assembly was wrong, but two things need to be said here: First, the problem is larger than neglecting those members. It has to do with how the party system was circumvented. Second, von Bogdandy does not really limit his praise of the proposal after acknowledging that it was not, in the end, as inclusive and accepted as it was claimed to be.

164 Issacharoff and Verdugo 2023.

165 See, e.g., Bhatia 2022; von Bogdandy 2023.

166 See, e.g., Gargarella 2022a.

to social demands with effective political and institutional means—true problems for any political system—the editorial lamented how weak judicial institutions were in the proposal.

The above issue triggers a paradox for ICCLA proponents. If they focus on social rights issues directly, they won't be solving the cause of the problem. But if they focus on the cause of the problem, they won't develop an explicit human rights agenda closer to what the ICCLA promotes. They could also do both. Nevertheless, it is unlikely that they will do that—as the example shows—because the emphasis of the ICCLA is inevitably on human rights and the judicialization of politics. The main problem is that their focus on the rights issues makes ICCLA inattentive to the dimensions of political projects that undermine or overlook the most effective ways to advance social reforms: the reorganization of the political institutions and of the political processes.

9.4.4 The Problems of Social Rights Enforcement

The ICCLA offers an ambitious and gradual path towards a court-centred strategy of social-rights jurisprudence that can be boosted by strategic litigation, following rights revolutions that can use domestic and regional judges in a common enterprise.[167] The previous sections have shown normative reasons to oppose, restrict, or modify this project. I have also shown how the ICCLA proponents have made counterproductive arguments. In this section, I argue that an excessive focus on the judicialization of social rights triggers a legitimacy and accountability problem and establishes an agenda with limited chances of success.

As I showed before with the examples of Ecuador—social rights as "bribes"—and Chile—social rights as "scapegoats" or as "utopia"—success in those aspects can distract from true attempts at responding to social rights demands within countries. Designing a more responsive political system, as Rosalind Dixon has tried to do in her recent work, even appealing to weak types of judicial review mechanisms and strategies,[168] should be the path to follow. Insisting on a version of constitutionalism that emphasizes legal obligations that courts should enforce means missing an important part of the picture. Sure, one could also argue that providing for a regional-based constitutional model would perhaps be more undemocratic than a narrower focus on human rights. However, the success of that type of argument should first answer whether a strong regional constitutionalism approach is necessary or desirable.[169]

Two additional points are relevant to the ICCLA project but have not been addressed sufficiently:

First, the judicial enforcement of social rights is contested from a normative perspective, and the debate also exists at the level of the IACtHR. The interpretation of

---

[167] The idea can be connected with Epp's classic work. See Epp 1998.

[168] Dixon 2017; Dixon 2022.

[169] See a related criticism against the IACtHR in Contesse 2017a.

Article 26 of the Convention remains elusive, unclear, and contested. Jorge Contesse has shown how concurring opinions of IACtHR judges claiming that the court is inappropriately expanding Article 26, are harming the court's authority, and the human rights framework.[170] Also, the new appointments made to the IACtHR and recent cases made the issue of social rights enforcement less predictable.[171] Thus, the legal foundations for the ICCLA project remain weak regarding an important aspect of its egalitarian agenda. If the ICCLA is committed to developing a regional project addressing social rights issues in a strong and court-centred way, it should achieve a sufficient level of consensus regarding Article 26.

Second, and perhaps more importantly, the evidence shows that the effectiveness of social rights is not necessarily connected with judicialization.[172] Arguably, the best case in Latin America for social rights enforcement (Colombia) shows mixed evidence of progress through litigation.[173] The judicialization of those rights can end up producing economically regressive consequences that can benefit the middle and high classes and neglect the lower socioeconomic classes[174]—those that are successful in litigation are those with more influence and better strategies at the judicial level, something that cannot be accounted for marginalized groups. For this reason, some scholars have suggested lowering the entry costs to the judicial system,[175] advancing collective legal claims, and empowering the courts to make them capable of addressing structural problems.[176] For the same reason, it makes sense for ICCLA proponents to encourage forms of strategic litigation. Nevertheless, even if we lack evidence to support these types of proposals for the region (most of the discussion comes from Colombia), these types of solutions might elevate the democratic-based criticisms against the ICCLA and social rights enforcement and create accountability issues that are likely to make the electoral procedures less meaningful, weakening the political rights of the voters in intolerable ways.

The evidence of social rights enforcement is mixed. Still, at least, one should conclude that (1) there is no strong evidence connecting the victories of social rights demands with the legal recognition of those demands; (2) funding, infrastructure, and politically sustainable policies are crucial to advance in social rights protections; (3) judges are poorly suited to provide for that funding, infrastructure, and politically sustainable policies; and (4) judges can perform a helpful but limited role in advancing those policies. Taking all of these considerations into account, one must conclude that achieving social reforms via the judicialization of politics is at least an insufficient

[170] Contesse 2021, pp. 1257–1258. The "winds against" the social rights enforcement agenda have been explored also in Reca Milanta 2024, pp. 38–40.

[171] The IACtHR seems to be taking an "unknown route". Reca Milanta 2024, pp. 41–42.

[172] For example, countries that recognize the right to healthcare and education do not necessarily increase their public spending in those areas. Ben-Bassat and Dahan 2008; Chilton and Versteeg 2016.

[173] Compare Uprimny and Durán 2014; Chilton and Versteeg 2020.

[174] See a discussion of the evidence in Brazil in Hoffman and Bentes 2008; Ferraz 2011; Brinks and Gauri 2014.

[175] See, e.g., Roa Roa 2020.

[176] See, e.g., Landau 2012.

strategy that can distract from the focus of promoting better political processes at the domestic level. Making that strategy the centre of the type of constitutionalism that the ICCLA proposes is then problematic and, in some cases, counterproductive. A constitutionalism that takes seriously the need to advance social reforms must change its main target, even if that implies weakening or replacing the regional approach based on convergence that the IACtHR encourages. Of course, this is not to say that the IACtHR should not play any role at all.

9.5 Conclusions

Even though many different constitutional schools of thought can be identified in Latin America, the ICCLA seems to grow in influence among judges and scholars. It is attractive, after all, because it offers a connection with liberal and democratic principles that present themselves as a reasonable and even moderate compared to the radicalism of, say, the New Latin American Constitutionalism. Nevertheless, the criticisms that the ICCLA has received should be taken seriously. If the ICCLA agenda is pursued, the threat of the judicialization of politics, the harming of ideas rooted in constitutional pluralism, and the rejection of valuable alternative variations of constitutionalism can make the ICCLA normatively weak. I have claimed that the agenda can also distract from the most effective means to advance social reforms and even become counterproductive in some cases. Choosing the judicialization of politics as the main instrument to achieve egalitarian goals may reduce the idea of constitutionalism to its legal and judicial dimension, can generate a democratic accountability problem, and may distract from finding different and targeted solutions in different areas of the region, and provide an argument to politicians as to why they haven't been able to advance on the protection of social rights. In this context, the ICCLA scholars should seriously discuss whether the means they offer are the best way to achieve the noble goals that inspire them.

Acknowledgements I thank Marcela Prieto, Jorge Contesse, James Fowkes, and an anonymous reviewer, for their helpful comments on an earlier version of this chapter.

References

Aguilar Riverat J A (2013) Multiculturalism and Constitutionalism in Latin America. Notre Dame Journal of International & Comparative Law 4:19–44

Aldunate E (2010) Aproximación Conceptual al Neoconstitucionalismo [Conceptual Approach to Neoconstitutionalism]. Revista de Derecho (Valdivia) XXIII (1):79–102

Alterio AM (2018) El Ius Constitutionale Commune Latinoamericanum y los desafíos de la judicialización de la política [The Ius Constitutionale Commune Latinoamericanum and the challenges of the judicialization of politics]. Estudios de Filosofía Práctica e Historia de las Ideas 20:1–21

Alterio AM (2019) La Suprema Corte de Justicia Mexicana en la Transformación Social [The Mexican Supreme Court of Justice in Social Transformation]. In: Niembro R, Verdugo S (eds) La Justicia Constitucional en Tiempos de Cambio. Suprema Corte de Justicia de la Nación
Alterio AM, Giménez FP (2018) Book Review: Transformative Constitutionalism in Latin America: the Emergence of a New Ius Commune. Verfassung in Recht und Übersee 51(1):115–120
Alterio AM, Ortega RN (eds) (2013) Constitucionalismo Popular en Latinoamérica [Popular Constitutionalism in Latin America]. Editorial Porrúa, Mexico
Arenas Catalán E (2021) Chile's New Constitution: What Right to Health? Hague Journal on the Rule of Law 13:295–314
Atria F (2013) La Constitución Tramposa [The Fraudulent Constitution]. LOM, Santiago.
Atria F (2016) La Forma del Derecho [The Form of Law]. Marcial Pons, Santiago
Atria F, Salgado C, Wilenmann J (2017) Constitución y Neutralización. Origen, desarrollo y solución de la crisis constitucional [Constitution and Neutralization. Origin, development and solution of the constitutional crisis]. LOM, Santiago
Barros R (2002) Constitutionalism and Dictatorship: Pinochet, the Junta, and the 1980 Constitution. Cambridge Studies in the Theory of Democracy. Cambridge University Press, New York
Barroso, LR (2016) Reason Without Vote: The Representative and Majoritarian Function of Constitutional Courts. In: Bustamante T, Gonçalves Fernandes B (eds) Democratizing Constitutional Law. Springer International Publishing, Cham/New York, pp 71–90
Bassa Mercado J, Aste Leiva B (2015) Mutación en los Criterios Jurisprudenciales de Protección de los Derechos a la Salud y al Trabajo en Chile [Change in the Jurisprudential Criteria for the Protection of the Rights to Health and Work in Chile]. Revista Chilena de Derecho 42(1):215–244
Bellamy R (2008) The Democratic Constitution: Why Europeans should Avoid American Style Constitutional Judicial Review. European Political Science 7(1):9–20
Bellamy R (2011) Political constitutionalism and the Human Rights Act. International Journal of Constitutional Law 9(1):86–111
Ben-Bassat A, Dahan M (2008) Social rights in the constitution and in practice. Journal of Comparative Economics 36(1):103–119
Bernal C (2013) Unconstitutional constitutional amendments in the case study of Colombia: An analysis of the justification and meaning of the constitutional replacement doctrine. International Journal of Constitutional Law 11(2):339–357
Bertelsen S (2021) A margin for the margin of appreciation: Deference in the Inter-American Court of Human Rights. International Journal of Constitutional Law 19(3):887–913
Bhatia G (2022) Chile marks a notch in global constitutionalism. The Hindu https://www.thehindu.com/opinion/lead/chile-marks-a-notch-in-global-constitutionalism/article65659006.ece
Binder C, Morales Antoniazzi M (2021) Toward Institutional Guarantees for Democratic Rotation. VerfBlog https://verfassungsblog.de/towards-institutional-guarantees-for-democratic-rotation/
Bonilla Maldonado D (2013) Constitutionalism of the Global South: The Activist Tribunals of India, South Africa and Colombia. Cambridge University Press, Cambridge
Brena Sesma I (2014) Interpretación del artículo 4.1 de la Convención Americana sobre la Protección de los Derechos Humanos, sentencia de la Corte Interamericana de Derechos Humanos, caso Artavia Murillo y otros (fecundación in vitro) vs. Costa Rica [Interpretation of Article 4.1 of the American Convention on the Protection of Human Rights, judgment of the Inter-American Court of Human Rights, case Artavia Murillo et al. (in vitro fertilization) vs. Costa Rica]. Cuestiones Constitucionales
Brinks DM, Gauri V (2014) The Law's Majestic Equality? The Distribution Impact of Judicializing Social and Economic Rights. Perspectives on Politics 12(2):375–393
Burgorgue-Larsen L (2017) The Added Values of the Inter-American Human Rights System. Comparative Thoughts. In: Ferrer Mac-Gregor E, Morales Antoniazzi M, Piovesan F, von Bogdandy A (eds) Transformative Constitutionalism in Latin America: The Emergence of a New Ius Commune. Oxford University Press, Oxford

Cardoso JV (2021) Judicialización de medicamentos huérfanos en Brasil: la justiciabilidad de un objeto políticamente "no palatable" [Judicialization of orphan drugs in Brazil: the justiciability of a politically "unpalatable" object]. International Journal of Constitutional Law 19(4):1322–1350
Carozza PG, González P (2017) The final word? Constitutional dialogue and the Inter-American Court of Human Rights: A reply to Jorge Contesse. International Journal of Constitutional Law 15(2):436–442
Castagnola A, Pérez-Liñán A (2011) Bolivia. The Rise (and Fall) of Judicial Review. In: Helmke G, Ríos-Figueroa J (eds) Courts in Latin America. Cambridge University Press, New York, pp 278–305
Celis Vela DA (2023) El Control de Conventionalidad y la Concurrencia de Intérpretes Autorizados de Disposiciones Constitucionales [Control of Conventionality and the Attendance of Authorized Interpreters of Constitutional Provisions]. International Journal of Constitutional Law 21(5): 1332–1359
Chilton A, Eyzaguirre C, Versteeg M (2023) Social Rights Scapegoating. Global Constitutionalism 13(1):220–227
Chilton AS, Versteeg M (2016) Rights Without Resources: The Impact on Constitutional Social Rights on Social Spending. University of Chicago Law School Working Papers.
Chilton A, Versteeg M (2020) How Constitutional Rights Matter. Oxford University Press, Oxford
Choudhry S (2013) The Commonwealth constitutional model or models? International Journal of Constitutional Law 11(4):1094–1099
Coddou Mc Manus A (2021) A critical account of Ius Constitutionale Commune in Latin America: An intellectual map of contemporary Latin American constitutionalism. Global Constitutionalism 1–29
Colón-Ríos J (2011) Carl Schmitt and Constituent Power in Latin American Courts: The Cases of Venezuela and Colombia. Constellations 18(3): 365–388
Colón-Ríos J (2014) A New Typology of Judicial Review of Legislation. Global Constitutionalism 3(2): 143–169
Conaghan CM (2011) Ecuador. Rafael Correa and the Citizens' Revolution. In: Levitsky S, Roberts K (eds) The Resurgence of the Latin American Left. The John Hopkins University Press, US, pp 260–282
Conaghan C M (2016) Ecuador Under Correa. Journal of Democracy 27(3):109–118
Contesse J (2017a) The international authority of the Inter-American Court of Human Rights: a critique of the conventionality control doctrine. The International Journal of Human Rights 22(9):1168–1191
Contesse J (2017b) The final word? Constitutional dialogue and the Inter-American Court of Human Rights. International Journal of Constitutional Law 15(2):414–435
Contesse J (2019) Resisting Inter-American Human Rights Law. Yale Journal of International Law 44
Contesse J (2021) Autoridad y disenso en la Corte Interamericana de Derechos Humanos [Authority and dissent in the Inter-American Court of Human Rights]. International Journal of Constitutional Law 19(4):1254–1260
Contesse J (2022) Human Rights as Transnational Law. AJIL Unbound 116:313–317
Contesse J (2024) The American Convention on Human Rights in Latin American National Courts. In: Bernal C, Choudhry S, O'Regan K (eds) Research Handbook on Constitutional Interpretation. Edward Elgar Publishing
Contreras P (2012) National Discretion and International Deference in the Restriction of Human Rights: A Comparison Between the Jurisprudence of the European and the Inter-American Court of Human Rights. Northwestern University Journal of International Human Rights 11(1):28–82
Contreras P (2014) Control de Convencionalidad, Deferencia Internacional y Discreción Nacional en la Jurisprudencia de la Corte Interamericana de Derechos Humanos [Conventionality Control, International Deference and National Discretion in the Jurisprudence of the Inter-American Court of Human Rights]. Ius Et Praxis 20(2):235–274
Couso J (2014) Radical Democracy and the "New Latin American Constitutionalism". SELA

de Sousa Santos B (2014) La refundación del Estado en América Latina [The refoundation of the State in Latin America]. Pehuén Editores
Díaz de Valdés J M, Verdugo S (2019) The ALBA constitutional project and political representation. International Journal of Constitutional Law 17(2):479–488
Dixon R (2017) The Core Case for Weak-Form Judicial Review. Cardozo Law Review 38:2193–2232
Dixon R (2018) Constitutional Rights as Bribes. Connecticut Law Review 50 (3):767–818
Dixon R (2022) Responsive Judicial Review. Democracy and Dysfunction in the Modern Age. Oxford University Press
Dixon R, Verdugo S (2021) Los derechos sociales y la reforma constitucional en Chile: hacia una implementación híbrida, legislativa y judicial [Social rights and constitutional reform in Chile: towards a hybrid, legislative and judicial implementation]. Estudios Públicos 162:31–73
Driscoll A, Nelson MJ (2012) The 2011 Judicial Elections in Bolivia. Electoral Studies 31:628–632
Driscoll A, Nelson MJ (2015) Judicial Selection and the Democratization of Justice: Lessons from the Bolivian Judicial Elections. Journal of Law and Courts 3(1):115–148
Dulitzky AE (2015a) An Alternative Approach to the Conventionality Control Doctrine. AJIL Unbound 109:100–108
Dulitzky AE (2015b) An Inter-American Constitutional Court? The Invention of the Conventionality Control by the Inter-American Court of Human Rights. The Texas International Law Journal 50(1):45–93
Dworkin R (1990) A Bill of Rights for Britain. Why Liberty Needs Protecting. Chatto Counter Blasts, London
Epp CR (1998) The Rights Revolution. Lawyers, Activists and Supreme Courts in Comparative Perspective. The University of Chicago Press, Chicago
Escoffier S, Vivaldi L (2023) Why Anti-Abortion Movements Fail: The Case of Chile. In: Payne LA, Zulver J, Escoffier S (eds) The Rights Against Rights in Latin America. Liverpool University Press
Escudero MC (2022) Making a Constituent Assembly in Chile: The Shifting Costs of Opposing Change. Bulletin of Latin American Research 41(4):641–656
Ferraz OLM (2011) Harming the Poor Through Social Rights Litigation: Lessons from Brazil. Texas Law Review 89:1643–1668
Ferrer Mac-Gregor E (2014) Hacia la formación jurisprudencial interamericana de un ius constitutionale commune americanum [Towards the inter-American jurisprudential formation of a ius constitutionale commune americanum]. In: von Bogdandy A, Morales Antoniazzi M, Fix Fierro H (eds) Ius constitutionale commune en América Latina. Rasgos, potencialidades y desafíos [Ius constitutionale commune in Latin America. Features, potential and challenges]. The University of Namibia
Ferrer Mac-Gregor E (2015) Conventionality Control: The New Doctrine of the Inter-American Court of Human Rights. AJIL Unbound 109:93–99
Ferrer Mac-Gregor E (2017) The Conventionality Control as a Core Mechanism of the Ius Constitutionale Commune. In: Ferrer Mac-Gregor E, Morales Antoniazzi M, Piovesan F, von Bogdandy A (eds) Transformative Constitutionalism in Latin America: The Emergence of a New Ius Commune. Oxford University Press, Oxford
Follesdal A (2017) Exporting the margin of appreciation: Lessons for the Inter-American Court of Human Rights. International Journal of Constitutional Law 15(2):359–371
Fowkes J (2024) Transformative process theory. Global Constitutionalism 1–21
Frishman O, Benvenisti E (2016) National Courts and Interpretative Approaches to International Law: The Case Against Convergence. In: Aust H P, Nolte G (eds) The Interpretation of International Law by Domestic Courts. Oxford University Press, Oxford
Fuentes Torrijo X, Farías D P (2018) El Efecto Directo del Derecho Internacional en el Derecho Chileno [The Direct Effect of International Law on Chilean Law]. Revista de Derecho (Coquimbo) 25(2):119–156

García JF, Verdugo S (2013) Activismo Judicial en Chile. ¿Hacia el Gobierno de los Jueces? Ediciones, Santiago
García Ramírez S (2017) The American Human Rights Navigation: Towards a Ius Commune. In: Ferrer Mac-Gregor E, Morales Antoniazzi M, Piovesan F, von Bogdandy A (eds) Transformative Constitutionalism in Latin America: The Emergence of a New Ius Commune. Oxford University Press, Oxford
García-Huidobro LE, Guidi S (2021) El espejismo de Baena: Luces y sombras de un derecho administrativo comparado latinoamericano [Baena's mirage: Lights and shades of comparative administrative law in Latin America]. International Journal of Constitutional Law 19(4):1291–1321
Gardbaum S (2011) Reassessing the New Commonwealth Model of Constitutionalism. International Journal of Constitutional Law 8 (2)
Gardbaum S (2013) The New Commonwealth Model of Constitutionalism. Theory and Practice. Cambridge University Press, New York.
Gardbaum S (2020) Comparative Political Process Theory. International Journal of Constitutional Law 18(4):1429–1457
Gargarella R (2010) The Legal Foundations of Inequality. Constitutionalism in the Americas, 1776–1860. Cambridge Studies in the Theory of Democracy. Cambridge University Press
Gargarella R (2013a) Latin American Constitutionalism 1810–2010. The Engine Room of the Constitution. Oxford University Press
Gargarella R (2013b) Latin American Constitutionalism: Social Rights and the 'Engine Room' of the Constitution. Notre Dame Journal of International & Comparative Law 4:9–18
Gargarella R (2015) Democracy and Rights in Gelman v. Uruguay. AJIL Unbound 109:115–119
Gargarella R (2017) The 'New' Latin American Constitutionalism: Old Wine in New Skins. In: Ferrer Mac-Gregor E, Morales Antoniazzi M, Piovesan F, von Bogdandy A (eds) Transformative Constitutionalism in Latin America: The Emergence of a New Ius Commune. Oxford University Press
Gargarella R (2021) La Corte Interamericana de Derechos Humanos y la "conversación entre iguales" [The Inter-American Human Rights Court and the "conversation among equals"]. International Journal of Constitutional Law 19(4):1223–1228
Gargarella R (2022a) Chile, después del plebiscito: el sí a una nueva Constitución. Clarín
Gargarella R (2022b) The Law As a Conversation among Equals. Cambridge University Press
Ginsburg T, Simpser A (2014) Constitutions in Authoritarian Regimes. Cambridge University Press, New York
Góngora-Mera M (2017) The block of constitutionality as the doctrinal pivot of a Ius Commune. In: Ferrer Mac-Gregor E, Morales Antoniazzi M, Piovesan F, von Bogdandy A (eds) Transformative Constitutionalism in Latin America: The Emergence of a New Ius Commune. Oxford University Press
González Bertomeu J (2011) Against the Core of the Case: Structuring the Evaluation of Judicial Review. Legal Theory 17(2):81–118
González-Jacome J (2017) From abusive constitutionalism to a multilayered understanding of constitutionalism: Lessons from Latin America. International Journal of Constitutional Law 15(2):447–468
Gonzalez-Ocantos E, Sandholtz W (2021) Constructing a regional human rights legal order: The Inter-American Court, national courts, and judicial dialogue, 1988–2014. International Journal of Constitutional Law 19(5):1559–1596
Henríquez Viñas M (2010) ¿Activismo judicial en la obtención de cobertura adicional para enfermedades catastróficas? Análisis jurisprudencial 2006–2009. [Judicial activism in obtaining additional coverage for catastrophic illnesses? Jurisprudential analysis 2006–2009]. Estudios constitucionales 8(1)
Herrera JC (2021) La idea de un derecho común en América Latina a la luz de sus críticas [The idea of a common law in Latin America in light of its criticisms]. International Journal of Constitutional Law 19(4):1385–1416

Hilbink L (2007) Judges beyond Politics in Democracy and Dictatorship: Lessons from Chile. Cambridge University Press
Hoffman F, Bentes F (2008) Accountability for social and economic rights in Brazil. In Courting Social Justice. Cambridge University Press
Hughes C (2019) The Transformative Potential of Constituent Power: A Revised Approach to the New Latin American Constitutionalism. Latin American Perspectives 46(6):73–91
Huneeus A (2011) Courts Resisting Courts: Lessons from the Inter-American Court's Struggle to Enforce Human Rights. Cornell International Law Journal 44:493–533
Issacharoff S, Verdugo S (2023) Populismo constituyente, democracia y promesas incumplidas: el caso de la Convención Constitucional Chilena (2021–2022) [Constituent populism, democracy and unfulfilled promises: the case of the Chilean Constitutional Convention (2021–2022)]. International Journal of Constitutional Law 21(5):1517–1548
Katz AS (2020) Taming the prince: Bringing presidential emergency powers under law in Colombia. International Journal of Constitutional Law 18(4):1201–1230
Katz AS (2023) Ninguna ley superior: El plebiscito uruguayo de 1980 como constituyente fallido [No higher law: The Uruguayan 1980 plebiscite as a failed constituent]. 21(5)
King P (2013) Neo-Bolivarian Constitutional Design. In: Galligan D J, Versteeg M (eds) Social and Political Foundations of Constitutions. Comparative Constitutional Law and Policy. Cambridge University Press, New York, pp 366–397
Kramer LD (2004) The People Themselves. Popular Constitutionalism and Judicial Review. Oxford University Press, New York
Kuo MS (2019) Against instantaneous democracy. International Journal of Constitutional Law 17(2):554–575
Landau D (2012) The Reality of Social Rights Enforcement. Harvard International Law Journal 53(1):190–247
Landau D (2013a) Abusive Constitutionalism. UC Davis Law Review 47:189–260
Landau D (2013b) Constitution-Making Gone Wrong. Alabama Law Review 64:924–980
Landau D (2014) Beyond Judicial Independence: The Construction of Judicial Power in Colombia. Harvard University, Cambridge, Massachusetts.
Landau D (2018) Constitution-Making and Authoritarianism in Venezuela. In: Graber M A, Levinson S, Tushnet M (eds) Constitutional Democracy in Crisis?. Oxford University Press, pp 161–175
Landau D, Dixon R (2020) Abusive Judicial Review: Courts Against Democracy. UC Davis Law Review 53:1313–1387
Landau D, Dixon R (2023a) Sobre fracaso constitucional, constitucionalismo transformador y utopismo [On constitutional failure, transformative constitutionalism and utopianism]. International Journal of Constitutional Law 25(4)
Landau D, Dixon R (2023b) Utopian constitutionalism in Chile. Global Constitutionalism 13(1):228–238
Larsen SR (2021) Varieties of Constitutionalism in the European Union. The Modern Law Review 84(3):477–502
Loughlin M (2022) Against constitutionalism. Harvard University Press, Cambridge, Massachusetts
Maués AM, Magalhães BB, Nassar PA, Sena R (2021) Judicial Dialogue Between National Courts and the Inter-American Court of Human Rights: A Comparative Study of Argentina, Brazil, Colombia and Mexico. Human Rights Law Review 21(1):108–131
Mendoza-Botelho M (2016) Revisiting Bolivia's Constituent Assembly: Lessons on the Quality of Democracy. Asian Journal of Latin American Studies 29(1):19–55
Meyer EPN (2021) Constitutional Erosion in Brazil. Hart Publishing
Morales Antoniazzi M, Alessandri PS (2017) Inter-Americanization: Its Legal Bases and Political Impact. In: Ferrer Mac-Gregor E, Morales Antoniazzi M, Piovesan F, von Bogdandy A (eds) Transformative Constitutionalism in Latin America: The Emergence of a New Ius Commune. Oxford University Press, Oxford

Muñoz León F (2014) Morning-After Decisions: Legal Mobilization Against Emergency Contraception in Chile. Michigan Journal of Gender and Law 21(1):123–175

Nunes RM (2010) Ideational Origins of Progressive Judicial Activism: The Colombian Constitutional Court and the Right to Health. Latin American Politics and Society 52(3):67–97

Núñez M (2010) El Neoconstitucionalismo y el Recurso a los Valores en la Jurisprudencia del Tribunal Constitucional Chileno [Neoconstitutionalism and the Appeal to Values in the Jurisprudence of the Chilean Constitutional Court]. Revista de Derecho (Valparaíso) XXXIV:523–541

O'Donnell G (1994) Democracia Delegativa. Journal of Democracy en Español 7–23

Palazzo N (2023) Fedotova and Others v. Russia: Dawn of a New Era for European LGBTQ families? Maastricht Journal of European and Comparative Law 30(2):216–228

Parra Vera O (2017) The Impact of Inter-American Judgments by Institutional Empowerment. In: Ferrer Mac-Gregor E, Morales Antoniazzi M, Piovesan F, von Bogdandy A (eds) Transformative Constitutionalism in Latin America: The Emergence of a New Ius Commune. Oxford University Press, Oxford

Paúl A (2012) Controversial Conceptions: The Unborn and the American Convention on Human Rights. Loyola University Chicago International Law Review 9(2):209–247

Paúl Díaz A (2013) La Corte Interamericana in Vitro: Comentarios sobre su Proceso de Toma de Decisiones a Propósito del caso Artavia [The Inter-American Court in Vitro: Comments on its Decision-Making Process Regarding the Artavia Case]. Derecho Público Iberoamericano 2:303–345

Piovesan F (2017) Ius Constitutionale Commune en América Latina [Context, Challenges, and Perspectives]. In: Ferrer Mac-Gregor E, Morales Antoniazzi M, Piovesan F, von Bogdandy A (eds) Transformative Constitutionalism in Latin America: The Emergence of a New Ius Commune. Oxford University Press, Oxford

Pisarello G (2014) Procesos Constituyentes. Caminos para la Ruptura Democrática. Editorial Trotta, Madrid

Post R, Siegel R (2004) Popular Constitutionalism, Departmentalism, and Judicial Supremacy. California Law Review 92(4):1027–1044

Ramírez CG (2024) Kelsen en el Mundo: La Influencia de la Teoría Pura del Derecho en Distintos Lugares [Kelsen in the World: The Influence of Pure Legal Theory in Different Places]. Universidad Externado de Colombia, Bogotá

Reca Milanta S (2024) La navegación de los DESCA en la jurisdicción interamericana [Navigation of ESCR in the inter-American jurisdiction]. Estudios Constitucionales 22(1):30–53

Roa J (2019) Justicia constitucional, deliberación y democracia en Colombia: Jeremy Waldron reflexivo en Bogotá [Constitutional justice, deliberation and democracy in Colombia: Jeremy Waldron reflects in Bogotá]. Revista Derecho del Estado 44:57–98

Roa Roa JE (2020) Control de constitucionalidad deliberativo. El ciudadano ante la justicia constitucional, la acción pública de inconstitucionalidad y la legitimidad democrática del control judicial al legislador [Deliberative constitutional control. The citizen before constitutional justice, the public action of unconstitutionality and the democratic legitimacy of judicial control over the legislator]. Universidad del Externado de Colombia, Bogotá

Rodiles A (2018) The great promise of comparative public law for Latin America: Towards ius commune americanum? In: Roberts A, Stephan P B, Verdier P H, Versteeg M (eds) Comparative International Law. Oxford University Press, pp 501–526

Sagüés N (2010) Obligaciones Internacionales y Control de Convencionalidad [International Obligations and Conventionality Control]. Estudios Constitucionales 8(1):117–136

Soley L (2017) The Transformative Dimension of Inter-American Jurisprudence. In: Ferrer Mac-Gregor E, Morales Antoniazzi M, Piovesan F, von Bogdandy A (eds) Transformative Constitutionalism in Latin America: The Emergence of a New Ius Commune. Oxford University Press, Oxford

Soley X, Steininger S (2018) Parting ways or lashing back? Withdrawals, backlash and the Inter-American Court of Human Rights. International Journal of Law in Context 14(2):237–257

The Economist (2023) How Nayib Bukele is breaking presidential term limits in El Salvador. The Economist https://www.economist.com/the-economist-explains/2023/12/06/how-nayib-bukele-is-breaking-presidential-term-limits-in-el-salvador
Tushnet M (2006) Popular Constitutionalism as Political Law. Chicago-Kent Law Review 81(3):991–1006
Tushnet M (2008) Weak Courts, Strong Rights. Judicial Review and Social Welfare in Comparative Constitutional Law. Princeton University Press, Princeton, New Jersey
Tushnet M (2011) The Rise of Weak-Form Judicial Review. In: Ginsburg T, Dixon R (eds) Comparative Constitutional Law. Edward Elgar, pp 321–333
Tushnet M (2014) Authoritarian Constitutionalism. Some Conceptual Issues. In: Ginsburg T, Simpser A (eds) Constitutions in Authoritarian Regimes. Comparative Constitutional Law and Policy. Cambridge University Press, New York, pp 36–49
Tushnet M (2015) Authoritarian Constitutionalism. Cornell Law Review 100(2):391–462
Tushnet M (2016) Varieties of Constitutionalism. International Journal of Constitutional Law 14(1):1–5
Tushnet M (2020) Varieties of Liberal Constitutionalism. In: Contiades X, Fotiadou A (eds) Routledge Handbook of Comparative Constitutional Change. Routledge, pp 101–114
Uprimny R, Durán J (2014) Equidad y protección judicial del derecho a la salud en Colombia [Equity and judicial protection of the right to health in Colombia]. Comisión Económica para América Latina y el Caribe
Valadés D (2017) The Presidential System in Latin America: A hallmark and challenge to a Latin American Ius Constitutionale Commune. In: Ferrer Mac-Gregor E, Morales Antoniazzi M, Piovesan F, von Bogdandy A (eds) Transformative Constitutionalism in Latin America: The Emergence of a New Ius Commune. Oxford University Press, Oxford
Venegas Maingón A, Muñoz VH (2019) Análisis de los Límites del Poder Constituyente [Analysis of the Limits of Constituent Power]. Derecho Global. Estudios sobre Derecho y Justicia 5(13):41–63
Verdugo S (2019) The Fall of the Constitution's Political Insurance. How the Morales Regime Broke the Insurance of the 2009 Bolivian Constitution. International Journal of Constitutional Law 17(4):1098–1124
Verdugo S (2021) Limited Democracy and Great Distrust. John Hart Ely in Chile and Bolivia. International Journal of Constitutional Law 19(2)
Verdugo S (2023) Is it time to abandon the theory of constituent power? International Journal of Constitutional Law 21(1):14–79
Verdugo S, Prieto M (2021) The Dual Aversion of Chile's Constitution Making Process: Between Bolivarian Constitutionalism and the Pinochet Constitution. International Journal of Constitutional Law 19(1)
Vilhena O, Baxi U, Viljoen F (2013) Transformative Constitutionalism: Comparing the Apex Courts of Brazil, India and South Africa. Pretoria University Law Press, Johannesburg
von Bogdandy A (2015a) Ius Constitutionale Commune en América Latina: Observations on Transformative Constitutionalism [Common Constitutional Law in Latin America: Observations on Transformative Constitutionalism]. AJIL Unbound 109:109–114
von Bogdandy A (2015b) Ius Constitutionale Commune en América Latina: una mirada al Constitucionalismo Transformador [Common Constitutional Law in Latin America: A Look at Transforming Constitutionalism]. Revista de Derecho del Estado 34:3–50
von Bogdandy A (2017) Ius Constitutionale Commune en América Latina: Observations on Transformative Constitutionalism. In: Ferrer Mac-Gregor E, Antoniazzi M M, Piovesan F, von Bogdandy A (eds) Transformative Constitutionalism in Latin America: the Emergence of a New Ius Commune. Oxford University Press, Oxford
von Bogdandy A (2023) Chilean Insights for Progressive Constitutionalism. Heidelberg Journal of International Law 83(1):1–10

von Bogdandy A, Ferrer Mac-Gregor E, Morales Antoniazzi M, Piovesan F (2017a) Transformative Constitutionalism in Latin America: The Emergence of a New Ius Commune. Oxford University Press, Oxford

von Bogdandy A, Ferrer Mac-Gregor E, Morales Antoniazzi M, Piovesan F, Soley X (2017b) Ius Constitutionale Commune en América Latina: A Regional Approach to Transformative Constitutionalism. In: von Bogdandy A, Ferrer Mac-Gregor E, Morales Antoniazzi M, Piovesan F (eds) Transformative Constitutionalism in Latin America: The Emergence of a New Ius Commune. Oxford University Press, Oxford

Waldron J (2006) The Core of the Case Against Judicial Review. The Yale Law Journal 115:1346–1406

Weale A (2018) The Will of the People. A Modern Myth. Polity Press

Werneck Arguelhes D (2019) Book Review: Transformative constitutionalism in Latin America: The Emergence of a New Ius Commune. International Journal of Constitutional Law 17:357–381

Wolff J (2012) New Constitutions and the Transformation of Democracy in Bolivia and Ecuador. In: Nolte D, Schilling-Vacaflor A (eds) New Constitutionalism in Latin America. Promises and Practices. Routledge, New York, pp 183–202

GPSR Compliance

The European Union's (EU) General Product Safety Regulation (GPSR) is a set of rules that requires consumer products to be safe and our obligations to ensure this.

If you have any concerns about our products, you can contact us on ProductSafety@springernature.com

In case Publisher is established outside the EU, the EU authorized representative is:

Springer Nature Customer Service Center GmbH
Europaplatz 3
69115 Heidelberg, Germany

Batch number: 10755292

Printed by Printforce, the Netherlands